Welco

THE
EVERYTHING
PARENT'S GUIDES ®

As a parent, you're swamped with conflicting advice and parenting techniques that tell you what is best for your child. THE EVERYTHING® PARENT'S GUIDES get right to the point about specific issues. They give you the most recent, up-to-date information on parenting trends, behavior issues, and health concerns—providing you with a detailed resource to help you ease your parenting anxieties.

THE EVERYTHING® PARENT'S GUIDES are an extension of the bestselling Everything® series in the parenting category. These family-friendly books are designed to be a one-stop guide for parents. If you want authoritative information on specific topics not fully covered in other books, THE EVERYTHING® PARENT'S GUIDES are the perfect resource to ensure that you raise a healthy, confident child.

Visit the entire Everything® series at *www.everything.com*

THE EVERYTHING
PARENT'S GUIDE TO
RAISING GIRLS

Dear Reader,

Many years ago, I came to this country as a young military wife with little money—and pregnant. When my first baby came—a daughter—she gave me a crash course in life. Through her—and her sister—I experienced life in abundance. Raising any child is wonderful but raising a daughter is special. In my case the impact was even greater since I had lost my mother at six and missed the important mother-daughter bond.

My daughters inspired me. I took classes, studied parenting, and devoted my whole life to it. For decades I taught school and worked with kids and their parents. I wrote newspaper columns and books on parenting, even a series just for girls. That's why I'm writing this book: to help guide you in raising your own girl with ease, skill, and confidence in today's challenging world.

My relationship with my daughters surpasses every other achievement I have made. Raising a daughter is the ultimate adventure. You are so lucky to be the parent of a girl, and she is lucky to have someone raising her who wants the best for her.

With love to both of you,

Sincerely,

Dr. Erika

THE

EVERYTHING®

PARENT'S GUIDE TO

RAISING GIRLS

A complete handbook to develop
confidence, promote self-esteem,
and improve communication

Erika V. Shearin Karres, Ed.D.
Technical Review by Rebecca Rutledge, Ph.D.

Adams Media
Avon, Massachusetts

To my mother, Barbara Schmelzer Vierling, who died when I was six. Now she lives again—in these pages.

• • •

Publisher: Gary M. Krebs
Managing Editor: Laura M. Daly
Associate Copy Chief: Sheila Zwiebel
Acquisitions Editor: Kerry Smith
Development Editor: Brett Palana-Shanahan
Associate Production Editor: Casey Ebert

Director of Manufacturing: Susan Beale
Associate Director of Production:
  Michelle Roy Kelly
Prepress: Erick DaCosta, Matt LeBlanc
Design and Layout: Heather Barrett,
Brewster Brownville, Colleen Cunningham,
Jennifer Oliveira

• • •

An Everything® Series Book.
Everything® and everything.com® are registered trademarks of F+W Publications, Inc.

Published by Adams Media, an F+W Publications Company
57 Littlefield Street, Avon, MA 02322 U.S.A.
www.adamsmedia.com

ISBN 10: 1-59869-247-X
ISBN 13: 978-1-59869-247-1

Printed in Canada.

J I H G F E D C B A

Library of Congress Cataloging-in-Publication Data
Karres, Erika V. Shearin.
  The everything parent's guide to raising girls / by Erika V.
Shearin Karres, with technical review by Rebecca Rutledge.
      p. cm. — (An everything series book)
  Includes bibliographical references and index.
      ISBN-13: 978-1-59869-247-1 (pbk.)
      ISBN-10: 1-59869-247-X (pbk.)
  1. Girls. 2. Parenting. 3. Parent and child. I. Title. II. Title: Parent's guide to raising girls.
      HQ777.K37 2007
      649'.133—dc22
                2007001125

This book is available at quantity discounts for bulk purchases.
For information, please call 1-800-289-0963.

All the examples and dialogues used in this book are fictional,
and have been created by the author to illustrate situations.

▶ girl (gurl) n.

1. A female child with an unlimited potential for giving, creating, and achieving. When mixed well with love, patience, and inspiration, she will turn into a strong, independent, and successful young woman with character, courage, and confidence. In short, a blessing to her family and community and a lifelong joy for her parents.

Acknowledgments

The Everything® Parent's Guide to Raising Girls is based on my thirty-five years of work, research, and the experiences of more than five thousand parents I have worked with. It builds on the premise that parenting is a science that can be studied, a skill that can be acquired, and an art that can be honed.

I want to thank my two daughters, Elizabeth Shearin Hounshell, R.N, and Dr. Mary D. Shearin, for their help, devotion, and love. Without them, this book would not exist. It is one thing to study parenting in the abstract, and another to put one's theories to the test. My wonderful daughters prove beyond a doubt that the thoughtful parenting of a daughter is a joy with happy consequences—over and over. Thank you so much, Elizabeth and Deesie. You are more than terrific friends. You are what is best in me reconfigured into the latest and shiniest models. I also want to thank my husband, Andy, for his great love and support.

• • •

Contents

Introduction

THERE IS NOTHING ON EARTH more important than raising a child. Just think for a moment about children collectively. If they were all raised properly, there would be no more discord or crime. Certainly we would still have illnesses and tragedy, even poverty, but this new generation of children would band together as adults, focus their attention on developing solutions, and implement them.

Even if the solutions were out of reach, humankind would still act like pleasant neighbors and take the sting out of the mishaps, mistakes, and misery of others. In fact, if everyone would do a great job raising their offspring, the world would be reborn almost in an instant. So raising a child is crucial not only for the individual but also for the community, especially now.

Why? Because these days, life is tougher, the pace is faster, tragic events occur with more frequency and severity, and crime is on the rise. Some people go so far as to say that these days our schools are dysfunctional, our families are falling apart, and the whole country is floundering.

That may be overstated, but it is a fact that parenting a child is of the utmost importance now. Yet, it's harder than ever before. There are so many more obstacles nowadays. Parents have less free time because society demands that their attention is focused more on economic concerns. Of course, less free time means

spending fewer hours with the kids, which leads to under-parenting (that is, the lack of parental supervision and guidance).

Besides that, these days there are more negative influences that rub off on our children at an earlier stage. It's not that society is going haywire as a whole, but too many problems seem to hit us all at once, not only in the national and international arena but also close at home. There are wars, terrorists, threats of missile attacks from foreign lands, new illnesses like the bird flu, global warming, skyrocketing gasoline prices, increasingly severe weather patterns such as hurricanes or tornadoes, and criminals who try to steal our identity, our money, or our children.

No wonder parents feel overwhelmed and don't know where to turn. Every aspect of life seems to have become more difficult, and raising kids can become a real nightmare. It's especially hard to raise a girl because it seems so many of the ugly facets of modern life target girls more often than boys.

As the parent or caregiver of a girl, you may feel like you're at your wit's end. First, you want your little girl to grow up healthy and safe and happy, and to be able to enjoy her childhood to the fullest. Next, you want her to become a strong, capable, and independent-minded teenager with hopes and dreams and a will to succeed. Finally, you want her to blossom into a confident and successful young woman with the whole world at her fingertips.

But wherever you look, whatever you read, whenever you turn on the radio or TV, you learn about another new and real threat—ranging from a new bad fad, to girls beating up girls, to Internet stalking, and so forth.

You can't bubble-wrap your little girl—you know that, so what should you do? Whom can you ask for advice?

You start to feel a little frantic because even the "experts" you decide to go to—through your reading or on the Net—seem to contradict themselves. All those programs and magazines entirely devoted to parenting offer nothing much that is new except new areas for concern. You didn't even know little girls can get depressed at age three or worry themselves sick over not having brand-name outfits to wear in kindergarten. You wonder longingly whatever happened to allowing your child to grow up like a little tree in the forest, without all the muss and fuss. The only thing you do know is that you love your daughter with all your heart.

Stop worrying. Stop searching far and wide for answers. Of course, your love for your little girl is enough, and you already have all the answers. You, only you, know your daughter and how best to raise her. You know what you envision for her future. You really have within yourself all the ingredients it takes to raise a wonderful daughter, even in the turbulence and uncertainty of today.

All you need is a simple step-by-step recipe that spells out how to blend the ingredients correctly: to let you know when to stir them, when to let them marinate, when to turn up the heat, and when to step back and wait for the result.

That recipe is this parent's guide. It's chock-full of all kinds of great suggestions, hints, choices, and solutions gathered from research, readings, and most of all from the hands-on experience of more than five thousand parents, parents just like you.

Here's the key point: You are capable of raising the most wonderful daughter and of helping her become a young woman who is strong, independent, loving, and successful, even in these difficult times.

The Everything® Parent's Guide to Raising Girls is going to be by your side every day with a menu of information, options, main points, and stories from which to choose whatever best fits your and your child's needs.

You know what you want for your daughter's future—and for your own. Make your hopes and wishes come true. You can, and you will.

CHAPTER 1

Your Infant Daughter

Congratulations! You are the parent of a baby girl! Sure, you may have a few hairy days early on, but soon you'll get a handle on your daughter's daily needs. You may even have a schedule of sorts. At any rate, after a few weeks or months, you can get more sleep and your energy level will bounce back. You feel that the toughest part physically of having a baby is over—and you are right! Now let the fun begin.

Developmental Factors

Your little girl is growing by leaps and bounds during her first year. Every day she surprises you with something brand-new she has learned, often more than one thing. Your heart almost bursts with joy as you observe her curiosity about all kinds of new things. You hardly dare blink for fear you'll miss something. In fact, when you consider just how much she will develop during the next twelve months, you feel like just placing her on a blanket on the floor and watching her all day long.

As you soak up your daughter's quick advancement, you want to be attuned to the four main areas that are the most noticeable.

Ability to Move Around

Around the age of six months, your baby girl can lift up her head and roll over. She can sit up if you support her back, bounce, and begin to put some weight on her legs. Six months later, she can crawl, perhaps pull herself up to a sitting then standing position, and take a step. After another half year has passed, she can walk, pick up a toy she dropped, and proceed up some steps if you hold her hand.

 **Fact**

The time from birth to twenty-four months is called infancy. During that time, a baby goes through many bursts of physical and emotional growth. Her development takes place in all facets of her existence and can happen so rapidly it seems almost instantaneous.

Your daughter's development from a helpless baby to one who scoots around so fast you can hardly keep up with her passes so quickly that you have what seems like a new miracle occur almost daily. More miracles occur in regard to her sight and hand movement.

Vision and Fine-Motor Skills

By the time your baby girl is six months old, she is able to follow a moving object—whether it is a twirling toy or you—with her eyes and can reach for an object. Once she manages to grab that object, her aim will be to bring it to her mouth. At the age of one year, she can grasp a small object and let go of it with ease. She can pick up a rattle with each hand and whack them together. Six months later, she can pile a few blocks on top of each other, turn a page in a big book, and start to show a preference for using one hand over the other.

Besides her growth spurts in locomotion and vision, your baby daughter also attains many new milestones in her auditory ability, her comprehension, and her oral communication skills.

Hearing and Speaking

At around six months of age, a baby girl can recognize her parent's tone of voice. She will turn her head to track where sounds come from and say her vowels. What is especially touching to observe is that now she can not only smile but also laugh, chuckle, and squeal with delight. Six months later, she knows her name, knows basic household objects and their use, and can babble to herself in her own language. She may even say a few recognizable words. At eighteen months, she can understand short sentences and has a vocabulary of up to twenty words. That burgeoning ability to interact verbally with others helps your little girl in the last big area of her development.

Alert!

Although all babies exhibit the acquisition of their most important skills in a similar order—for example, babies learn to roll over before they sit up—the speed at which these skills are gained can vary enormously. A sudden change in the baby's environment can also slow her developmental rate.

Playing and Socializing

While at the age of six months, your baby can be shy around strangers, she enjoys looking at herself in the mirror and playing peek-a-boo with you. Before long, however, she will learn to wave goodbye, clap her hands, and look for a toy that is hidden, thereby exhibiting the first signs of developing a memory. At one year, she will enjoy dropping objects or putting them into a box. She will like playing patty-cake and being around you and any other adult she knows and can snuggle with. Six months later, she will set out to explore her complete living quarters, use a spoon and cup, and alternate from being too clingy to wanting to be set down on the floor—now.

Be sure to take your little girl to her regular checkups and have her get the recommended immunizations. Always take a small notepad that is filled with questions that occur to you, dealing with your daughter's development, and even more important, to record what the pediatrician tells you. Many parents are in such a rush at the doctor's office that they do not remember later what they were told. A few pertinent notes will keep them on track.

Fact

There are several causes for what is called developmental delay, meaning a baby has not mastered the expected new skills within the normal time frame. Some causes are a lack of bonding with the parent, a lack of stimulation, and the existence of a physical problem ranging from vision disorders to hearing loss and other impairments.

As you can tell, the various skills cited under the four broad developmental areas are only a partial list. Many more and complex abilities need to be mastered by your baby girl and you, the parent or caregiver, want to be able to assist her in that process. How? It is simple—just tune into your daughter's world.

Your Baby's World

For a moment, put yourself into your baby's position and realize just how much she has to learn and how quickly. There is not another period in her life when she has to amass such a mountain of knowledge and attain so many developmental milestones. She has to do it by herself, but you can help by providing her with what it takes to make her monumental task easier. Of course she continues to need all the basics: food, her little bed, and fresh diapers. Beyond that, there are other objects that help her develop her potential at the speed that is optimal for her.

Babyproofing

Before rushing to buy out the toy store, first babyproof your home by lying on the floor and examining the furniture, walls, and bric-a-brac for safety issues. Then cover the electrical outlets, remove any valuables, and pad the sharp corners of the living room table and any other pieces of dangerous furniture. Crawl around and see what you have missed. Then stock up on baby toys that are safe, but do not introduce them to her all at once.

Toy by Toy

One new toy at a time is sufficient. Let your little girl examine it, absorb its shape and color, handle it, and get familiar with it. Let her form an attachment to it and to you. Also, too many new things can overwhelm your little daughter.

 *Essential*

As much as your baby needs stimulation from toys, she needs quiet time even more. In addition to sleeping, she enjoys being placed on the floor and taking in her home environment—all the colors, shapes, and pieces of furniture. Placing her into a playpen can keep her from wandering.

But besides her toys and her chance to observe the world around her through the screen or the bars of her playpen, your baby daughter needs something else: you. She will make the most strides with your help. So hold her, help her to sit up, support her as she tries to stand for the first time—and smile and tell her how well she is doing every step of the way. It is your encouragement, your praise, and your smile that will spur her on as she learns to crawl, to walk tentatively holding onto the sofa with her feet spread apart, and then finally to walk nicely with her feet closer together as if to say, "Look out, world, here I come."

Maintain a Routine

When your baby girl was only a few weeks old, you entertained her with your conversation and song, but it was primarily a one-sided process. Now that she is able to make sounds such as *Da-da* and *Ma-ma*, you want to capitalize on her newly learned early speech capabilities and encourage them as best you can.

 **Fact**

The average baby walks between thirteen and eighteen months of age; some babies start before a year and others wait until a year and a half. Many girls are early walkers. The late walkers sometimes make up for it by turning immediately into runners who are hard to keep up with.

One quick way to do that is incorporate books into her life. That works best if you do the following:

- **Set a regular time aside for reading to her.** This time may be right before her nap or before she goes to bed at night—and, you hope, sleeps until morning!
- **Have books on hand that are geared to her age.** Your neighborhood bookstore or public library has a list of the best books for babies and small children.
- **Read the same book over and over to her, allowing her to point to the duck or the kitten as you read about them, so that before long she can "read" the story back to you.**

As far as music, you probably have already found out that your little girl likes certain CDs played at a low volume as her favorite lullabies. Now is the time to get a song book and sing your childhood favorites with her. Have her sit on your lap and sing to your heart's content.

To your baby's ears, your voice will sound better than the most acclaimed singer in the world. Again, start with an easy song or a well-known rhyming ditty. Before too long, your baby will clap along, bounce on your lap, or hum along with you. What makes the reading and singing habit especially beneficial for your little daughter is that even if your—and her—day gets crazy, the established routine will show her all is well anyway. Babies, as much as they tend to make us overturn our regular schedules, thrive on the sameness of something they enjoy.

Alert!

Be sure to have on hand books to enjoy with your baby, including a collection of nursery rhymes with big pictures, a baby book of lullabies with pictures, and a book of settle-down activities. Add to the collection as much as you can by buying smaller books your child can hold in her own hands.

When you have to change your days because you are going back to work, the customary twenty minutes with you or the other caregiver that is devoted to books and/or music is like a handrail for your little girl. With it she can move ahead in her development, knowing that you can be relied on at all times.

Fun Time as a Routine

Even when a parent is a full-time parent, unavoidable changes can occur in the household, such as a relative coming to live with the family, a parent going on a business trip, or a move to a bigger apartment. Your little girl will weather these changes much better if her fun times with you stay exactly the same, and you will feel content that while the surroundings or circumstances of your family are in flux, her world's foundation remains solidly in place.

Her Care and Needs

As your baby grows, so do her requirements and needs. They do not become more difficult, only different. No longer do you feel as if you have to hover over her every minute. At other times, you can carry your little girl with you from room to room in her baby seat. It is then that you notice she's heavier. Her weight increases along with her growth, and both change very quickly during her infancy. Although baby boys grow faster than girls during the first seven months, girls take off after that and continue to grow more rapidly until about age four. No matter how speedily your daughter grows, her needs continue to increase in two vital areas—the physical and the emotional—and her care demands that you keep both aspects of her development in mind.

Physical Needs

On the physical front, your baby daughter outgrows her outfits often as fast as you can replace them. You will also notice the change in her body's proportions. During her first year, her head grows almost to its adult size.

 **Fact**

A baby's body shape changes because her various parts grow at different rates. Although her head is unusually large at birth—as compared to the rest of her body—her body catches up before too long. During early childhood, her arms and legs grow faster than her trunk, but the whole growth process balances itself out thereafter.

Your little girl's appetite also increases as does her wish for, and ability to digest, solid foods. By the time she is four months old, you may start introducing her to one or two teaspoons of cereal, puréed fruit, or vegetables. Ask your pediatrician what he or she recommends for your baby girl; no two babies are ever the same. But before long she will indicate by her facial expressions if the jar of split peas tasted as good to her as the applesauce. Of course, her nutrition is important as is her medical care and any environmental factors that could have a negative impact on her.

For example, if you live in an older house, you may want to have the water quality checked. Unacceptable lead levels due to old pipes have been reported in apartments and homes built more than two decades ago. Lead has also been found in old paint. Children who lick or eat paint that contains high lead levels can suffer from lead poisoning, which does not produce physical effects but can lead to mental impairment

Question?

Both my parents smoke, and I'm afraid to let them spend too much time around my baby. Am I wrong?
No, you're not wrong. But don't let this issue keep the grandparents from spending time with your baby. Before their next visit, have your pediatrician write a note stating that secondary smoke is especially harmful to a baby's lungs. Then make sure the doctor's advice is followed.

Emotional Needs

Your baby daughter may be able to say "Down," meaning, "Put me down," by the time she is one year old, but she always wants you close by. So keep spending as much time as you can with her and continue to hug, kiss, and show your love for her. Also when you promise her you will do something, follow through. Especially if you have to be separated from your little girl, you have to make sure to reattach with her emotionally each evening. A warm and trusting relationship with your daughter is a requirement that takes a little effort every day but brings enormous benefits. Babies who are neglected emotionally grow up to crave attention at all costs, often cannot cope with frustrating events, and may even show a delay in their overall development, according to studies backed by the American Medical Association's *Encyclopedia of Medicine.*

Even if you work at a job with long hours, you can meet the emotional needs of your baby daughter. Every evening when you come home, focus on her first thing. Many research studies prove that infants do very well with more that one primary caregiver. All that is required is a person who is loving and consistent and fills in capably for you while you are gone.

Alert!

Most experts agree that a baby should be taken care of at home if the mother decides to go back to work. So try your best to find a warm and reliable caregiver to come to your house. Or maybe you and a friend can share an experienced caregiver. Do not leave your baby with someone who has more than two infants to look after.

As with so many aspects of parenting, your baby's care becomes easier the older she gets. Her needs are less difficult to meet when she is able to express what she wants or what is bothering her. Sometimes, however, even after she has learned to say a few words, she still cannot tell you exactly what is wrong.

The Fussy Baby

Not all babies are placid and easily entertained and looked after during their first year. Some babies have such fine-tuned systems that they resemble extremely complicated mechanisms that can have many breakdowns. So you, the parent, have a lot on your plate, trying to adjust to a newborn baby with a high susceptibility to colds, earaches, or the flu, or one who has allergies, for example. You find yourself going to the pediatrician every week and constantly filling the prescriptions she gives you. Then you try to figure out how to make your daughter swallow the medicine, which, of course, she detests.

Or your baby may experience almost constant episodes of crying that are not due to an obvious illness. This type of baby is called "fussy" because she can cause a constant fuss, and these periods of crying do not abate even when you try the usual means of comforting her, such as feeding her, changing her diaper, or just cuddling her. What is worse, the periods of excessive screaming are more prolonged in the evenings when you are exhausted, having done a full day's work running the household or the office. Therefore, your fussy little girl presents an extra challenge, and one you may not have counted on, but you can manage it by using the following measures:

1. Keep a record of when the irritable periods occur in your baby's day. What preceded them?
2. Observe what she does while she's crying. Does she draw up her feet or otherwise indicate that her tummy hurts?
3. Do not feed the baby every time she cries. Many fussy babies have immature digestive tracts and a bloated stomach makes the condition worse.

Most pediatricians use the word *colic* to describe the spasmodic pain that may very well be the cause of your little girl's fussiness.

But no matter what the doctor's diagnosis is, your baby is not a happy camper. Soon you will find to your dismay that you are not a happy camper either. The good news is that your little girl will outgrow the condition at least by the time she is six months old, although some babies—just like some adults—have a more sensitive digestive system that may be theirs for life. So while your daughter suffers from this common but harmless colicky state that occurs in roughly one in ten infants, you want to do what you can to help her feel better.

Fact

The word *colic* comes from the Greek *kolikos* and means suffering in the colon, which is the major part of the large intestine. The colon's function is to absorb water from the material that is passing through and to compact the indigestible waste.

Some things you can try include:

- Taking her for a ride in your car
- Playing some soothing music
- Putting her facedown on your knees while stroking her back
- Giving her a pacifier
- Rocking her in a rocking chair

Know that simply waiting until she gets older will also help, especially if you turn to your network of family and friends and share your concerns.

Draw on Your Network

Being a parent to a baby girl—whether she is the calm or the fussy type—is made so much easier if you have a network of other people in place who can come in and relieve you when your nerves get frayed. Many experts warn parents not to get too exhausted because exhaustion makes even easy baby chores, such as feeding or bathing, much more difficult. Therefore, have your phone handy. Have on speed-dial all those people who can help you not only with the chores related to your infant but also with bringing in groceries and lifting your mood. Revel in the feeling that your sisters and brothers, and your mom and dad circle around you more closely now.

Enjoy Baby Joys

Enjoy being the center of your extended family's attention; be sure to inform each member of your little daughter's progress. Don't think you are shamelessly using them when you ask them to pick up the dry cleaning, make a run to the grocery store, load the dishwasher, and bring on the diapers.

Alert!

You can be a hero but not if it means you feel as though you have to shoulder all the responsibilities that come along with an infant girl. When you drive a car, you have to stop and pull over when you are sleepy to avoid an accident. The same concept applies with your baby. Ask someone for help before you collapse from fatigue or reach the end of your rope.

Being pampered as a parent is also important. Imagine a new mother whose baby girl goes through a relatively easy few weeks and then develops a stretch of irritability. Imagine her calling her parents before she and her partner are at their wits' end. Her family will not be able to do enough for her by bringing home-cooked meals and taking dirty laundry away only to return it washed and folded. Neighbors stop by as well and bring fresh flowers and the suggestion that a soothing bath for the baby might do the trick.

Ask for Help

Babies respond well to different calming techniques on different days, although not according to what you have in mind. Sometimes just putting your baby into the loving arms of another person—your grandmother, uncle, or cousin—distracts her enough to be able to sleep.

When the well-being of your baby is at stake, you have to ask other people to assist you. You cannot drive yourself until there is nothing left in you. That is why you must also call on another network—your close and personal one. Just like your baby girl, your close and personal network cannot thrive without your looking after it and its needs. You do that by making sure its various segments are never neglected.

Faith and Friends

The first segment is your faith and passion. Keep your faith strong and indulge in what you are passionate about. Next, remember your friends, no matter how far away. Keep in touch with them by sending them a picture of your baby girl or a dozen. Then tend to your own mind. If you read a book a week before the baby came, get back to that relaxing pursuit and to your news magazines and your puzzles.

Your Physical Health

The biggest part of your close and personal network is your relationship with your own body. Breathe deeply, stretch, and start exercising. Your muscles will be grateful to you, your pants will fit better, and your energy level will skyrocket. Your little girl will be so proud of you as she watches you and even tries to imitate you. You and your spouse can then enjoy all aspects of being a wonderful family. If you are a single parent, you should be extra proud of the way you are evolving.

CHAPTER 2

Your Toddler Daughter

As you are beginning to realize, as your little girl grows older and becomes a toddler, looking after her becomes easier. There are two reasons for that. First, her increasing size makes her less fragile to handle. Second, she learns to communicate better with you, so she can better tell you what might be wrong with her. Therefore, you have so many more child-rearing options, and what a joy it is to use them.

Girl Playgroups and Toys

One option you have is to widen the circle of interactions for your little girl. Up until now, this circle may have included only the parents, other close relatives, and/or the babysitter or caregiver. But now your little girl is ready to meet new people—her peers. For that reason, you now want to investigate all appropriate playgroups in your area.

Of course, if your daughter already spends the time you are at work in day care, she may already have a playgroup. Then just add visits to the park and the playground there, with you choosing carefully what types of play equipment your little girl is ready for. Keep in mind that toddlers have mastered many skills and enjoy playing with all sorts of toys. They can:

- Climb up stairs—with two feet to a step—and benches, and back down.
- Throw and kick a ball and retrieve it.

- Pull a doll in a carriage and carry their favorite stuffed animal everywhere.
- Build towers with many blocks and ride a tricycle.

 **Fact**

A playgroup is a group of children, ranging from at least two to many that is organized for the purpose of meeting and playing under appropriate supervision. These meetings can be held in a commercial, church, or private setting.

So give your daughter a chance to try out her new play skills in a group setting. If you are a stay-at-home parent, however, and your little girl hasn't been exposed to many other children, you need to go more slowly. Introduce other little girls and boys to your daughter one at a time and starting with short periods. Many mothers of toddlers form an informal group that meets, for example, three times a week, on a rotating basis. While the parents watch and visit, the small children play alongside each other or—as they mature—with each other. The most beneficial playgroup arrangement is one that includes the following:

- Your daughter gets to spend some time in her home environment.
- The supervision is along a one-to-one ratio.
- The parents benefit, too, as they have a chance to air their frustrations and share their baby girl joys.
- The cost is usually minimal. There may be a small cost for the refreshments.

When you select a playgroup in a commercial or faith-based setting, you may have the assurance that the staff is well trained, but the ratio of kids to supervisors may be less than ideal—three or four toddlers to an adult, when two is a handful. Also the cost may be prohibitive, as well as the driving time. Still, check out all possibilities.

Pick 'n' Choose Playgroups

Of course, you know what will work best for you and your circumstances. But whatever choice you make, go slowly with the playgroup. Stay with your little girl until she is comfortable in her new setting. Depending on the degree of comfort you have with the playgroup you have selected, that may mean you will always be in the same room with your little girl, or at least close by.

Alert!

Never drop off your little girl in a new playgroup and leave—no matter how highly recommended that group may be. The success of your daughter's fit into the group depends on the group and your daughter's ability to adjust. Start with a trial period of a few minutes and lengthen that a few minutes at a time, with you present.

Your best guideline to a playgroup is your little girl's reaction. If she eagerly anticipates going to play with her new friends again, all is well. But if she is reluctant to attend the group, do not push her. Some toddler girls are not ready for group play. It overwhelms them. Others can sense a lack of warmth and love for children in the supervisors and while they cannot explain the negative "vibes," parents must trust their child's feelings, and either find another playgroup, hold off for a while longer, or start one themselves.

Tough Playgroups

Sometimes, the children in a playgroup are older than your little girl; they may be more rowdy, more demanding, even aggressive. Make sure the other little girls and boys are the types of children you want your little girl to emulate. You do not want her suddenly coming home saying bad words and starting to hit other children. Once you investigate what is going on, you will find that the other toddlers are not "bad." No one has taken the time to teach them how to act. You hope that somebody will—and soon. Somebody really needs to teach them a few basics.

Essential

From the age of nine months on, babies can understand the meaning of the words *no* and *yes*. After hearing "no" every time they do something that is not acceptable, they associate the word with something they should not do and "yes" with something they should do.

But unfortunately you cannot take all the toddlers in your neighborhood under your wing. The best you can do is to express your concerns and reasons for leaving one playgroup and joining another. You already have much to do. Raising your little girl is a full-time job that fills whatever hours you have available, especially during the year from age two to age three.

The Terrific Twos

In the past, the period between twenty-four months and thirty-six months in a child's life used to be called "the terrible twos" because with the development of a child's ability to speak, she could suddenly seem much more demanding—and at quite a loud volume. Furthermore, this was the same time when most parents were ready for a little respite from the nonstop baby care and suddenly their quiet and easily pacified bundle of joy had turned into a little person who banged the top of her high chair with her fist, wanted something now, and kept asking for it until she got it. If this took a little while, she stomped her feet and screamed so loud it made their heads ring.

Your Two-Year-Old's World

The reason for the terrible twos perception was that many parents did not understand the normal stages of their child's development. At approximately two years of age, the child sees her world opening up with so much on the horizon that she cannot yet have. By then she has also learned that her parents can be manipulated by simply showing her displeasure—and the more obvious the better. Now she can use many words, but she doesn't necessarily understand their meanings completely. All she is good at is making demands. Plus, she is filled with questions and fires them off, one after the other. Also while she has developed an either left-handed or right-handedness by now and can undo her buttons and untie her shoes, she cannot yet close her buttons or tie her laces. Nor can she do other things that seem so simple to adults. So she is boiling over with frustration and impatience.

Be Prepared

None of these characteristics are negative, however, unless the parent is not prepared. In fact, your little girl's demanding attitude and hurry-up manner are an opportunity to teach her how to act acceptably. All you have to do is expect her increased impatience, demands, and questioning and have a plan to deal with them. Slowly and surely, you will make progress with her.

 *Question?*

Ever since my little girl turned two, she refuses to do anything I tell her. What am I doing wrong?

Nothing, but age two is a hard time for a child and her parents. Remember she is not intentionally trying to be rebellious or defiant, she is just trying to express her growing independence, but she doesn't yet have adequate verbal skills to do so. Know that this won't last and that your little girl will outgrow this phase.

What helps is that by now your daughter has learned to follow simple instructions. Therefore, make your instructions to her as simple and to the point as you can and expect them to be followed. No explanations need to be given about why you want her to drink her milk or get her coat besides, "Because I said so." In years to come you will want to give a reason for your instructions and rules, but now is too early for your little girl to understand whatever deeper implications there might be.

 **Fact**

Pediatrician Dr. Alan Greene, who is on the faculty of Stanford University School of Medicine, prefers to call the terrible twos—which may begin before that age and may continue after age three—the "first adolescence" because it is the first time in a child's life when she exhibits oppositional—that is, disagreeable—behavior.

But if you give directions to your little girl in a kind but firm tone, you will get results. So, do not start screaming or moping over your hurt feelings when she balks. Your daughter does not mean to upset you. She is just going through a stage. Also there is no need for you to jump every time she expresses a wish. Calmly do what seems reasonable, after explaining to her that she has to ask nicely and not be demanding. Also, help her understand that raising her voice will not make you run to her side unless she is hurt. Only then is it all right—even necessary—to scream.

There are several practices that ensure the terrible twos turn into the terrific twos, which they can if that is what you want. First, be forewarned and do not take the sudden disagreeableness in your little girl as a sign you have made a mistake. Take it as an opportunity to expand your parenting skills. The following hints have been tried by many parents and they work, if you use them on a consistent basis with your girl:

- Avoid asking her a question that can be answered with no, such as, "Do you want to wear the blue top?"
- Give her two choices: "Would you like to wear the pink top or the yellow one?"
- Have a regular routine for naps, meals, and so on, and try to stick to it each day.
- If there are two things she needs to do, allow her to decide which she wants to do first, as in, "Do you want to pick up your toys first or take your bath first?"

Various other methods may occasionally work for parents of a little girl caught in the throes of the confrontational twos, but calmness and consistency always work—after a while. So keep at it.

Parenting Growth

Furthermore, discuss with other mothers and fathers what works for them and take notes. Also remember what you've tried that has the best result for you. Then roll up your sleeves, feel confident in your parenting, and enjoy this terrific time in your daughter's life. She is becoming quite a little person now with a preference to dress up and play imaginatively. Or she will line up her stuffed animals and give them a talking to. She certainly makes your coming home from work a joy every evening and gives you a reason to live. As a mom or dad of a toddler girl, you never wonder why you are here. You know your purpose is to raise this smart and beautiful little girl to the best of your ability.

In the process of rearing your daughter, you continue to grow as well. The more she challenges you with her developmental stages—some smooth, some rocky—the more chances you have to be resourceful and draw out innate parenting abilities you never knew you possessed.

Your Girl Learns to Listen

The underlying purpose of all parenting is to enable the child to have an easier life. That is the reason for teaching your little girl one of the most important skills she can possess: how to listen and listen well. Once she has mastered this skill, all other childhood tasks are so much easier for her to grasp and for you to teach.

One thing that can get in the way of your little girl's learning to listen is the TV. So often this appliance has become a second parent. In too many households, it is turned on the moment someone gets up or comes home. Yet unlike a mom or a dad, TV never demands anything of your child. It is filled nonstop with changing images, music, and bright colors, but it does not demand your child's full attention.

Even if you do not have the TV on constantly, being exposed to it for a few hours daily—or being exposed to lots of DVDs or CDs, even age-appropriate ones—tends to draw your baby girl's focus away from the voice of a parent or caregiver. Then she will tune out her mom's or dad's messages.

Listening Test

Give your daughter a quick listening test. Ask her to do a simple task such as take off her muddy tennis shoes. If your little girl does whatever small task you asked her to carry out right away, you have managed to instill good listening habits in her. But if you have to ask her more than once and if you have to trot out the one-two-three method of making sure you have been heard, you need to work on that skill with her. It will come in handy throughout her life.

Make a game out of teaching your daughter to listen. While she is in the middle of playing with her dolls or her toy cars, ask her—in a normal tone of voice—to bring you your purse. Then time her to see how long it takes. If she responds quickly, all is well. But if your daughter takes forever to comply, tell her how important it is for her to drop everything and do just what you told her. Count the seconds it takes her, write them down, and on the following day, try the experiment again. The response time should get shorter. Practice with her until she learns to set aside immediately whatever occupies her and to carry out the task you gave her promptly. "Do what Mommy or Daddy says" must be her motto.

Clear Voice

While you are teaching your little girl to listen better and to act at once when you call her, you have to speak clearly, especially when you proceed to tell her to do more than one thing. Observe her as she next gets her coat and your purse. After that ask her to do three things and see how well she listened to your instructions. Can she remember all the little tasks you asked her to perform?

Of course, you must model good listening. When she tells you something, concentrate on her story. Answer her questions, even if she peppers you with them. Even better, alternate the questioning and listening. She can ask you something and you respond carefully. Then you ask her something and expect a complete answer from her—as much as she can give you one. Shrugs are to be avoided. Next, work on having her listen to what someone else says. Take her to story time at the library, and ask her to listen to the narrator carefully. On the way home, ask her what the story was about, and listen to her tell you all sorts of details you might have missed. As a consequence, she will learn to listen better.

Clear Understanding

Your daughter will grow up with the knowledge that you will always listen to her, whatever she has on her mind, if you prove it to her early on. As a result, she will remember that Mom and Dad are the rocks she can depend on to hear her out. But for now, just being able to listen to her parents diminishes many of the troubles a little girl might get into because she will automatically absorb what you have told her not to do and mind you—or not.

Tantrums and Time-Outs

Even if you have made it a point of raising a good listener, there are always a few times when even the best-trained child does not hear her mom or dad. Most often that happens when your little girl had a bad day. Maybe it was filled with all sorts of frustrations. Suddenly she does something she has never done before. She throws a fit—otherwise known as a tantrum. These emotional eruptions can come out of nowhere like lightning out of the blue sky. These outbursts can be frustrating and draining for the parents, but with consistency, determination, and understanding, even the worst tantrums can be overcome.

Tantrums

Tantrums can come on suddenly and seemingly for no apparent reason. But you, the aware and well-prepared parent, will know how to handle the situation. Again, as in most parental quandaries, once you know what a tantrum is and why it occurs, you have practically disarmed it. A tantrum is most often described as an outburst of bad temper. While the origin of this word is unknown, you know exactly where it comes from in your household. Your normally sweet little girl throws herself on the floor, yells for no reason, and bangs her head against the wall.

 **Fact**

Roughly 75 percent of all school instruction is delivered via oral communication. In the workplace most people devote more than one-third of their working hours to face-to-face talking. So even with all the electronic devices we now use to communicate and exchange messages, being able to listen is crucial.

According to Kay Albrecht, executive director of Heartshome Early Learning Center, temper tantrums erupt because the toddler cannot express herself as well as she would like to even though her vocabulary can be quite large at that time, consisting of up to 300 words. What makes parents especially frustrated is that no matter how many times they tell their child to stop, even when they raise their voice, she will not. Later, when they ask their little girl what that was all about, she probably is not able to tell them because she has been on frustration overload. So understand that this is a tough time for your girl and for you, but do not lose your own temper.

Alert!

Never spank a child who has a temper tantrum. First, it does not work because she is unreachable during the tantrum, and second, she will then be encouraged to continue to have a tantrum—but only when you are not present. Use other methods to calm her down.

It is best to ignore a tantrum when it occurs at home. Just steel yourself, go about your work, and ignore the little tantrum thrower. Or you can try to talk to your little girl, and tell her, "I know you're upset because you can't have a Popsicle right now. When you're through being upset, come and sit with me, and we'll discuss it."

But when the tantrum occurs in a public place, ignoring it won't work. Therefore a different method has to be used. If her temper outburst happens while you are shopping at the grocery store or when you are walking in the park together, do the following:

1. Stop whatever you are doing and take your daughter home immediately. You may have to carry her—kicking and screaming—to the car. Do it anyway.
2. When she has calmed down, tell her that she will have to stay home from now on when you go shopping or walking.
3. Then do exactly what you said—leave her at home the next time you head out. That may cause another tantrum, which you calmly ignore.

In a few weeks, try another outing with her. Usually one or two harsh changes of plans will cure the problem, especially if you are watchful and immediately take her home again at the slightest sign of another outburst. Think of a temper tantrum as a weed sprouting in your garden. If it dares to crop up between your prized tomato plants or show roses, you will root it out immediately. Your little daughter has to learn how to act and express herself without causing an uproar, and the sooner the better.

Time-Outs

Many parents prefer using time-outs with toddlers who have tantrums or refuse to listen. The concept of the time-out is that the toddler will stop what she is doing—literally take "time out" from her activity—and have to think about the bad or inappropriate behavior she has just displayed. What is great about time-outs is that they are easily adaptable to any location. All you need is a chair, or a corner, or a sofa. When your daughter has a tantrum, have her sit in the designated time-out spot you have chosen and stay there until you tell her that her time-out is over.

The instigation of the time-out concept is a time to make another paradigm shift. The first shift you made was when your daughter was born, and you went from looking after one—yourself—to looking after two—her and you. Now you need to step back and take charge by combining what is best for her with imbuing in her trust in you as a parent and by trusting yourself.

Some parents recommend a minute of time-out for every year of age. Two or three minutes can seem like a long time for your child to sit by herself and usually has an effect on her. Although it may take a long period for the time-outs to work, your little girl will catch on if this consequence is carried out consistently. A haphazard use of time-outs will achieve nothing, but using the same chair or corner every time and making the time-outs last longer will bring results. When your girl gets older, she can go to her room, but for now when you send her to her room, you or someone else needs to accompany her. Take something to read with you.

Trust Parenting Instincts

During this frustrating phase of raising your girl, you need to trust yourself. You have already come so far in raising this precious human being. Now build on that trust and stay strong. Gone are the early days when your little girl was like an appendage to you. Now she is coming more and more into her own, and it is you who must cut the cord. Take over and stop feeling bad when your little girl gets disagreeable; this is not about you. It is her attempt to learn how to grow up and thrive. With each new skill she masters, she feels productive and proud. Do not stand in her way by denying her new achievements. Allow her to conquer all the challenges of being a toddler. She will make so much progress, with you being loving and firm and expecting the best results in a timely manner. Two more accomplishments are waiting for her now: potty training and switching to a big bed.

Potty Training

Training a little girl to say goodbye to her diapers and to use the potty is much easier than training a little boy. The difference may be due to the fact that boys mature a bit more slowly than girls and are often more active and less compliant. As the parent of a girl, the most important gender-specific potty-training tip to remember to tell your daughter is to wipe from front to back, thereby helping to prevent bacteria from infecting the sensitive skin of the vagina.

 **Essential**

Some people believe that using training pants that the child can pull up can slow the toilet-training process. They feel that the child will feel a bigger sense of accomplishment going right into regular underwear. But others believe these training pants are a necessary midstage to help the child make a gradual switch from diapers to underpants. Always do what feels right for you and your child.

There are many methods for toilet training; some focus on a speedy switchover and some condone making a more gradual switch. But whatever training method you choose, remember that every child is different with a unique personality and rate of development. If you have other children, keep in mind that what worked for one child may not work for another. Therefore, being flexible is the key.

Fact

The American Academy of Pediatrics suggests waiting until two years of age to potty-train a child, but watch your child for signs of readiness (an awareness of needing to go, the motor skills to dress and undress herself, the cognitive ability to understand directions) and interest in potty training. Some children may be ready to train even earlier than at two years, and some may need more time.

When your baby girl learned to crawl, you removed fragile and dangerous objects so she would not break them or bump her head. Now you'll want to remove the Oriental rug or other expensive floor covering, or swathe them with plastic. There will be accidents—count on it!

Next, build some excitement for the process with your daughter. Tell her that her body is smart and knows how to eliminate waste. But just like you put trash in the trashcan, she has to put her body's waste in a special place: the potty. Take your daughter with you to buy the new potty-chair and let her choose which model she prefers. Having a say will create excitement over the potty and make your daughter more interested in using it. You could also get your daughter a book on potty training so she will have an idea of what to expect, or have your daughter watch you or an older sibling use the potty so she can have an understanding of the process.

There are several potty-training methods you can use, but you'll want to use the one that you are most comfortable with. Whatever your decision is, be consistent and know the following steps can help you:

- Explain the functions of her body to your daughter.
- Have her help you with the cleanup when she makes a mess.
- Motivate her to be part of this wonderful new adventure.
- Be consistent. Potty training is a process.

From Crib to Bed

Before you undertake switching your little girl from her crib to a big bed, rehearse in your mind the steps you want to follow. They include knowing what is best for your daughter, making a plan, and sticking to it. Again there is a speedy switchover and a slower method, but once you understand the basic procedure of moving her from a small, enclosed sleeping space that she is comfortable with to one that is new, is larger, and has no restraints, you are getting there.

Getting Ready

Be confident that you can help her make the transition in a time span of about three weeks. So set a date, get the bedroom transformed, and childproof her bedroom. Don't overlook the electrical outlets, drapes, small toys, and any piece of furniture that might topple if she climbs on it. Install a night-light and a safe, sturdy gate. Have your little girl participate in all the exciting preparations and have her practice taking a nap in the big bed with the gate open. Later the gate will be closed, of course.

Alert!

Little girls are good climbers and can figure out many ways to make it across the gate. Praise your daughter for how long she manages to stay in her room. It may only be an hour at first. Each time she shows up in your bedroom during the night, take her back at once.

A good night routine that is soothing and includes reading a story, singing a song, giving plenty of hugs and kisses, and allowing one—repeat, one!—drink of water helps. Tell your little girl how proud of her you are. Tell her that her body needs its rest and that sleeping in a big bed is a sign she is growing up.

Trust your daughter to be able to adjust to her new sleeping arrangements. If she feels that trust from you and that special confidence you have in her, she will not disappoint you. On the contrary, she will run to her room and close the gate herself when she is ready to go to bed because you have made her feel safe and protected and have helped her succeed in what she needs to learn.

Record Her Successes, and Yours Too

Each time your little girl learns a new skill, record her success. You want to take pictures of her, videotape her, fill in facts and dates in her baby book, send e-mails about her progress to family and friends—even plaster the door of your refrigerator with photos of her beaming after her potty training was achieved, and her big bed switch was completed. All these milestones in her life are crucial, and she couldn't have done them without her parents and caregivers being so supportive, loving but firm, and steadfast in their high expectations.

Record your successes as parents as well in your journal or in a log you keep. You know that all the successes your little girl is experiencing are yours as well. But yours go beyond that. It is one thing to be a woman or a man—another thing to be a mother or father. You have made the profound change. So, celebrate in ways that reflect your great accomplishment. You have raised your baby girl into a smart little daughter who is well on her way to becoming a confident, courageous girl with character. That is your special reward. So, revel in the joy.

CHAPTER 3

Your Preschool Daughter

The joy of raising a girl grows constantly because there's so much more she has to learn about the world and so much more you want to teach her. Furthermore, some of the pesky basics you had to instill in her are now history. So if some glitches developed during the process, you can now recoup and fine-tune your skills. The next couple of years in your little girl's life will be a great time to continue with your strong parenting and enjoy seeing her develop more and more.

Developmental Factors

Your little daughter is now four or five years old. What a pleasure it is to watch her bounce out of bed every morning when you tell her it is time to get up. Even if she drags into the kitchen and has to be prodded into saying "good morning," she soon comes fully awake and is ready for another exciting day.

At the preschool age, energy abounds in little girls. They can do so many things and want to show you what those are. You are their audience and it is you they tell what is on their minds. As you are busy setting out the cereal bowls one morning, your little daughter is probably bubbling over about what will happen at preschool today. She is excited about the fact that her teacher will bring in a kitten. As your daughter tells you all about it, you will catch your

breath for a moment because you realize how well she can now speak. You notice that she can:

- Speak fluently and has trouble only with longer words. Once you correct her pronunciation, she will not forget.
- Use correct grammar, except for a making a minor mistake now and then. She knows her full name, address, age, telephone and cell phone numbers, and where her parents work.
- Tell you a long story about the kitten that uses more fantasy than fact and ends with her telling you what she wants for her next birthday—a puppy.

Alert!

Watch how your preschool girl acts first thing in the morning. If she has a hard time waking up every day and seems sleep-deprived, she is. Make sure she goes to bed half an hour earlier from then on. Lack of sleep can cause her not only to be grouchy but also not to thrive as she should and could.

In fact, your little girl is becoming quite the conversationalist. You can almost see her brain working as she switches to yet another topic, using words that amaze you in their complexity.

She can also do so much more now. In her coloring book, she finds a picture of cats and dogs and colors them correctly. She may go outside the lines now and then, but overall she does quite a neat job. She knows all her colors and can draw pictures of many things, including a picture of you with the major body parts in place and even a face that can be recognized.

It's hard to believe, but your daughter will also begin to write. In these beginning stages, she may only copy letters—mainly, the easy ones such as an O or a V—but in no time she will tackle all of them.

Essential

Many preschools offer programs that introduce language, math, and science to preschoolers in a sequential manner by using thematic units to develop the children's skills. While first-grade teachers welcome those early gains in education, it is more important that a child's curiosity is awakened and she gets excited about learning.

When you ask your little girl to put her book aside and help you, she will fly to the task. Pleasing you is tops on her list. She may skip as she gets the paper napkins or spoons, or dance, run, walk on tiptoes, or hop on one foot. When she comes home from preschool, she will dash to her room and emerge with an amazing number of toys. How wonderful it is to see her be able to amuse herself. When she runs out of games to play by herself, she will listen to your suggestions and start on something else with an eagerness that is heartwarming.

While a child's brain grows very quickly during the early years, by age five, it reaches most of its adult weight—nine-tenths of it. Therefore, after age five, the rate of growth of the child's brain slows noticeably.

Her Toys and Hobbies

Does your little daughter have her own library? If she does not, encourage her to set one up. Her love of books is paramount. Reading is the most important of all school skills, and the more you read to her, and she to you—mainly, by retelling to you and embellishing what she remembers you having read to her previously—the more her reading readiness increases. Soon she will start to recognize words that recur and trace them. Her love for letters will extend beyond her tracing them on a sheet of paper or trying to write her name in capital letters. When you drive with her on the highway, she will now point to billboards and greet the large letters on them like long-lost friends.

Besides your daughter's books, tapes, and DVDs, her toy collection will include a variety of items that reflect her special likes and hobbies. She will probably have many dolls and doll furniture, sets of miniature dishes, a little oven, and dress-up items like princess outfits and little high heels and all kinds of baubles and beads. She will use her toys to act out her stories. But she may also have a collection of dinosaurs or fake creepy crawlers and move them around the house to pretend-caves or to a forest made up of stacks of building blocks.

 **Essential**

Many preschool children have a favorite book that they want you to read to them every night, just as they have a favorite blanket or stuffed toy. Try to introduce your daughter to a wider selection of age-appropriate stories by reading something new at the beginning of your nightly ritual and ending up with her most beloved book.

When it is time for her to get a present, allow your daughter to select what she wants at the toy store at the mall, rather than force her to get something you like. In short, approve of the developing interests of your daughter while guiding her toward what you feel is suitable, without stifling her unique personality. She may fall in love with the latest version of the same toys you had at her age, or she may choose the exact opposite. She may be thrilled to hold in her arms the baby doll you played with that Grandma saved, or she may hand it back to you at once.

Educational Programs

Of course, how and where your little girl spends her day will influence some of her toy choices and hobbies. Often what she sees at preschool—or on TV—is something she will clamor for when you are close. Many children advance from a preschool program to regular kindergarten in a public, private, or church setting. You will want to encourage a similar program at home. Quite a few of these programs introduce a child to the use of a computer.

Alert!

Child experts agree that it is more important for a child to learn to play with toys that require more physical involvement beyond just sitting in front of a screen, whether it is a computer or a TV screen. Basic computer skills can be taught in thirty minutes, but too many childhood hours spent glued to a screen can negatively affect kids.

Read carefully the curricula—the listings of instructional goals—of the kindergarten program your daughter attends. Ask for an explanation of the terms you do not understand. These days, many kindergarten teachers speak "educationese" in an attempt to align their programs with first grade. Many of their programs are impressive and barely resemble the kindergarten you remember attending.

Now much more academic pressure has been placed on the early years in a child's education, so that she will be completely ready once she enters first grade. Kindergarten offerings reflect that shift. But once you understand their goals, you can shore up at home what your little girl is introduced to away from home and what she seems to enjoy most.

Fortunately, your daughter is now old enough to tell you what activities she thinks are fun. When you ask her what she would like to do on a free afternoon, most often she will opt for playing with her friends.

Social Interactions

One thing that makes your preschool daughter happy is playing with other children. It may come as something of a surprise to you, but children have to learn how to play. Their earliest playmates may be the daughters and sons of your neighbors or friends, or classmates from preschool or kindergarten. If your daughter has developed a liking for one or two of them, give her a chance to trot out her toys and interact with her cohorts as often as you can arrange it. She is now at an age when she needs to play with other children, so she can learn to share.

Language and Play

Social skills are among the many things children must learn, and if you've ever tried to encourage three- or four-year-olds to share, you know how challenging the process can sometimes be. Children must learn how to get along with others and to gain a sense of what others are feeling and thinking. The process takes time and a great deal of patience and coaching from parents.

 **Fact**

The first kindergarten, meaning "children's garden," was started in the 1830s by Friedrich Froebel (1782–1852). He believed that children have unique needs and capabilities, and he set out to create a system of education based on that belief. Froebel is credited with recognizing the great importance of activities in a child's learning.

Very young children engage is what is called parallel play. That is, they tend to sit together, each playing independently. They are in the same space, and they are playing—but they are not playing together. Eventually, a child will begin to notice other children and to express curiosity about these strange beings. A little girl is likely to explore her new acquaintance by touching or poking him or by grabbing at a toy to see what he will do.

Not surprisingly, social relationships tend to work out better when a child has learned to use her words. It also helps when a child has acquired some emotional skills and can read faces and body language to understand whether to approach a new person. Several studies have noted that girls tend to be more collaborative in their play; they talk and make rules together about how their game will go. Boys often form groups with a leader, and the chosen activity is usually physical.

Your daughter will need time and opportunity to practice her social skills. Be sure you offer her opportunities to be with children her own age. When things go awry (and they inevitably will), don't punish or scold; instead, take time to explore with your daughter what happened, what made it happen, and what she could do to get a better result next time. Parents can help with the development of social skills by coaching children with their friends, rather than intervening.

Learning to Share

Learning to share is important because from birth on, children are self-centered and develop a strong desire to want something. Whenever they see something new, they want it, no matter how many stuffed animals they already possess. Also from about age two on, they see the world in regards to personal ownership. They talk about "my" house (where your family lives), "my" car (the car you drive), and "my" swimming pool (where you take your little girl to splash in the water). To a little girl, her bed and her room and her toys matter—a lot. She sees these items in terms of herself, and the word *mine* crops up often in her conversation.

Little girls do not automatically know how to share, but they can learn quickly if you explain some basic rules to your daughter and her playmates, and use them systematically. Here are some sharing rules many parents use and explain to their children and their little visitors:

- **Do not grab another child's toy unless you get permission first.** Ask every time you come over, and don't assume the permission gotten once lasts for more than one visit.

- **Rather than saying no when someone asks to play with your toys, give him some hope.** Say something like, "You can play with it next," or "In five minutes" (while Mom sets the kitchen timer), or "Sure, if you let me play with your toy."
- **Treat others as you want to be treated.** That goes for their possessions, too. If you break something they own, you must offer to replace it. The same goes for them.
- **Change the rules as the play situations change.** The main thing is to teach respect for other children and treat them as you would like to be treated.

It helps a lot when all parents agree on the "sharing" rules. But even if they do not, you can always inform your little girl's friends that in your house there are rules for playing with each other inside as well as outside. Children have to learn to take turns at the swings and when hitting a ball. But what a wonderful sight it is to see your little girl and three, four, or five other children playing peacefully and imaginatively.

Curiosity and Your Preschooler

During the preschool years, even the best little girl will struggle to comply with adult expectations. There's just too much else going on in her world. You will be far more successful at setting limits, communicating, and getting along with your daughter when you take time to be curious about who she is becoming and what her world is like. Here are some things to ponder:

- **Preschoolers do not experience time in the same way adults do.** Five minutes for you may feel like an hour for your daughter. If you expect patience, you will both be disappointed in the results.
- **Preschoolers are far more interested in the process than the product.** You may want a painting to hang on your refrigerator; your daughter may have found smearing the paint with

her fingers satisfying enough and may never get around to the final product.

- **Preschoolers cannot tell fantasy from reality the way you can.** If it happens on the movie screen or on television, it's "real" and no amount of debate can convince her otherwise. (This fact is a good reason to exercise caution where the media is concerned.)
- **Preschoolers love to ask questions.** While the constant stream of why and how-come can be exhausting, questions are truly how little children learn. Be sure to take time to listen to your daughter.

Developmental psychologist Erik Erikson said there are two stages in children's emotional development during preschool years. At two, they learn autonomy, which is why two-year-olds love the word *no*. At three, they begin to practice initiative, the ability to make and carry out their own plans. Both of these stages create challenges for parents. Remember that it's normal development, and it is not about you.

Curiosity about your daughter's perceptions, her feelings, and her ideas is always a good place to begin as you solve problems and face challenges together. Take time to express curiosity before passing judgment: It will always help you parent your daughter wisely.

Fostering Healthful Habits

In addition to play, there are other healthful habits you want to instill in your daughter. Anything that promotes her physical and mental health falls under this category, including eating right and exercising. These healthful habits can be small changes in what you already teach her, or they can be major. But nothing is wasted on your daughter, especially if you practice what you propose. If she picks up the being-active habit now, she will keep it up in the years to come.

Eating Right

Another healthful habit for your little daughter is eating healthfully. Examine the foods you serve her carefully. Think of the meals you offer her as her physical building blocks. Her body cannot grow strong and "bug"-repellent unless the building material you provide is of top quality.

These basic food guidelines will help to get you started. Examine what your daughter eats with them in mind. The basic guidelines are as follows:

- Fresh fruits are crucial. Make sure that every so often you introduce your little girl to some new choices besides the bananas and apple slices she already eats with gusto.
- Of course, fresh vegetables should be part of her menu as well. Let her select what she wants to add to the salad she eats with her dinner.
- Whole-grain breads are a must, but they don't have to be boring. Vary the format of the breads, even the size of the servings. For example, whole-wheat pancakes made in the shape of a bunny taste better to your little girl than the usual ones.

Again, your daughter's tendency to imitate her parents comes in very handy. If you and your spouse eat a health-conscious diet, your little girl will follow along. So make a game of shopping with her for groceries. Get your daughter involved in meal planning, shopping, and food preparation. Children love to be invited; they usually resist being commanded. When your daughter is old enough, invite her to help you plan meals. You can give your daughter her own short grocery list (use pictures if she cannot read yet) and help her shop. Even toddlers can rinse lettuce, put cheese slices on hamburger buns, and set the table. Your daughter is more likely to eat something she has helped prepare. Have her become savvy at an early age about what is good for her little body and what is not.

Young children and their parents often disagree about eating. Parents tend to like the idea of three meals a day; they want their children to eat healthful food, to eat what is put in front of them without complaining, and to cooperate about snacks and other food choices. Eating is actually much simpler than most parents make it: You should eat when you are hungry and stop when you are full. When parents force children to eat, punish them for avoiding certain foods, provide sugary snacks, or cook meals on demand, they usually interfere with the natural process of eating.

Essential

Your job as a parent is to make good food available; your daughter's job is to eat it. A little junk food won't damage her permanently (you don't need to take away her Halloween candy, for instance), but do limit the amount of fatty, sugary treats available. Instead, provide fruits, vegetables, dairy, and other acceptable snacks.

Of course, you worry about your daughter's eating because you want her to be healthy. It may help you relax to know that children usually eat what they need over time. In other words, your daughter may not eat all of the food groups every day. In fact, she may want to live on macaroni and cheese for days at a time. But if your daughter is active and healthy, she will usually choose to eat what she needs—eventually.

Healthful eating can be a fun experience for kids. Together come up with a list of foods that are good for you and post it where the whole family can see it. You and your daughter can then pull out from the refrigerator the snack items and sandwich fixings you bought together judiciously and pack health-conscious lunches together. You will laugh when she discovers that you're trying to sneak some Oreos into your stash. "Not on the list," she may say, pointing to the posted sheet that both of you developed.

"Cookies once a week are okay," you inform her because they are. Even the most health-oriented household has to make allowances for someone's sweet tooth now and then. It is that friendly give-and-take between your daughter and you, with plenty of laughter added, that will make her feel good about her eating habits.

Teaching Your Daughter Happiness

In addition to encouraging your little girl's development of healthful habits, you want to ensure her attitude is positive. While it is unnatural to be happy every second—after all, there are tragic events in everyone's life at some time—you want to instill in her a deep sense of optimism. Teach her that she may not be able to control what happens at kindergarten or with her friends, but she can control her response to what happens.

"Humor" Your Girl

Your everyday expression will imprint itself on your girl's mind and heart. In this, she is a mirror image of you, so erase your negative look and try your best to smile or laugh. Giggle with your daughter, tell funny stories, and read a book of goofy jokes or riddles together. The various things that make you happy make her happy, too. So, model happiness as often as you can consistently and be sure to include the following important joy components by sharing with her:

1. **An ability to lessen stress.** Having a place for everything helps. Provide her with a bookcase and other storage space for her toys, papers, and favorite must-haves. Not being able to find her "blankie" can make a little girl very stressed. Also teach her to soak in a warm tub, and play with her bath toys while soothing music wafts in from another room.
2. **An ability to listen.** Every afternoon in some countries, there is tea time. In golf, there is tee time. What you want to do is start talk time. Every evening after supper and right before your little girl goes to sleep, ask her about her day, and let her talk about whatever is on her mind. When she is close-mouthed, get her to open up.

3. **Faith.** Your spirituality will be a lodestar for her. So expose her to the religion of your choice, take her to the services with you, let her lift her little voice in prayer or song, and talk to her about the tenets of your belief, making sure her spiritual foundation is strong and solid.

That is how you make your daughter happy and productive. This process will be of great help as you guide her on to the next stage of her development—starting school.

Getting Ready for School

What great excitement is in the air as you introduce your daughter to the most important childhood career there is—being a student. This career may be longer than that of grown-up people. Your daughter may go to school for twelve, sixteen, eighteen, or even twenty or more years, depending on what graduate program, if any, she will eventually choose.

For now, you want her to have the best start to school that is possible. That begins with building her enthusiasm. Tell her about the thrilling time that is ahead for her. Mention the many new things she will learn and the many new children she will meet. Long before school starts, take her on a visit to the school she will attend.

 **Fact**

Children spend seven or eight hours a day at school. After their home, the school building, grounds, and staff are their most important environment. After discounting all the hours children spend sleeping and after adding the time they spend on homework and class projects, it is easy to see how important school is to a child.

You want your little daughter to have a "homey" feeling about her school. So, go by the office and let her meet the secretary, the assistant principal, and the principal. That process can also be accomplished during the school's Open House, but then there will be swarms of parents and kids, and the sheer size of the building can be alarming.

Ease School Anxiety

Depending on your girl's wishes, let her visit her future school complex at a quiet time. Let her walk the halls, count the classroom doors, maybe even go into the cafeteria and peek around. Now that talk time you have put in place will come in especially handy. At your next short session, ask your girl what she wants to know about first grade. Tell her what fun lessons she will experience. The next time you swing by the school, let her lead you. Does she remember where the bathrooms and the library are?

Long before the first bell rings, try to erase whatever little anxious thoughts she has. During the week before school starts, have her meet her new teacher—after e-mailing first to find out what time would be best.

Alert!

Never pop into a classroom unannounced. Always communicate with the teacher before you come to visit. Even though your girl's school may loudly proclaim its open-door policy, no teacher wants to be interrupted during work.

While getting your daughter acclimated to her school before the opening day, review with her listening and sharing skills. Most important, tell her that her teacher is similar to her parent. At home the motto is "do what Mom or Dad tells you." At school, it is "do what the teacher tells you."

Reap School Riches

Just imagine how much this new chapter in your little daughter's life will enrich your household. Every day she will come home excited about having learned some new skill, fact, or idea. Before long, she will inform you about things you have forgotten or never knew. Your child's drive to learn so much will inspire you as well. You may start taking a new class.

According to columnist Joyce Maynard, "It is not only children who grow. Parents do too. As much as we want to see what our children do with their lives, they are watching us to see what we do with ours. I can't tell my children to reach for the sun. All I can do is reach for it, myself."

You are showing your little girl that you are going after your top goal. Every day as you raise her with thoughtfulness, you are indeed reaching your top goal more often—that of being the finest mom or dad you can be.

CHAPTER 4

Rules and Consequences

A family resembles a factory. While the factory turns out inanimate products, a family turns out animate products: children. In both cases, rules are required. They may be numerous or few, written or understood, but any time a group of human beings interacts, order has to prevail. Otherwise, nothing gets done and chaos ensues. You, the parent of a little girl, need a few rules to make your and her days run smoothly. Along with rules, you want some consequences because even the best-behaved little girl can occasionally slip.

Management Styles

In times past, the term *discipline* was a hot topic. It denoted strict, prescribed conduct by a child and a stern taskmaster as her parent or caregiver who saw to it that the demanded conduct was exhibited at all times. Children were treated like little soldiers who had to be drilled into behaving with military precision.

Drill Sergeant?

In the past, parents were the drill sergeants who spanked or delivered other forms of punishment. Words such as *fear* and *penalties* were in vogue in child-rearing circles. Back then, however, not much was understood about the behavior of children. They were mainly seen as miniature adults who needed whipping into shape.

Many child-rearing exercises went terribly wrong, and too many children were disciplined much too harshly. Thankfully, theories on child rearing have changed tremendously during the past decades.

 **Fact**

> One pioneer in early parenting behaviors was the Austrian psychiatrist and educator Rudolf Dreikurs (1897–1972) who moved to the United States to continue his groundbreaking work. He found out that children's actions are based on their need for power, attention, revenge, and avoidance of failure.

Therefore these days, many people prefer to use the expression *child management*. That is a method of raising children that is based on science combined with practicality and tempered with love. But you know you love your girl deeply. Is that not sufficient?

Love Is Important

Love is very important in raising your daughter. But when applied to a child—a young person in the process of growing into what she can become—it lacks structure and direction. Love by itself is an emotion that has no road map. Just one example: Some parents shower their children with a warehouse of toys. Others deny them any frills and criticize them harshly—yet all of them do it in the name of love. In either case, the child may go astray and not reach her great potential because there was little parental thought involved. Indeed, the most exquisite pampering and the most egregious punishing can harm your daughter. So it is not the parents' depth of love for their offspring that is at fault. It is love without a backbone that can get in the way of your girl's proper development.

Love Plus Structure

Love plus control structure means you love your little girl with a special kind of love. Some experts call this empathetic love. In other words, as a parent, you understand the feelings and motives of your daughter but love her so profoundly that you are willing to add some courage and structure into the mix, which will guide her and give her a framework of conduct and a direction. In other words, you love her with a plan in mind.

Model Character

Think of your daughter's future. In the years to come, she has to be able to take the solid behaviors and values you taught her first to school and later to life when you are not with her. You cannot, and do not want to, accompany her forever, so by modeling character you will pass on to her now what builds her character. Start as soon as you can by expecting her to act her best every day.

Alert!

Be sure to have a few rules in place as soon as your little girl is two or three years old. Starting with kindergarten, children like to brag about what they can and cannot do at home. They feel proud when they can recite three or four things their parents will never let them do. Don't inundate your little girl with too many rules, but give her a few important ones to go by.

Having been reared with love and control, your daughter will feel the security of being showered with affection plus being trained to do the right thing, so her future is a bright path. While she may not always be in an environment where she is surrounded by love, she will always be in an environment where her ability to conform to society's rules is crucial. So you want to prepare her for the realities of life. That is what is so great about your parenting: With each stage in your daughter's development, you become more proactive; that is, instead of waiting until a problem occurs, you are prepared for it ahead of time. You know what rules and consequences are the best practices for your girl, and you know that you cannot give her a greater gift than to raise her with rules and consequences in place.

Talking It Over and Apologizing

One main rule to instill in your daughter is to take responsibility for her actions. That begins by teaching her to be able to talk about what happened and then to apologize for her mistakes. This process begins when she is small, when her "oops, sorry" for a glass of spilled water may suffice. As your daughter grows and her sphere of activity widens, she needs to be able to examine her choices and make good ones. When she makes a bad choice, and we all do, she needs to learn to acknowledge her error in judgment and do what she can to "right" the wrong. In most instances, that means to express her regret for her error and mean it. What a great girl-raising moment for you to show her how that is done.

 **Essential**

Always practice what you teach. When you make a mistake—such as forgetting an appointment, burning dinner, or denting your car—explain why you did what you did to your spouse and your daughter, apologize for it, and fix the problem to the best of your ability.

During the discussion, make eye contact with her, crouch down so that you are on the same level with her, and take time to listen to her explain what her reasons were for her conduct. Examine the way you talk to your daughter. Be sure to delete the following types of comments from your vocabulary:

- Sarcastic ones, such as "Aren't you a pretty sight!" when she is dirt-streaked from top to toe.
- Demeaning ones, such as "You're always so clumsy," when she breaks a piece of china.
- Threatening ones, such as "If you do that again, you'll be sorry," when she bursts into laughter at a funeral.
- Over-punishing ones, such as "Go to bed right now and no supper," when all she did was sneeze with flair, without using a tissue.

Also, remember that little girls are the best imitators in the world and that they have excellent ears. So make sure your daughter overhears you whenever you tell Grandma or Granddad about the time she realized she made a faux pas—big or small—and corrected it by apologizing, and then making sure it would not happen again.

Treat your girl in such a way that she knows you are always on her side. That requires patience. Children's memories are not as well developed as ours. Their attention span is shorter, too, and they have such a plethora of new things to learn and digest that they can get overloaded. Verbal reminders should do the trick if you acknowledge your daughter's feelings and deliver the reminders with understanding and love.

Question?

My daughter constantly says she's sorry, even before she does something wrong. What should I do?
Tell her you appreciate her trying so hard, but that "sorry" is not a permission slip to do something wrong. It is like a bandage that is used after an injury. It makes a mistake better but does not undo it.

Taking out a notepad and writing down what you notice about your girl's developing conduct is useful. It signals to her that she is important and that you plan to devise a solution for what went wrong, if anything did. Trust and be confident that you do possess the solutions. This can-do attitude will rub off on your little girl. She will be so proud of your relationship with her. She will feel an ever-strengthening commitment from you to her in requiring her best deportment, and from her to you in showing her best side.

Teaching Delayed Gratification

Many times, visual reminders work better with your girl than verbal ones. They are like cue cards for her and help to keep her on track, and they are also a record of the tremendous progress she is making in learning how to behave. Also just as in a play, these cue cards are frequently needed only at the beginning of the performance, or in your case, the beginning stages of managing your child. You will be out of this important part of your parenting job before long.

Delayed Gratification Tools

It is so much easier for your daughter to learn what you want her to if she can see with her own eyes what it is she needs to absorb and how far she has already come. When trying to instill in her the ability to wait for something, she may need a little help. Often a note with a smiley face tucked into her hand works after she has shown increased patience. Or post a calendar on the refrigerator and have her mark off each day that she gets closer to that beach trip she has been begging for. When she can see the proximity of her desired goal, she can see that her waiting without making a big fuss is paying off.

Patience

Expect some difficulty in teaching your daughter to be patient. No profound new learning can take place without a change in behavior, and that can be hard and is often resisted. Also wanting something "right now!" is as normal for a child as expecting to be fed every time she screams is for a newborn. But not learning that skill early in life will have many negative side effects for your daughter later. She will become a very demanding girl who may go on to demand more and more—now.

Children who have not learned to accept the word *later* often have a more difficult time than others. In school, they will be clamoring for the teacher's attention incessantly, which can affect their progress. Later in life, they may max out their credit cards because they never learned to postpone expensive purchases until they could afford them. They may even engage in adult behaviors long before they are appropriate. But with your friendly guidance, your daughter can learn to increase her level of patience, delay her wishes and wait for something until the time is right.

 **Fact**

The famous psychologist Dr. Haim Ginott started his work as a teacher in his home country, Israel. Later, in the United States, he gained enormous attention with his bestseller *Between Parent and Child*. According to him, children are our enemies and we don't know it, while we are their friends, and they don't know it.

Make sure you make the effort to help your daughter overcome her impatience. As you do, keep in mind that girls have a tendency to rebel not as openly as boys do; they show their aggravation in other ways. Try and provide your daughter with the keys to success by:

1. **Verbalizing her feelings:** "You are angry because you can't have that toy now."
2. **Responding to her irritation without anger:** "I think I understand why."
3. **Teaching her what change is needed:** "Here is a solution."

Your daughter's trust in you and your validation of her feelings plus her certainty that you know how to further her emotional growth will pay great dividends. Every day your gentle but firm manner will add to the solid foundation she is building as she becomes a young woman. Wimpy, wishy-washy, or wrathful parenting styles are not for you because you want to use the best style of parenting. Raising your daughter is not a practice run. It is real and forever.

R-E-S-P-E-C-T

The most basic rule dealing with behavior for your little girl is always to treat others with respect. That means she should show appreciation and consideration for others. If everyone in the world would adhere to that rule, society would run along kinder and gentler lines. But one look at the everyday climate among people makes it evident that mutual respect has fallen by the wayside. The younger generation often treats its members and their elders with disrespect. Yet with a few good lessons you can teach your daughter that respect matters—a lot.

Mutual Respect

The best way you teach your girl to respect others is by treating her and all other people you come in contact with respectfully. It is much easier for her to learn this important character quality if you exhibit it daily as a way of life and expect her to follow suit. Tell her that respect is a two-way street. In order for her to command it, she must show it.

To facilitate the process, lay down a few rules that will encourage her to act with more consideration for others. Explain to her that it is not just the spoken words but also the accompanying imitations and gestures that can convey a lack of respect. In fact, her body language should match her appreciative comments and not disagree with them.

Louder than Words

There are several universal ways little girls can express their disrespectfulness without saying a word. Root them out before they set in and become a habit for her that will be hard to get rid of later and could diminish her future success. The disrespectful actions include rolling her eyes, exaggerated and prolonged sighing, and slamming the door or throwing books or other objects.

One way to exorcise these behaviors at the start is to list them on a note, with the admonition, "Do not," and stick the note on your girl's bathroom mirror as a daily reminder. Even better, use this opportunity to reinforce your lessons for delaying her instant gratification. When your daughter begs for a new pair of expensive jeans, ask her to draw a picture of them. Cut the paper into four pieces and for each week that she manages to show respect, she can tack a piece on a bulletin board. When she has collected all four pieces, take her to the mall.

Use this piecemeal approach only in a positive manner, not as punishment. You want to highlight your daughter's progress, rather than emphasize her shortcomings. Your girl depends on you to find solutions and put them to use, so that she can develop a good attitude and character, not resentment.

Alert!

Don't micromanage your little girl's life. Her facial expressions and gestures are uniquely hers. Don't demand that she suppress her emotions completely, but do caution her about making overly negative gestures in public. Trying to be the center of attention with disapproving hand motions shows selfishness, which you want to discourage.

Another behavior that can become a problem at home, in school, and in life is a tendency to whine. When a car whines, it needs something—a checkup, lubricant, or an overhaul. When a little girl whines, she needs an adjustment as well. Maybe she has learned that her plaintive utterances get big results, but in the long run, whiners are annoying and people avoid them. Therefore, teach your daughter to delete the whining tone from her voice before it becomes permanent and brands her as a child who never grew up. You do not want to retard your precious daughter's growth in any way, be it physical, mental, or emotional, or in her relationships with others.

Developing Good Manners

What a thrill it was for you when you first heard your little girl say thank you, or please, or excuse me. You beamed because you knew you were on the right track. Those basic expressions of common courtesy were fairly easy to instill. Now as she grows older, you want to add to your daughter's well-mannered behavior and make sure she can acquit herself admirably at all occasions: from visiting the playground to having tea at the White House. It is best to instruct her by your example, which makes child rearing so special. You must always make sure that you achieve what you teach your daughter.

Many girls, much more so than boys, are interested in their manners and like to work on them. Often they are fascinated with fine table behaviors and the various utensils and dishes associated with dinner parties. They enjoy watching you set a pretty table and either help you with the task, or arrange your dining-room table in a similar fashion by themselves the next time. Give your daughter plenty of chances to practice her table manners by taking her to a fancy restaurant as soon as you feel she is ready for the test, and always praise her eagerness to learn how to conduct herself properly.

Tea for Three
How quickly your daughter develops in her manners can be observed in her play. Watch her as she pretend-serves a meal to her teddy bear with her toy china. Make sure she invites you to the party now and then. Many established hotels have afternoon teas. Take her to one and enjoy observing her in action. Even better, have her invite some of her friends and serve the "tea"—refreshments that she decides on—at your house one weekend afternoon.

 *Fact*

Miss Manners, whose real name is Judith Martin, is one of America's eminent etiquette authorities. Since 1978, her columns on the importance of good manners and the elements of politeness have appeared in more than 200 newspapers worldwide. In 2005 she was honored with a National Humanities Medal.

Always compliment your daughter on her good behavior even if it does not yet quite measure up. At home, praise the way she arranged the carnations as a centerpiece or how creatively she folded the napkins for supper. Away from home, remark on how pleased you are with her growing confidence in various social situations. Be sure to repeat to her all the comments other adults make about her impeccable manners.

Haute Tips

Society constantly changes while it clings to many old-fashioned modes of behavior. If possible, recall a time when you were unsure of how to act at a dinner or other formal event and mention it to your daughter. Laugh with her over a past dilemma when you did not know whether to bow, curtsey, or run when you were faced with someone eminent. Be glad that each day you have a great opportunity to clue her in to your best social tips and hot hints—things that have taken you decades to learn that you can now pass on to your girl in a few minutes. Think of them as your special heirlooms to hand down to your daughter and maybe someday—through her—to future generations.

Polish and Practice

Working on polishing your daughter's manners, little by little, is rewarding and so much fun—for her and her parents. You have a chance to see your finest work in progress—your little girl—

becoming more poised every day. Her social awkwardness will fade in no time, and she will welcome the opportunity to shine at whatever function she attends. Even if she is not a social butterfly, just knowing that she is prepared for all eventualities will give you peace of mind. Also the process of imbuing good manners in her affords you an opportunity to examine your own manners.

Politeness and Proper Language

People tend to become careless with their manners over the years. They are in a hurry, and politeness and proper language fall by the wayside. They forget to send thank-you notes or snap out a phrase they later regret. Most often this is not because they do not care but because their minds are focused on too many things they just have to get done.

As a parent, however, you want to be in top form as far as behavior is concerned. Your daughter will learn so much by the way she sees you act every waking moment. So by example show her how to be as polite as you can and suppress the tendency to curse. This can be a challenge, but the end result is that you—and your daughter—will be empowered by your solicitude.

An informal survey conducted by several diverse parenting groups in 2004 in North Carolina showed that most kids, when asked, admitted having trouble with the following:

- Interrupting adults
- Introductions
- Avoiding profanity

So tackle these three topics as soon as you can. If your daughter interrupts you while you are having a conversation with another adult or are talking on the phone, designate a signal just for her. Holding up one hand could mean you need five more minutes. Teach her to set the kitchen timer for that period. Then she can learn to wait patiently until the bell goes off.

As for introductions, teach your little girl to step up to the person in question, use a polite form of greeting, say she is glad to meet them, and add, "My name is…" Train her by practicing different scenarios at home and always give her a gentle reminder before she is to meet someone new.

Essential

Check out the many new books your library has on "kid etiquette." It helps when your daughter has a chance to select one that appeals to her. By working with her, you can be sure she will master all the potential sticky situations that may crop up. While society acts as if good manners don't matter, they're more important than ever.

Curse Control

In regard to profanity, help your daughter devise a list of substitute words, such as *darn* and *rats* for the four-letter words that seem so commonplace these days. You may think that rudeness and bad language are like an avalanche, coming at you with no let-up. In fact, you may be appalled by the way you hear young people speak to each other and the cursing on TV, even in programs meant for audiences of all ages.

Be heartened. Just as one falling rock can start a landslide, shoring up a levee can stop a flood. The same is true for coarse language. As much as possible, avoid using it. You do not want your daughter to have less respect for her parents because you cannot control your tongue. In fact, every time you rein in your outbursts of profanity you rise in your daughter's esteem.

Your daughter will be so proud of you for remaining "cool" and polite even during the most trying circumstances. You show her how you keep calm under pressure. Each time you model a civilized manner, you add to your daughter's mastery of conduct, in word and deed. What a jewel in her crown—and yours.

CHAPTER 5

The School Years

Raising a girl means you always have the best years yet ahead because her progress goes from awesome to absolutely amazing, but only if you take advantage of your parenting opportunities. One of those opportunities occurs when your daughter enters school. The progress you have observed her making so far is nothing compared to what you will see as she advances up the ladder from grade one to grade twelve. With you guiding her, she may not only climb up step by step but may skip up the various rungs.

Getting Along with Others

To facilitate your girl's successful journey through her school years, you want to prepare her before she enters first grade. To begin with, teach her how to get along with all kinds of other children who might turn out to be her fellow travelers. That may be a little scary at first because there will be so many new children your daughter will meet. Many of these kids will be from her neighborhood, but some may be from other parts of town. Even in the school cafeteria, she may be assigned to a lunch table alphabetically or be asked to share a book with a child who does not speak her language.

No matter what type of school your daughter attends, she is in for much novelty. But what a real education this will be for your little girl. She will have a chance to meet children with a connection to various other parts of the

United States or to foreign countries without ever leaving home. She will be able to mix and mingle with the offspring of all the wonderful ethnic groups that combine to make our country so great.

Beanbag Travel

So teach your daughter to enjoy the smorgasbord of girls and boys in her class as she sits next to them in the casual reading corner. When she comes home and mentions a girl or boy who is from Pennsylvania, a state different than hers, or from Panama, a country different than hers, look at a map or atlas with her. Show her those places and answer her questions. This is exactly what you want your girl to develop, a curiosity about people and places that interest her.

 *Fact*

A 2006 study by the U.S. Department of Education found that students in public schools perform as well or better than students in private schools in every area of study, except in eighth-grade reading. The study was conducted by the world's largest private educational group, the Educational Testing Service.

Books and Beyond

Think of your daughter's school as a microcosm of the world and of her association with her new classmates as her beginning to understand other people and cultures. This is a great opportunity for her to expand her understanding of the globe. In addition to meeting these youngsters in person, it will be fun for her to:

- Read about children with different backgrounds
- Meet these youngsters in person
- Get an insight into what motivates them

Education goes beyond book learning. It includes learning about real people, places, and things.

Alert!

During the first few weeks of school, watch out for any changes in your daughter. If she develops a sudden dislike for school, investigate the reasons fully. Schools will honor a parent's request for another classroom assignment but only if the reasons are valid. Your pediatrician will be your best ally here.

Besides just noticing the diversity in her classroom, your daughter gets to practice her sharing skills. Remind her to be willing to wait in line, wait her turn, and raise her hand if she wants the teacher to call on her. Getting along with others is especially important in school because an orderly classroom where rapid learning takes place cannot exist without the cooperation of all the children.

Essential

Designate a corner in your kitchen, den, or living room as your daughter's homework zone. Don't send her off to her room to do her homework, at least not during her first few school years. You want to intervene should she get frustrated with an assignment. Also an encouraging word from you may lead to less dawdling. Make homework a family endeavor.

With every successful school day that passes, your daughter will take another sure step on her path to her best school career possible. So remove any early stumbling blocks that might crop up with patience and humor. Share with her some stories about when you first went to school and had to learn everything from scratch. Tell her about some of your elementary school teachers, your early assignments, and favorite books. Do you have any school mementoes to show her? Show and tell is not just an enjoyable classroom activity. It is useful at home too. If possible, drive by your old school and let her take a peek, so that she can see where your drive and striving first sprang into being.

 **Fact**

In today's society, girls are thought to be less advanced in the subjects of math and science compared to boys of the same age. But science in particular has not always been a male domain. In the early nineteenth century, science was considered a "girl's subject." There was a greater percentage of girls' schools offering equally difficult and complicated classes in physics, chemistry, and astronomy than comparable boys' schools.

Girls and School Culture

American schools have a long and varied history. They have their roots in the enormous challenges the settlers faced. During those early years of our country, several unique factors influenced our educational system, including the existing Native American child-rearing practices, the settlers' home cultures, and an emerging sense of nationality.

As our school systems progressed and came into their own, the idea of practicality was most important. It was for that reason that early on, much learning was gained in the school of hard work. Later, as towns and school districts began to emerge, boys in many parts of the new country received a rudimentary education but girls were generally excluded. While this practice changed gradually, most often girls were only admitted to the public schools many years after the boys. This practice had a detrimental effect on girls' scholastic achievements.

Even when school attendance for all children finally became mandatory, girls did not fare as well overall as they should have. They were often channeled into less academically rigorous classes, such as home economics. They were caught up in the enormous bureaucracy that comprises today's public schools, which 90 percent of all American children now attend. Like all huge bureaucracies, schools are slow to change.

Alert!

Any time your daughter's grades drop more than half a letter grade on her report card, for example from an A to a B, you want to find out what the problem is. Don't delay. While all children do not excel in every subject, you want to be alert to any negative pattern in her school progress.

Does Quiet Equal Good?

Even today quite a few schools still show traces of the belief that boys are more deserving of an education than girls. This attitude does not show itself in pupil attendance, which is usually higher among female students than among male students, but it does reveal itself in lowered expectations for many girls. For example, when boys show a disinterest in schoolwork, they are often the subject of emergency meetings by the school faculty. The male students' parents are notified at once and extra lessons are advised.

When girls follow a similar pattern and lose interest in school, they are allowed to slide—just as long as they behave in class. One underlying reason is that our schools are sensitive to the potential of violence, and in boys that potential is often accompanied by dropping grades. In girls with falling grades, the violence potential is less prominent. As of yet, there have been no Columbine-style tragedies instigated by girls.

What works extremely well is your networking with other parents. Join the PTA and other supportive parent groups. As you work within those organizations, you will meet parents with high-achieving girls. Feel free to ask them for their advice. Too often, parents feel they have to reinvent the wheel when all they have to do is connect with other parents who have already successfully shepherded their daughters through a particular school system.

Fact

Underperforming schools exist in many communities. Keep up with the annual achievement scores of your daughter's school, especially the reading scores. If you are not satisfied, ask about alternatives. Some systems allow for a transfer to a high-performing school. Attending the school board meetings and asking questions are civic duties that pay off.

Another option is to join an informal parent group or to start one. Put a note into the PTA newsletter asking all parents of girls to e-mail or otherwise contact you. Brainstorm with the correspondents about methods you can implement to ensure that the culture at your daughter's school changes.

Nix the Negatives

You want the lingering vulture culture in our schools that robs girls of a chance to excel to turn into one that offers a menu of meaningful opportunities for your daughter and all the others. Discuss your concerns with the principal and start a speaker program by inviting outstanding women achievers in your community to come to the school and talk to the girls. Rest assured that any small change you bring about in the school climate can help your daughter.

Teachers as Mentors

It's important to remember that you, as parents, are not working in isolation. You can present a united front that is fortified by your capable coworkers—the staff at your daughter's school—who will do all they can to facilitate your girl's swift and smooth rise to the top of her school experience. Working hand in hand with your daughter's teachers, you become a team that is dedicated to bringing out the best in children, yours among them. What they bring to the table, you supplement, and they complement what you have already instilled in your girl. In fact, your child's teachers can mentor your daughter to such a degree that she will blossom in school and outside.

To kick off the spirit of cooperation between you and your daughter's teacher mentors, you want to know more about what they do, so you can bolster their efforts at home. Teachers have several areas of expertise that dominate their time. Some of the most important areas include:

- Planning and preparing. Teachers spend a great deal of time planning their lessons, organizing the material, and getting ready for students' individual differences.
- Having the appropriate teaching materials at hand and presenting the information in an engaging manner.
- Managing the behavior of their students and dealing with all disruptions.
- Checking homework, giving feedback, and testing for advanced skills and increased knowledge.
- Interacting with other staff members.

Knowing the teachers' main duties, you can readily fill in at home what your daughter might be lacking in her educational background and in-class behavior.

To maximize her teachers' work, make sure your daughter is 100 percent ready for learning every day by:

- Being prepared for each school day with her books and signed notes tucked into her book bag the night before.
- Having the right school supplies with her, and being ready to listen and pay attention in class.
- Being well-behaved in class and causing no unnecessary interruptions in the learning process.
- Always having her homework done and being prepared for all quizzes, tests, and exams.
- Insisting your girl goes by the dress code and looks like a student ready to acquire new knowledge.

Having your daughter and her teachers on the same page can double her gains in achievement, and knowing that her parents care about her education will add an extra boost to her desire to learn. Additionally, her teachers will feel gratified that you understand their tough job and are doing your best to support them. Thus, they will step up and feel more energized in their work. They will accept their mission wholeheartedly and inspire their students, your eager daughter among them.

Essential

Much work in school revolves around note-taking. Work with your daughter on that skill. Even in first grade, she should be able to pick out the main points of a short talk. Tell her about your plans for the upcoming holidays, for example, and see if she can write down a few key items. Never mind her spelling. Praise her for trying.

Why Girls Excel . . . or Fail

Girls, like all youngsters, rise to meet our expectations. When you have high hopes for your daughter, she will know it and have them too. But when you expect less of your daughter, in all likelihood, she will produce less.

Alert!

Do not turn into the proverbial stage parent who hovers in the wings, or in this case, behind the school water cooler for a chance to peek into her daughter's classroom, follow her every move, and break into a loud cheer whenever she spells a word correctly. You want to strengthen her academic growth, not stymie it.

Make sure you tell your daughter every so often that only the sky is the limit for her. Tell her how lucky she is—and you are—to enjoy so many opportunities that were missing in the past. Do not push her, but do nudge and encourage her. Begin early, before her school years start officially. Do not let your girl express a girl-negative attitude without setting her straight. Find extra opportunities for her in her schoolwork and toss out many ideas as springboards. Point out great academic heights, and then watch her climb to the scholastic platform.

Perfectionism Is Overrated

Perfectionism is the process of trying to do the best you can, and still being displeased with the result; it is not a final destination. The word comes from the Latin *perfectus* and means "finished" or "completed," but it does not have to mean "impeccable." That distinction is especially important for girls as they work their way through school. Too many girls latch on to the idea that whatever they do—from a social studies project to a term paper—has to be flawless. Often that quest for perfection preoccupies them to the exclusion of everything else. Or it can paralyze them and keep them from getting started on a school assignment.

Therefore, teach your daughter that perfection in scholastic work is completely overrated. Nothing should ever be "faultless to a fault." Inform her that you expect her to make good grades, but she should not obsess over each tiny percentile. That is why a range of numbers is assigned to each letter grade: for example, A ranges from 93 to 100, B ranges from 85 to 92, and so on. Explain to your daughter that aiming for a grade range is a good thing. Tell her to do all her assignments as well as she can, and then put them out of her mind and go on to the next task.

Question?

My daughter gets so stressed. What can I do to help her?
Help her do a little work each day before the due date of her project, and get her excited about some other activities, such as some of the extracurricular activities at her school. They will provide a good balance for her.

The best way to lessen the importance of perfection for your daughter is to relax your own standards somewhat. This really is a great time to examine your own behavior. Do you worry too much about every tiny detail at work or at home? If so, schedule a session with yourself about your obsession to be perfect—and let your daughter in on the process. Tell her to remind you when you stress out over trifles. As the old Chinese proverb says, "Tell me, I forget. Show me, I remember. Involve me, I understand."

Extracurricular Activities

The extracurricular activities at your daughter's school do so much more than encourage her to participate in a sport or club. They give her a chance to balance her mental training with her physical training. Plus, they give her confidence, increase her circle of friends, and offer her a chance to show some leadership.

Start-up Clubs

While the elementary school years do not provide as many choices in extracurricular activities as the middle and high school years, most schools have some start-up clubs in art, drama, or science. Some schools also provide after-school meetings for students interested in computers or musical instruments, but the choices can be few and far between for first- through fifth-graders.

School Groups

To find out about your daughter's school's after-school activities, ask the office for a list. Read the list carefully and ask if there are some informal clubs or groups not mentioned in the listing. Some schools have a "Library Committee" or a "Guidance Assistants Group" that meets only a few times a year to get student input. In general, see if there is an extracurricular activity at your girl's school that might interest her.

Then follow these steps:

- Speak to the club sponsor or coach to find out what the extra-curricular activity entails.
- Ask your girl to attend at least one meeting before deciding whether she likes it or not.
- Ask the principal of your daughter's school if you can be a cosponsor for a club or start a brand-new one, tailored to your girl's special interests.

Once your daughter attends middle or high school, she will be swamped with school sports options. Then she may have to make some tough choices about which athletic teams she will join or try out for. The offerings of clubs will also be staggering. Some high school handbooks list dozens of available clubs with an amazing array of student involvement possibilities.

Listen Up!

Many girls fear being the center of attention and feel embarrassed because of it. So no matter what other after-school activities you investigate for her, make sure she is involved in a group that demands her stating an opinion and making decisions. Most PTAs have a student auxiliary that kids can join. Encourage your daughter to get involved with that. Whether the group raises funds or works on a school beautification project, your girl can discuss the options on the table, weigh the pros and cons, and make her opinions heard. She will find herself speaking to a group of her peers and to adults and get used to expressing herself in public.

 **Fact**

Many centuries ago, the Greek orator Isocrates came up with a sure-fire method to prepare students to become outstanding orators who could serve in government or other high-ranking positions. He taught classes in rhetoric and politics. By studying extraordinary orations and practicing public speaking, his students were able to become great leaders and have a lasting influence.

With your encouragement, your daughter may run for office in her grade-level class council or later in the student government. Attending meetings and speaking up is a life skill, not just a school skill, and has immeasurable benefits. It will make her feel secure, needed, and honored, and can lead to her becoming a very productive and involved citizen.

CHAPTER 6

Developing Your Girl's Talents

E very girl possesses a multitude of talents. It is your opportunity to explore with her what they are—and there are many avenues available. Many of her talents can be fostered in school. All you have to do is encourage your daughter to show some of her flair and then let whatever school or after-school extracurricular training she gets involved in do the hard work for you. In effect, you were just hired as a talent scout. Your first job is to see what natural abilities your girl has.

Expose Your Daughter to Varied Activities

By exposing your daughter from early childhood to all kinds of activities, you can see if she has an interest in them. It is not just her natural talent that matters; it is also her liking for that talent that is important. For example, some girls may have the build of a long-distance runner—a lean physique and long legs—but if they despise running, they may not follow up on that talent. Therefore, you have to be open to introduce your girl to what you would consider obvious choices for her, as well as to some that are not so obvious.

Some families have a long-standing tradition of producing girls who excel in tennis (athletic talent) or have a gift for painting in oils (artistic talent). If you are part of that type of family, it is only natural that you expect your daughter to show an ability and penchant for those activities as well.

New Traditions

Other families want to break with tradition. Perhaps some members had a less-than-perfect experience trying to follow in their parents' footsteps, as far as their talents were concerned. So they want to strike out in new directions and guide their girls into new territories. What helps in this case is to understand that talent is affected by both nature and nurture. Added to that must be an opportunity to express whatever talent a daughter has. Practical considerations are also involved, such as what your daughter might prefer and what special training is offered in your area that your daughter can benefit from and that you can afford—in terms of time and money.

 **Fact**

The word *talent* comes from the Latin *talentum*, meaning a unit of weight or money. Later the word changed in definition to denote a mental or physical aptitude. Both definitions, however different, agree in one sense. Having "talent" is definitely an asset.

Besides the various athletic or artistic talents you may already have discovered in your daughter, take a closer look at her performance in school where her giftedness may already be evident. In many school systems across the country, talented students are classified according to the following gifted and talented categories:

- **Overall Intellectual Talent:** These children have a large vocabulary and a high IQ. They make excellent grades and are very good in whatever subject they choose.
- **Specific Academic Talent:** These children are talented in one or two subject areas and perform extremely well in them while making only average progress in others.

- **Visual Arts Talent:** These children demonstrate a high potential in drawing, painting, and sculpting, and possess a high degree of creativity.
- **Performing Arts Talent:** These children have an exceptional ability in acting, singing, playing a musical instrument, composing music, and writing lyrics.
- **Creative Talent:** These children show their creative abilities in oral, written, and nonverbal expression and have many original ideas. Their thinking is complex and their imagination is boundless.
- **Leadership Talent:** These children demonstrate an outstanding ability to organize, influence, and lead others. They are often recognized by their peers as goal achievers and have personality traits that attract followers.

As manifested by these talent areas, giftedness is recognized early by our schools.

Gifted and Talented Programs

Does your daughter fit into one of these categories? If so, make sure she is placed into a gifted and talented program—often referred to as G/T education—in her school. If there is not one, maybe you and the other parents of talented girls and boys can get one started. You begin the process by conducting a survey to see if there is a need, besides your own, and presenting your findings to the school board. Keep in mind that, as a general rule, usually 8 to 10 percent of students exhibit some type of remarkable giftedness.

Besides the documented areas of giftedness that may show up in your daughter, other factors can influence her and the emergence of her talents. Some girls have a unique personality that you need to honor.

Best Personality

Your daughter's personality may not be the personality you wished for, if you could, but it is her best personality, so rejoice over it. What personality is exactly has been much debated. However, most experts agree that it consists of a person's traits, habits, and experiences.

Although a child's personality arises out of the interplay of her heredity and environment, it encompasses the following aspects:

- Intelligence
- Temperament
- Motivation
- Emotion

Alert!

Many gifted school programs base their admission criteria on IQ scores. Children from well-to-do families usually have higher-tested IQs, but a child can have a lower-tested IQ and still be gifted and talented in other areas. Be sure to have your daughter placed into an enriching class in her area of talent.

The aspect of intelligence and its various areas of manifestation in school children were discussed earlier. As for temperament, the different natures and responses of children must be taken into consideration. For example, some girls are easily upset over nothing while others shrug off most annoyances, even major ones.

In regard to motivation and emotion, you must consider your daughter's hopes, likes and dislikes, and feelings. Her likes and feelings come into play the older she gets and the more her individual preferences emerge. These preferences may influence how she acts.

The Tomboy or Tough Girl

No matter if you call her a tomboy or a tough girl, there is little that is subtle about her. If your daughter has tomboy tendencies, she makes herself seen and heard from early on. In most people's opinions, she acts more like a boy than a girl. From the moment she gets up, there is commotion since she rarely tiptoes. Usually she jumps over a chair on her way into any room. She prefers to play with a ball or a toy dump truck rather than with dolls. But if you insist on giving her a doll, she rigs up a catapult out of twigs and rubber bands, and sends her shooting through the yard.

 **Fact**

In medieval physiology, the four main fluids of the body—blood, phlegm, choler, and bile—were thought to determine character and disposition. Therefore, people were classified accordingly into choleric (bad-tempered), melancholic (depressed), sanguine (cheerful), and phlegmatic (sluggish) types of human beings.

Wilted Blossom

You should accept her with open arms and make sure her teachers do too. You tell her she makes you happy just the way she is. But watch out. If she has brothers, she may engage in rough-and-tumble play with them; not being as big and strong as they are, she may get hurt more quickly. Or she may best them in various kinds of physical contests, so be prepared for her brothers' expressions of dismay.

As far as your tomboy's appearance, she may get just as dirty as boys, or more so, and revel in the process. Often a tomboy prefers wearing blue jeans and T-shirts to skirts and dresses, which can be a benefit. Buy her the clothes she wants. They are usually easier to take care of than girly outfits, may be less costly, and last longer.

Essential

No matter how tomboyish your daughter is, instill in her the appropriateness of dress. Depending on the occasion, she should always wear a suitable outfit. That does not necessarily mean a skirt and blouse or a dress, but can be a dressy pants ensemble.

Many parents agree on a compromise when it comes to the clothing of a tomboy. They have an every-other-day rule in place. That means on some days they choose their daughter's attire. On others, she is free to wear her favorite sweatshirt and ripped jeans. For her birthday or holiday gifts, asks her what she wants. Whether it is overalls or a toolbox filled with the latest tools, fulfill her heart's desire.

Alert!

Be alert to the fact that tomboys can get teased not only by girls but also by boys. Teach her a few handy come-back phrases, such as, in regard to her outfits, "It's the latest style," or in regards to her rough playing, "I'm into acrobatics" or "Don't you wish you could be like me?"

Many tomboys go through developmental stages that may include:

- A slow but steady increased liking for activities, clothing, and behaviors usually associated with boys.
- A peak period when she may wear her hair in a boyish style, prefer to play only with boys, and insist on being called by a unisex form of her name, such as Alex for Alexandra or Sam for Samantha.

- A switchback to more middle-of-the road behaviors such as acting like a traditional girl some times and like a boy at other times.

Not all tomboys go through stages. Some tough girls stay the way they developed from early on and grow into confident, independent-thinking, success-oriented young women. As adults, former tomboys can be much in demand because they are usually strong-willed, are high achievers, and can do so many useful things from changing the oil in a car to installing a new sink, thereby saving money and time. Most of all, they are empowered in all situations. Wow—what an asset.

The Ballerina or Skater

One of the best things you can do for your daughter is to help her discover what is deep inside her and to encourage her to grow into what she is meant to be. Remember the words of Oscar Levant: "It's not what you are, but what you don't become that hurts." Therefore, you will never know what your daughter could become unless you validate her early wishes and accompany her as she tries to follow the path of her innermost passions. In the case of a girl who is drawn to being a ballerina or skater, you are fortunate. You simply supply what she needs and watch her advance.

 **Fact**

More than three centuries ago, the French courts started a formal ballet tradition, which prompted Louis XIV (1643–1715), who was a great dancer himself, to establish the first Academie Royale de Danse in 1661.

Turns and Axels

There are so many ways in which you can foster your girl's interest in dance steps or skates, whether they're meant for an ice rink or a skate park. Classes abound in ballet, jazz, rhythm, tap, modern dance, and all forms of skating. The great thing about getting your girl involved in these activities is that they increase her flexibility, poise, and gracefulness. Her body, and her self-confidence, benefit greatly as well. Another plus is that these activities are available in many locations in your community. Thus, if your daughter enjoys them, check out the many dance schools and sports complexes in your area. Then allow her to take a trial class.

Alert!

Do not insist that your daughter continue to take dance or skating lessons if she loses interest. Children change their minds about what they like many times, so it is always best not to pay for a program far in advance. Go with a week-to-week payment plan and have another activity in mind that you can introduce.

Costumes for dancing and skating can cost huge amounts, not including the fees required for the various lessons. No matter how determined your girl seems in wanting to be a great dancer or skater, start slowly. Often after-school programs offer introductory movement classes. In middle school, dance may be offered as a subject, and she can try her skating flair at a public ice rink before getting too deeply involved. Always leave the door open for your daughter to develop an interest in something entirely new. So much has to do with the development of her body and spirit. Growth in a girl's talents is rarely straightforward. It may involve side paths to other interests. But that is what makes parenting so fascinating. It broadens you just as your daughter broadens her interests. She may decide that dancing and skating are not for her. Instead, she may suddenly want to take up tae kwon do or some other sport.

The Athlete or Outdoor Girl

If your girl has some or a lot of athletic ability, you are again fortunate because there so many opportunities for her to practice what she likes. Whether it is tae kwon do, soccer, or lacrosse, you should be glad your girl can find something she is passionate about.

What heightens your joy is that most athletic programs at school offer such a variety of choices that your girl can always discover something that piques her interest. Since the sport training is school-sponsored, you do not have to worry about her coaches not being qualified. Besides, you, the parent, will most likely be "volunteered" by your daughter as a chaperone for whatever meets or events are scheduled away from school. Or maybe you will be asked to provide the transportation.

 *Essential*

If you home-school your girl, ask the public schools if she can participate in an organized sport with children her age. The camaraderie with the other kids plus the social skills she can pick up by being with her peers an hour or two in the afternoons can make her home-schooling experience much fuller.

The best way to motivate your athletic girl is by taking her to places where kids participate in sports. Besides the usual sports venues in the schools, most communities have YMCAs that offer a large menu of activities that fall under leisure (for fun) or enrichment (more advanced skills) categories. Girls are divided into groups based on age, grade level, and interests and abilities. For very little money, they can find out if they have any interest at all in basketball, volleyball, softball, field hockey, and other team sports.

Individual sports such as diving may also be offered, in addition to swimming. Your daughter can have a whole array of athletic pursuits to explore before she decides on cross-country running or downhill skiing, since she likes being outdoors.

As long as she enjoys her choice of sports and is not overcommitted, you can relax; not that there will be much free time for you to do so. Parents of budding female athletes frequently have to make sacrifices. When the tryouts for the various teams are over and your girl has been chosen, her schedule may change, as may yours.

Sports Take Commitment

Before your daughter decides to pursue an indoor or outdoor sport wholeheartedly, explain to her the time commitment it may take to become her best. Not only does it require hours and hours of training, but every athletic endeavor has the potential of injury. Some of these injuries can have lifelong consequences. Also there is no guarantee that even the longest, hardest, and most painful training program will result in her winning major recognition in that sport. Tell her that she should pursue athletics because sports will help:

- Energize her, increase her fitness, and make her healthier.
- Release stress and fuel her passion.
- Make use of her special talents that should not be wasted.

Your girl should not only go after athletics because she wants an Olympic gold medal. If she has decided to play on a school or community team, her daily routine will definitely change. She will have longer hours than her classmates, and her athletic obligations will become the centerpiece of your family life. You will feel the pride well up in you even as you realize that your free time has shrunk to almost zero.

No matter how "free" being on the school's track team, for instance, is supposed to be for your daughter, there are always hidden costs, such as team pictures, special camps, and extra food for your girl and her teammates who drop in to celebrate a victory at your house. You welcome them, glad your daughter has found an arena in which to showcase her extra abilities, but you will see your cash reserves take a hit.

Many parents go beyond spending money that is not allocated in the budget. They move to a school district where a top-notch coach works. They free up weekends for practice at a special sports facility and take their vacations around national sports events their girl wants to see. They give their best effort to encouraging their daughter in whatever athletic interest she develops. As a result, their daughter flourishes.

 **Fact**

Michelle Wie, born in 1989 in Honolulu, is a well-known American golf phenomenon and one of the world's best young players. She started playing at age four, routinely practices four hours a day, and seven on the weekend. So far, she has had a record-breaking career, surpassing all expectations.

The Artist or Crafts Enthusiast

Not every girl likes chasing after a ball or cycling her heart out. Many enjoy various forms of arts or crafts activities. They may be content to sit in the den and doodle, sketch, or write. Or they fashion objects out of Play-Doh, or stitch together a new outfit for their stuffed toys. Their hobby occupies them and brings them joy. Girls with this wonderful ability to entertain themselves are easy to satisfy. Paper and crayons are easy to come by. Modeling clay and cloth remnants cost almost nothing. All you need to do is give your young artist or crafts enthusiast a corner in your house as a hobby station, and she is in business.

She's Got Talent

Art as a subject is taught in most schools, often from the middle grades on up. Some schools also hold monthly art exhibits. Others schedule performances where your artistic daughter can read her poetry or show off her blossoming acting talent or the props she painted for the drama club. If your girl's school is underfunded in the art department, check out the art center in your community. Research the best after-school programs for your creative daughter and her interests. The wonderful thing about having a daughter who is talented in arts and crafts is that she is never bored.

Very Crafty

Your arts and crafts–oriented girl can always find something enjoyable and useful to do. Just giving her a box of buttons, pieces of different colored ribbons, construction paper, and glue can get her started. Before long she will be able to:

- Design and print greeting cards for the family.
- Update her old T-shirts with velvet cutouts and sparkles.
- Dash off a short story and illustrate it for the kindergarten class in her school.

To know that you are raising such a productive and self-sufficient girl who has a wealth of creative talent is a special joy.

Private Lessons

As mentioned earlier, talent—in order to come to fruition—needs opportunity. Your job as a parent is to provide that. Give your girl a chance to explore her gifts to the fullest, whatever they may be. You can do that by investigating what the school system offers. Next, check the various community programs and low-fee associations. After that, contact the closest university. Graduate students can always use extra money and may turn out to be excellent private teachers or coaches.

You want to turn to professionals only after exhausting all other possibilities. Hiring a professional coach or performing artist to instruct your daughter in the area of her unique talent can be expensive.

Alert!

Before signing up for private lessons, get recommendations from other parents. Also let your daughter spend some time with the professional to find out if their personalities mesh. You don't want her to stop playing the violin because her new teacher is overly critical or just not good with children.

Sometimes all it takes is one meeting with a retired professional dancer, actor, athlete, or coach to find out just how much creative or athletic promise your daughter has. In conversation with the former Broadway star or world-class athlete, your girl will reveal to what extent she is willing to devote herself to the development of her talent.

Winding Road

Think of the talent exploration in your girl as a journey that is usually not on a straight path. Nevertheless, walk confidently down that path with her. See if your daughter has the fire in her that it takes to advance her talent, or if this is just a hobby. Keep in mind that even hobbies should never be discounted. A hobby may become a lifelong pursuit or lead to a rewarding career. A commitment to a sport or creative bent may also have long-range implications. It may develop into an overriding passion that will continue in high school and college and end up as a life-changing endeavor. Each child is different, and girls especially vary tremendously in their choices of activities and options.

CHAPTER 7

Girls at Home

I n order for your daughter to become a responsible citizen now and later, you need to start training. From the time she is two or three years old, have her do small but meaningful chores. She can pick up her toys and put them away, take fresh towels to the bathroom, or put some groceries on low pantry shelves. The older she gets, the more she can contribute to your family by doing more tasks, and the more she contributes to her home and family, the better citizen she becomes.

Responsibility to Home and Family

To make your daughter a responsible citizen, make her a full participant not only by allowing her to share in the privileges of your home and family but also by allowing her to share in the duties that running your household requires. Only by being denied neither the pleasures nor the pains that come with the daily management of your hearth and home can she develop fully in her capacity to pitch in when needed.

Increase Her Responsibility

If you do not allow your girl to contribute to the making and keeping of your home, she will feel useless. If she is expected only to consume food and clean laundry without helping out in the preparing or supplying of either, she will feel left out of the joys of being productive.

Her sense of nonproductivity will negatively impact her. Why strive to become more responsible when there is no growth expected?

Easy Workout

Besides, after a long day at school where your girl's mind gets a workout, her body needs a workout too. Watching TV or playing video games for hours leads to a couch-potato mentality and lazy lifestyle, which you do not want for your girl. Her body requires frequent periods of movement every day or the calories pile on. These days, preteen and teenage girls tend to be heavier than in the past, so getting her moving is key.

 **Fact**

A 2005 study by the Kaiser Family Foundation found that third-graders through twelfth-graders spend—on the average—almost six and a half hours per day watching TV and videos, listening to music, playing video games, and using the computer.

Of course, some downtime is necessary for your growing girl but doing routine household chores can be an activity that combines work and fun. Your daughter can dispatch her housekeeping tasks while listening to the radio, for example. Or she can plug in her headset and listen to her music, humming along as she loads or empties the dishwasher. Allow her to organize her list of to-dos any way she wants to, just as long as she completes her jobs.

A special plus in assigning chores from the time she is little is that it lessens the burden on you. If you do all the work at home without anyone helping you, you become resentful. Parents who are martyrs may think they are saintly when in reality they fall short of what parenting should be: raising a child who is encouraged to do his or her best, not only at school but also at home. You want your girl to help out and do her part.

Helping with Household Chores

By being expected to do her share around the house, your daughter will blossom. She will feel needed and look forward to getting busy. So help your daughter to become responsible and productive at home.

Be sure to assign some daily chores to her from early on, such as making her bed, hanging up her clothes, and folding and putting away her laundry.

The older your daughter gets, the more she should be expected to do around the home and yard. By the time she is six or seven, she can help prepare meals, mop the floors, dust and vacuum, and sweep walkways and help collect leaves.

By age ten or eleven, there will be few household chores your girl cannot accomplish, or at least assist you with. As time passes, it may turn out that she can bake better fudge brownies than you ever dreamed of or scrub a tub more efficiently than you can. Praise her for her contribution to the household and enthusiastic tackling of her chores.

Alert!

Do not burden your daughter by making her do all the housework. Girls who feel as if they are "the maid" resent that role and either do a sloppy job, come to hate housework, or develop a desire to "escape" from your house as soon as possible, or all three.

Do not get irritated if your daughter does not do all her chores perfectly to start with, or if she needs reminding. Be patient in teaching her how to fold sheets and towels and how to clean a mirror without streaks. Once a week discuss what needs to be changed in the chore schedule. Maybe you and your daughter can switch, or alternate, tasks neither of you likes, or delegate the toilet detail to whoever picks the shortest straw.

Essential

Be sure both parents have household chores on a regular basis. You don't want your girl to grow up thinking that doing housework is exclusively a woman's job. The same goes for other tasks around the home and yard, such as gardening or washing the car.

Tackling the care and management your home needs as a team consisting of you and your daughter may turn into a good time for all of you. A pleasant routine can develop that makes order out of chaos and keeps the dirt and grime under control as much as possible. When your daughter leaves for college, she will thank you for having taught her the household basics, from simple meal-preparation to cleaning and doing laundry.

If you are in the habit of giving your house an annual or biannual cleaning, be sure to involve your daughter. What a great feeling to have your home sparkling and fresh-smelling, even if just for one day. The feeling of accomplishment for both of you will be heightened if you treat her and yourself to something special afterward. It is much fun planning beforehand what that special something will be. By teaching your daughter to help you take care of the house, she will learn to develop that same appreciative attitude in regard to her own possessions.

Taking Care of Her Belongings

Your daughter's belongings and her room matter a lot to her, so encourage her to take good care of them. Teach her how to hang up her clothes, store her shoes and purses, organize her dresser drawers so she can quickly locate what she needs, and designate a place for her toys, games, books, and keepsakes. Show your daughter how you stay organized and pass on your best tips.

Make Organizing Fun

Many girls want to keep everything, from the tests they made a 100 on to the ticket stub of a movie they saw and loved, to a snapshot of themselves and their best friends. Teaching your daughter how to sort through all the piles of papers, programs, and pictures she stacks on her desk every week will help her to toss some of them and treasure others even more.

 **Fact**

Scrapbook-making kits for kids are available in many bookstores, and many of them are suitable for kindergarten age and up. They contain everything your girl needs for this useful organizing process. The numerous appropriate stencils, stickers, and design ideas in the kits can be a starting point for her as she learns to deal with the avalanche of papers and pictures in her life.

The easiest filing system to buy for your daughter is some attractive boxes in which she can place the items she wants to keep. She can trim the boxes, embellish them with markers, and decoupage them. There she can also keep swatches of her favorite but outgrown pajamas or T-shirts, newspaper clippings and cartoons that interested her, and postcards from her traveling aunts.

Room Makeovers

Another way to get your daughter more interested in looking after her stuff is to let her fix up her room. Getting your girl excited about decorating her room has many advantages. She can scout through some magazines for ideas, and then roll up her sleeves and get started. She may settle on just changing the paper she uses to line her dresser drawers, or she may ask for new sheets and a new bedspread. Or she may get very ambitious and paint her bedroom furniture, if the pieces are worn but not antiques. She may redo one wall or apply a border to it, or with your help, paint a favorite motif all over the room.

It will be fun for both of you to visit a home-improvement or department store and amble up and down the aisles to see what she is drawn to, and what you can steer her toward that makes sense in terms of suitability and price. Even if you do not like all the ruffles and valances she may opt for, appreciate the fact that she is experimenting with her decorating ideas and skills. How can she learn to look after her room and belongings if she is not allowed to feel ownership of them, which may include making a mistake now and then?

Mine by Design

One disadvantage of letting your daughter have a lot of freedom in redoing her home space may be all the pinks and purples, floral and heart designs she is crazy about. Or worse—she may crave animal prints to plaster her room with or hang collages of "teen hunks" torn from movie magazines from her ceiling. As long as her decorating scheme is not offensive, let her go ahead and express herself. It is her room after all, so withhold any comments unless she asks for them.

Instead, help her with installing the new shelves or show her how to make her own picture frames. Every few months assist her with sorting through her clothes and tossing what she has outgrown. If she tends to misplace things, teach her to label certain segments in her closet, or sections of drawers or shelves, and then put her items where they belong.

Pizza Party

Once a week, schedule a clutter-freeing night when you and she make it a point to wade through everything that has accumulated in the nooks and crannies of your home. Combine it with thirty minutes of speed-cleaning, then go out for pizza—all of you, and enjoy staying on top of your never-ending housework. This workload increases even more when a new member—one belonging to the animal king-dom—joins your family.

Girls and Their Pets

Another great way for your daughter to learn responsibility is to allow her to have a pet. Since puppies, kittens, and little girls seem to go together almost naturally, do not be surprised if before long, your daughter wants a pet. Besides teaching her to be accountable, a pet teaches her something far more important: love. Your daughter's ability to love begins with your love, which she returns in huge measure. She may also love some close relatives and her stuffed-animal collection, but loving and caring for a pet is different.

Alert!

Do not let your daughter have a pet that is "cute" only when it is small but not when it is grown. Always consider your living arrangements before buying a pet, ask for the advice of pet-store staff, and read up on all the needs of the pet you are considering beforehand.

Having a pet and looking after it may turn out to be a forerunner of your girl's loving relationship with another human being when she is grown. In fact, each time she is allowed to experience a different type of love, she will increase her capacity to become a loving young woman. So try to accommodate her if you can by letting her have a puppy or a kitten, but only if she is old enough to handle the responsibilities. How can you know that?

- Take her to a pet store and let her hold a kitten or puppy to see how she reacts.

- Take her to an animal shelter to check out what animals are in need of adoption and have an attendant explain to her what is involved in owning a pet.
- Let her look after a neighbor's pet for a few days to see how mature she is in taking over the care of a living thing.

If you decide to go ahead with the pet project, be sure to pet-proof your house first. Buy slipcovers for the sofa and chairs, inexpensive sheets for the bed the pet may jump on, and establish a schedule for your daughter to feed (and walk) the new arrival in your home regularly. Sometimes brightly colored fish in an aquarium will suffice, or a hamster in a cage, even a hermit crab, if not as a final pet for your girl, then at least as a first one. But if at all possible, honor your girl's wishes when it comes to a pet, because although there are trial pets, there are no trial children. You only have a few fleeting years to teach her how to love something and to treat her the best way you can.

Relating to Siblings

When there are other children in the family, your little daughter may fit right in, depending on the circumstances. Some families incorporate a new little girl as a matter of course. Other families have to go through a process of shifting and changing until the roles of each member are redefined to everyone's liking.

 **Question?**

My two sons and my daughter are arguing every day. What do I do?

Tell them you love all three of them best and expect no more arguing. The first time they start arguing again, put all three in time-out, no matter who started it. Your kids need to learn how to get along.

If your daughter is the oldest child in your brood, she may be a great help to you as the younger children come along. Having a well-trained, obedient girl as the eldest offspring can acclimate the rest of the children to a smooth-running household. Her example often rubs off automatically on the younger kids. In effect, once you have your oldest child on the same page with you, the rest of the siblings will follow suit.

Parenting Checkup

If you find constant squabbles arising among your children, look at how they interact objectively and see where the conflicts originate. It is always better to eradicate problems before they become ingrained. Also scan your parenting style for any counterproductive tendencies that might have crept in. You want to stick to what works: being firm and flexible in dealing with your children, playing no favorites, and training all of them to become productive and responsible adults.

Responsibilities

Abigail Van Buren said, "If you want children to keep their feet on the ground, put some responsibility on their shoulders." Be sure to have plenty of organized time to discuss what is going well with your household, what needs to be improved, and what needs to be made fairer in regard to home duties. Let all the kids have a say, not just the older ones. Have a family bulletin board with a list of chores for your children, your daughter included.

To Pay or Not to Pay

Many experts say that paying a girl for her chores amounts to "bribing" her. She should be encouraged to pitch in with what needs to get done without getting an allowance. Parents do not get an allowance for running the household, so why should children? Other experts say you should teach children the value of money from early on and giving them an allowance and tying it to their chores is the only way to go.

The best way may be a compromise. For the routine making of beds and keeping her room straight, no money needs to change hands. For other chores, you could give an allowance. That means you have to stay on top of what she does and check up on her chores. Then once a week—for instance, on Saturday morning—have a "pay day." If she completes her work, she gets the full amount of her allowance; if not, no allowance.

Essential

You might consider giving your girl one dollar a week for each year of her age, as many parents do these days. Each birthday she automatically gets a raise and has something to look forward to as she gets older.

This system of household management equates children with employees. Very few employees do a good job without getting paid. Very few students would study for a test if there were no grading system and report cards. So just as in school students do some things routinely—such as lining up, attending class, and remaining quiet unless told to speak up—children should have a few basic chores as a matter of course. For bigger chores, an allowance tie-in can work very well (more about your daughter and money matters in the next section).

However you handle the chore challenges at your house, the decision is yours, as long as you make sure your daughter has a few jobs around the house.

Learning to Handle Money

What a thrill it is to teach your girl all you know about handling money, and more. This is such a gratifying process with nothing but huge advantages. There are no downsides. Even if your daughter learns only a small part of money management at a time, each tiny bit she absorbs will bring her interest—not just in her financial skill level but also in cash. In fact, every hint you pass on to her now can save her thousands of dollars in the future, and you as well—right now.

Cash Know-How

While you are teaching your girl the "common-cents" basics, you get a chance to review your own money management. This is an intergenerational lesson you can both benefit from enormously. Start as soon as you can to discuss money matters with her.

 **Fact**

In a 2004 survey conducted by Visa USA, only about a third of all girls ages thirteen to seventeen were able to define six common financial terms such as interest, IRA (Individual Retirement Account), and APR (Annual Percentage Rate), but girls who frequently discussed money issues with their parents scored much higher.

Involve your daughter in financial dealings as soon as you begin giving her an allowance. Teach her how to budget her money. Fill her in—in a general way—on your budget. Show her the monthly bills that come in. Discuss the price of hamburgers, movies, and gasoline with her. Let her make some informed choices at the grocery store—generic foods versus brand foods. Is it better to buy two more expensive muffins advertised "for the price of one," or cheaper ones, priced individually? Also teach her that usually you get what you pay for. Sometimes things are more expensive for a good reason.

Cash Inflow

Teaching your girl about money is easy because she can see it, hold it in her hands, go to a bank with you, and watch the transactions there. Show her your paycheck, if you can, and how you handle depositing it into your account. This is a concrete lesson with many levels of knowledge. Have your daughter follow the trail of your money and see how much is left after your expenses have been met and what you do with the leftover amount. Tell her savings are wonderful, and have her deposit some of her allowance in her own savings account. Some parents ask their daughters to keep a money journal in which the girls record what they spend their allowance on. Other parents match their daughter's savings—dollar for dollar. Do what works best for you.

Money Growth

Tell your daughter a little—or a lot—about investments and growing money. The daily paper offers opportunities to study financial trends in its business or advertisement sections, and runs articles by financial planners to advise parents on saving money for college. Should your girl want to get into the stock market, tell her to use only money she can afford to play with—not her regular allowance. So what money can she use? Well, help her to develop an entrepreneurial spirit. If she sees a job around the house—or at her grandparents' home or in the neighborhood—have her "bid" on it. Let her come up with the job and let her work out the details. Then she can use her extra money to try her hand in the stock market—one share at a time.

 *Essential*

Close to two-thirds of a group of girls interviewed by Visa USA recently said they would like to know more about personal finances. Only about 40 percent of them said they had discussed family finances with their parents, and only 13 percent had ever written a budget for themselves.

Make discussing money a hot topic with your girl. If possible, take her to a mint or a coin collector, and show her old silver dollars and buffalo nickels. Let her see some Civil War money and give her a few euros. Talk to her about some of the more unusual forms of currency—which comes from the Latin *currentia* and means "a flowing"—such as a farthing, a former British coin worth one-fourth of a penny. How would she like to have her allowance in farthings? Then, depending on your daughter's age, be sure to move on to discussing the advantages and disadvantages of the following items with her:

- **Personal checking account.** Help her set up her own account at your bank, help her balance her checkbook, and keep up with her statements.
- **ATM card.** Many girls prefer using the automatic teller machine to get quick cash out of their accounts. Warn her to use hers only at a supervised location and during daylight hours.
- **Debit card.** Although a debit card limits her to the cash she has in her account and she cannot overspend easily, she does not need one until she goes to college but should understand what it is.
- **Credit card.** This is an expensive way to delay paying for her purchases, but it can help build a good credit record for her, has more protection, and is safer than a debit card.

Even if your girl gets a scholarship or a great financial aid package, and earns her own cash during her summers, she needs fiscal advice long before she leaves your home. The sooner you talk with her about every possible money issue that might come up, the better. Warn your daughter about the dangers of losing her checkbook or credit card. Teach her this motto: "If you can't pay it off at the end of the month, don't buy it."

Make mulling over money a lot of fun for your girl. Teach her to be careful with every hard-earned buck, to bank her birthday checks, and to be miserly with her balance—to a healthy extent. Take her on a visit to Wall Street. Tell her that at the moment men dominate the world of corporate finance, but not for much longer with smart girls like yours coming up through the ranks.

Help your daughter to secure an internship at a financial institution—maybe a lending business or a mortgage company. Officially welcome her to the high-pressure atmosphere where hushed tones and hundreds of thousands—no millions!—of dollars rule.

Alert!

Jane Bryant Quinn, the money expert who writes a column for *Newsweek*, advises against using debit cards on the Web for any group, not just girls. Since the payment comes directly from the person's bank account, using a debit card can in fact open an account on the Internet and could give access to it to cyber crooks.

Learning to Share and Care

You want your daughter to realize that not everyone is as lucky as she is. Even if she lives in modest surroundings and money is not in abundance, she has you—parents who do their utmost to raise her right. So she is rich, no matter what your bank balance might indicate. Unfortunately, many other children do not have that. Therefore, talk to your girl about her many blessings and help her feel grateful for all she has. This feeling of gratitude may translate into her being willing to open her eyes to other people who are less fortunate.

Whenever your daughter mentions someone who has experienced a misfortune—when she sees on the news a family without insurance whose house burned down or notices a picture in the paper of a girl whose school was destroyed in a war zone—let your daughter express her feelings of compassion.

Ask her the following questions, or similar ones, to explore her developing sense of sympathy:

• What do you think about those people?
• Can you imagine what is going through their minds?
• Would you like to do something to help them?

By focusing on the lives of other people, she will learn to become less selfish, and by acting on her unselfishness, she will learn to do some good for other human beings. Also, she will join the ranks of many other kids these days who from early on support people in their neighborhoods who are down on their luck, classmates whose families experience sudden hardships, or homeless people living in their communities.

 **Essential**

While parents are the main source of advice about money management for their teenagers, 50 percent of girls say they received most advice from their mothers, and only 27 percent say they received most advice from their fathers, according to a Harris Poll.

Giving Lessons

One good way to teach your daughter to share and care is to give her an allowance. Having a little money gives your girl something tangible to share—the fruits of her work around the house and yard. After she receives her weekly amount, she can hold the quarters or dollar bills in her hands and decide to contribute part of it to a worthy cause of her choice.

One rule many parents swear by is the "thirds" rule, which encourages your daughter to make sharing a part of her life. It states that one-third of her allowance goes into her savings account, another third is hers to spend as she wants to, and the last third goes to benefit other people in the form of a contribution to a charity she selects.

A Kind Heart

Let your daughter choose a cause that speaks to her heart. There are many charitable organizations and events, from the Red Cross to school-sponsored fundraisers, to drives sponsored by your place of worship that need your girl's compassionate contributions. They do not only need her financial help but also her time and her kind heart. That means, you have a choice—either you become involved in her volunteer efforts, or she accompanies you in the volunteer work you do.

Do not force your daughter to give up and donate a cherished blanket or teddy bear to charity unless she is ready to part with it. Coercing a girl to become more charitable can backfire and make her less willing to share anything. Do not send some of her money to a fundraising group without first getting her permission.

It does your girl good to see her mom and dad spending time working in a soup kitchen once a month, or contributing to a toy drive for underprivileged children. She will be excited to go to the store with you to buy new school supplies for students in this country or a continent away who are returning to their flood-damaged schools after a hurricane or tsunami.

Giving Love

Ask your daughter to pack up all her outgrown clothes and old toys to be dropped off at a shelter for abused women and children. Ask her if she can find it in her heart to include one of her "best" games or books. Sharing with others does not mean giving them something shabby, broken, or useless. It can be tough to part with a new toy; but if you set an example, your daughter will get the idea. Sharing an item we love is sharing love.

Maybe your daughter and her friends can come up with an activity that brings in a healthy sum. Or they can hold a yard sale and donate the proceeds to a needy foundation, or even start their own.

 **Fact**

Alexandra Scott was four years old when she started Alex's Lemonade Stand. It was her way to raise funds for pediatric cancer research. She was diagnosed with cancer before her first birthday and by the time she died in 2004, word of her efforts had spread around the world and raised millions for her cause.

Your daughter can also make use of her arts and crafts talents to brighten someone's days. She can make colorful placemats for the nearest rest home or bake cupcakes for a shut-in. The possibilities for her to care and share are endless. With you as a role model, she can be a force for good from childhood on. Contributing to the world will make your girl feel just as productive as contributing to your household does. As you observe her, you will find her love toward others growing, her heart opening to the world's needs, and her gratitude shooting through the roof. As a result many other people—her age and older—may benefit from her caring and sharing spirit, now and for years to come.

CHAPTER 8

Education and Achievement

With world events and the economy being unsettled these days and with family patterns changing, you cannot prepare your daughter better for the challenges her lifetime may bring than to provide her with an excellent education. It will serve as her admission ticket to a fulfilling and financially rewarding career. To give her a special boost in this area, help her get excited over her education and academic achievement, and give her every early advantage you can.

Building Excitement

Think of your daughter's future in increments of five years. Envision her proceeding through her school years—at five, ten, fifteen, and twenty years of age—so smoothly that she will excel in many subjects, gain knowledge to the best of her ability, and enjoy the process. That is your underlying goal: to help her succeed in scholastics and develop her character. To achieve your goal, be willing to provide her with every opportunity possible.

Character Triumphs

Character trumps academics every time. For that reason, teach your daughter about it constantly and stress its significance, but not only at home. Also make sure she receives many fine character lessons at your house of worship. Every time you notice her showing

signs of inner strength and integrity, praise your girl. Thus, this important aspect of your girl's total development is being developed.

Having a good character and high morals, however, does not automatically equal future career success. It is most important for her as she goes through life, and if she has her own family. But even the strongest value system should be enhanced by strong school skills. To have your girl's inner beauty and backbone underlined by her brilliance should be on your agenda. That combination will definitely make your daughter the complete package.

Fact

Noah Webster (1758–1843) was a pioneer in the field of dictionaries. A man of many and varied interests, he spent more than twenty years studying and researching the English language and compiling spelling books. He ranks as the greatest of American lexicographers (writers of dictionaries).

A Home Library

To facilitate this goal and make it fun, buy the following three books and place them on a table in the middle of your den, living room, or kitchen—wherever you and your daughter spend the most time:

- An unabridged—that is, not condensed—dictionary recommended for older students, preferably of high school age
- An atlas of the United States and the world, plus a globe if space permits
- A thesaurus (a book containing synonyms, words with similar meanings; and antonyms, words with opposite meanings)

Then the academic excitement can begin. Use these books like board games with your daughter and have her delve into them several times a week. Circle new words in the newspaper and have her find the definitions.

Another great option is to play Home Travel Channel with your daughter. Every time she hears a city or country mentioned on the news, ask her to find it in the atlas. After that, play word treasure hunt. Mention a simple word like *go*, and ask your girl to list all the words she knows that have the same meaning, such as *move, drift, flow, travel*, or *sashay*. Then look in the thesaurus with her to see if she missed any important or unusual words. Soon she will return the favor and laugh when you have to scramble for words that escape you. You daughter will find it exciting to try to best you with word games of her own invention. She may make up an impossible word list for you to memorize or even invent a new language. The excitement that builds with each little academic activity will be contagious.

The Library as Home

From the time you start reading to your daughter, take her with you to the public library, so that by the time she is three or four, she will feel at home there. Help her discover a quiet corner in that building that she can call her nook and always gravitate to as if it were in her own home.

Alert!

Never treat the public library as a babysitter. Sadly and too frequently, some parents have dropped their little girls at the public library during a teacher workday only to find out that this location may be a magnet for all kinds of people of questionable character or intent.

Once your daughter feels welcome at the public library or a "commercial" one—otherwise known as the mega bookstore in the mall—she can settle in and flip through the pages of a children's book. Later she will scan several "chapter" books by a favorite author before settling on one to read immediately and saving the others for later.

As soon as your girl is old enough, make sure she gets her own library card. It should look worn from frequent use. Besides letting her browse in the fiction section in search of more thrilling stories, tell her about the American librarian Melvil Dewey (1851–1931). He invented the Dewey Decimal System that divides all publications into ten major areas, from encyclopedias, to engineering books, to essays, and so forth.

 **Fact**

The Library of Congress is the oldest U.S. federal cultural institution and the largest library in the world. It houses more than 130 million items and more than 530 miles of bookshelves. Besides books, it has millions of recordings, photos, maps, and rare manuscripts and is an exciting place for girls to visit in Washington, D.C.

At home, help your daughter organize her growing book collection, according to her own system. The more she bonds with her books, the more excited she will be to read voraciously. Mark Twain said, "The person who does not read has no advantage over the person who cannot read." You want your daughter to have every advantage possible.

Alleviate School Fears

Just as you familiarize your daughter with the library, do the same with her school, so that she is ready to learn without being beset by fear, which could limit her capacity for absorbing new knowledge. A 2006 survey conducted by guidance counselors in several states revealed that girls, no matter what age, have similar fears about starting school, transitioning from one school system to another, or advancing from elementary to middle school.

These fears center on:

- Not knowing any other children
- Forgetting their books or locker combinations
- Getting lost in a much larger building

Even elementary schools vary greatly in size, and middle schools are often two or three times the size of an elementary school. High schools top that in size. So ask your girl what fears, if any, she might have and then ease them. Make sure she goes to school without jitters. Only then can the academic excitement you have created in your daughter away from school continue at school. It should also permeate the way she tackles the assignments she receives as homework.

Help with Homework

Homework is an extension of work your daughter does in class and can be an overnight academic exercise or a major project that will take her a week or several to complete. But no matter how involved or lengthy, homework allows your girl to develop a better understanding of the topic at hand or to explore it further. Through a deeper immersion in any subject, she can experience the fun of learning and discover her academic strengths, especially if you help her.

To position your daughter best vis-à-vis her homework duties is a snap.

- Turn off the TV.
- Provide your daughter with a "homework haven."
- Pass your best study skills on to her.

Turning off the TV during homework time stops the distractions that might interfere with your girl's learning. No matter how much she pleads her case by pointing out the volume is on low or the program is "educational," any disruption can negatively affect the way she learns.

Single-Tasking Is Key

Multitasking while studying degrades learning, a 2006 study proves. According to Russell A. Poldrack, a psychology professor at the University of California, Los Angeles, "Even if you can learn while distracted, it changes how you learn to make it less efficient and useful." Therefore, explain to your girl that watching TV will drag out her homework, whereas with the TV off, she will zip right through it.

Homework Haven

Any corner in your house can be designated as the homework haven. Many parents set up a small desk in the kitchen while their daughters are young, so they can get started on their work—doing math—while their parents get started on theirs—fixing dinner. When your girl reaches middle or high school, she will then be trained well enough to follow her homework routine by herself in the den or even her room. But for the beginning learner, doing her paperwork under mom's or dad's supervision is a big plus. Weaving their daughter's vocabulary words into their conversation or reciting the multiplication tables or the names of the fifty states with her, while tossing the salad, shows her how much her parents care about her homework.

Study Smarts

When it comes to the efficient completion of homework assignments, you are a walking fountain of knowledge for your daughter. Since you finished your formal schooling, you are the expert on homework hints. Hand them out to your daughter while she starts her book report or fills in her social studies worksheet.

When your girl is finished with her homework assignment, review it with her. Point out where she might have made a mistake and encourage her to correct her spelling errors. Tell her neatness counts. If her teacher sees just how much effort your daughter puts into her writing, a special recognition is sure to follow.

Question?

Should I help my daughter with her homework?
Help her by finding the part in her book where the answer is, by teaching her study shortcuts—such as reading the first and last paragraphs of a chapter—and by brainstorming with her for project ideas. Assist her in gathering materials and type her reports, but only if she dictates them to you. Do *not* do her homework for her.

Testing 1, 2, 3

Another part of doing homework is getting ready for an upcoming test. To prepare your daughter for it, give her a short practice quiz the day before the real one. Teach her to study short sections of her work long before a big academic checkup comes her way. Studying and reading ahead in a textbook should become part of her homework routine so that she is not overwhelmed on the day before a major exam. A calendar posted prominently in your home should list your daughter's big tests far in advance, so she can prepare herself. To be up on these dates, you want to establish good lines of communication with her teachers from the moment she steps into their classrooms.

Connecting with Teachers and Coaches

Being a teacher, coach, or other school staff member is difficult these days. Not only is it challenging to have twenty-five or more students or budding athletes to instruct simultaneously, but the quality of parenting has gone down in many cases. Kids today are not what they used to be, and many parents have less respect for the public school system than in the past.

Additionally, our changing population and constantly fluctuating society, plus our rising expectations and push for school accountability, have placed extra stress on educators. As a consequence, be careful not to add more pressure to their already arduous jobs. Instead, try to communicate with the staff at your daughter's school in an efficient, helpful, and friendly manner that honors them for the hard work they do every day.

 **Fact**

Approximately 100,000 parents support an educational program called "unschooling" or "child-driven learning" that lets kids—not parents and teachers—choose what they want to study. It's a legal option in all fifty states but is controversial because no studies of its long-range effectiveness exist.

Teacher Notes

As soon as possible, establish a way of getting in touch with your daughter's teachers, according to their preference. At the school open house, find out how they want to be contacted. Some teachers prefer old-fashioned written notes sent via your daughter. Others want to be called in the evening during a specific hour, and still others want to be e-mailed any time. Once you know how to contact your girl's teachers, do not use their permission to contact them about every small item. Ralph Ellison said, "Education is a matter of building bridges." Do not destroy them, or your daughter will feel the effect.

Grade Parents

To connect better with the teachers who have such a huge influence on your girl's success, volunteer to help out in their classrooms. Most elementary and middle schools ask parents or caregivers to volunteer as grade parents and help with special events or activities.

Become one of those grade parents and offer your assistance with the preparation of a bulletin board or with research on a specific topic. Collect magazines for your girl and her classmates to use as supplemental materials, or serve as one of the judges in the science fair for a grade level your daughter is not in. Find out what special addition to the classroom would make the teacher's job easier, then get busy and supply it. If your time is limited, you can volunteer for one of the following duties:

- The reminder parent who calls up the students to remind them of an upcoming exam or other important dates
- The makeup parent who helps to get a child who was out sick caught up
- The unpaid substitute who spends one lunch hour per week supervising the cafeteria so the teacher can eat in peace

Be sure to ask your daughter what she wants you to volunteer for at her school, and she will tell you. On the days you visit her class, ask her if she wants you to speak to her in front of her classmates or just wave to her. Remember the school is your daughter's second home and she knows the rules there better than you do.

Honor Teachers

When you see up close just how much teachers do every day above and beyond their regular duties, you will want to recognize them for their special dedication. Sit down with your daughter and discuss the teacher's hard work, his patience, and the positive influence he has not only on your daughter but on all the kids in his room and maybe even the young teacher next door. Then decide together how you and your daughter can honor her teacher and his coworkers—all of whom are your parenting allies. With them by your side, you can truly inspire your girl.

Here are some options for recognizing outstanding teachers:

- Send a fruit platter, flowers, or fresh bagels with a selection of spreads—and a thank-you note written by your daughter and other students—to the teachers' lounge.
- Write a letter of commendation for the teacher and send copies to the principal and superintendent.
- Have your daughter write a paragraph praising her teachers and send it to the newspaper to be printed as an open letter for the whole community to see.

Or do all three. Society can never thank teachers enough, and your daughter needs to learn to show her appreciation to the people who help guide her.

After-School Tutoring

No two students ever learn at the same rate. So even if your older child—or you—breezed through a certain class, your daughter may have trouble with it or say she does not like it, which is a sure indication that she will not do her best in this subject. What a perfect opportunity this is for you to investigate what is going on, and then come up with a solution, which may be after-school tutoring.

Tutor Time

Most schools have a list of tutors, so start with a conference with your daughter's teachers any time she brings home a grade lower than a B-minus on her report card. Of course, before that, talk to her about it. Sometimes just a little more time spent on a subject can raise the score.

Also encourage her to ask her teacher for a retest, more practice sheets and homework, or an extra-credit project.

Teachers enjoy seeing students take the initiative to teach themselves more about a topic and often will provide them with an alternate textbook, quizzes from a previous year, and a chance to come in at lunch and redo a unit of work that was bungled.

But sometimes after-school tutoring is the best option. It can be remedial or enriching and should be used early as intervention, after an educational evaluation has taken place. If, for example, your girl has missed acquiring some early-grade skill basics, they need to be dealt with first before she can advance at full steam.

Tutor Types

Tutors are like teachers in that they specialize: Some will work with your girl according to subjects such as reading or writing. Others focus mainly on teaching study skills and getting your daughter organized. Still others can test for, or identify, learning disabilities, such as attention deficit and dyslexia, or help ease the transition from one grade level to another.

Alert!

The hours from three to six have been dubbed the "danger hours" for kids, meaning that this is the time period when kids most often get into trouble. The reason is that these are the hours when most school programs are over and many parents are still at work. Make sure your daughter has regularly scheduled activities in place for that time span.

In fact, you will find that tutors can teach foreign languages or ESL (English as a second language), prepare your daughter for AP (Advanced Placement) classes, and assist you if you home-school your girl or if she is homebound due to an illness. They can also be your best support group in revving up your daughter's skills in the two school subjects that matter tremendously for girls but are too often neglected.

Math and Science Matter

Throughout the past decades, society has expected boys to excel in the "harder" classes (science and math) and girls in the "easier" ones (language and social studies). The fact is all areas of study can be hard or easy, depending on the individual child and her attitude. Another fact is that when it comes to the job market, college graduates with a math or science background can usually find better-paying jobs in more abundance. Women applicants, equipped with advanced math or science skills—especially in computer science—can often write their own tickets.

 **Fact**

While the number of science and engineering bachelor's degrees obtained by women has increased, the number has decreased in computer science. In 1985 women earned 36 percent of those degrees, but in 1995 they earned only 28 percent. In 1999, only 17 percent of the high school students taking the Advanced Placement Computer Science Test were female.

Today's world is one where math and science are becoming ever more important, especially for girls and their future career choices. The clock cannot be turned back, but parents can step up and make sure their daughters are prepared for that challenge. That means they first have to lay the foundation for their girls to be math- and science-ready every day. It all starts with you, the parent. Yet no matter how gung-ho you are about math and science, begin with what your daughter truly likes. It does no good cramming a liking for those subjects down her throat when she has a love for literature or history. This is about **her** life and **her** gifts.

Physically Ready for Math and Science

Studying math and science takes a girl's full and nonstop concentration. There are no lulls in those classes as there may be in English when a teacher is likely to instruct his students to quietly read Act I of *Romeo and Juliet* or the next scenes in Lorraine Hansberry's work. So just as you would give your car a close checkup to ensure it is ready for a road trip, check to see if your daughter is at her best physically every day when she faces what could be her more difficult classes. You do that by closely examining the following:

- **Sleep schedule.** Establish your girl's proper sleep pattern two weeks before school starts. Tired girls cannot concentrate as well as those who are well rested.
- **Breakfast choices.** Girls who eat a healthy breakfast perform better in schools than those who do not eat one, or eat nothing but sugary cereals and candy.
- **Physical condition.** Make sure her height, weight, and body mass index fall within a normal range.

Use your resourcefulness in handling any issues that crop up along those lines. Girls can take naps after school to add to their rest time. They can eat leftover cheese pizza—made with low-fat cheese—or a turkey sandwich with lettuce and tomato for breakfast. Or pack some food for later—to eat during break—if their stomach hasn't woken up yet. You don't have to limit her to the traditional breakfast foods. A daily quick jog around the block can do wonders physically, for both you and her.

 *Question?*

Should I send my daughter to school when she is sick?
Check your daughter's school policy, but generally speaking, she can go to school with some minor conditions such as a slight cold or a slight temperature up to 100.5 degrees if there are no other symptoms, according to the American Academy of Pediatrics. If you are unsure about how serious her cold or temperature is, keep her home.

In short, the healthier and more energetic your girl is, the more she is off to a great start when tackling her math and science courses.

Mentally Ready for Math and Science

Any time your daughter says something negative about science or math, counter it immediately with a positive statement. If she says, "I'm just not good in science and math," say, "Nobody knows how good they are in anything unless they try their best. Let me help you."

Then choose a deliberate course of action that may include the following plans:

- Encourage her to join her school's math or science clubs. This works best if she and a friend sign up together.
- Urge your daughter to become a lab assistant in her chemistry or physics class. Girls rarely volunteer, so challenge her to get out of her comfort zone.
- Provide her with a role model, a "cool" mathematician or scientist who can mentor her.

If all else fails, you can "bribe" your daughter. Tell her to be daring in math and science and sign up for the hardest courses. You and she can negotiate on the payoff, but why not? Does your company not provide bonuses for extra-brilliant performance? Yet, at the same time, please be realistic. Not every girl is mentally geared toward these courses, so take into consideration your daughter's abilities and desires.

Good Grades Grow Careers

A 2005 survey, reported in parenting circles around the world, asked what most parents wanted for their daughters to get out of their schooling. The answer was universal: to be prepared for a good career. So consider your girl's first few years of school as skill builders. They form the building blocks of her future success in the workplace. Make sure she has been instructed well in the basics. It does no good to have her lacking in the prerequisites for the more rigorous courses.

Keep up with your daughter's grades, plus the scores she makes on local and state tests. Have her show her academic prowess in whatever arena she can. Encourage her to enter math contests and participate in science summer camps. These days there are specialized programs for girls who are into ladybugs, spiders, and frogs, or snakes and alligators. Or perhaps your daughter is curious about lemurs or red wolves.

Whenever she is undecided about taking honors classes in school, encourage her to go for it. It is better to make a lower grade in an advanced class where she is challenged than to make a top grade in an easier class where she may be bored.

Expect your girl to try to make the honor roll every year. Teach her to respect her teachers and to follow their advice. They can help her with awards, honors, and recommendations in the future, plus they can point her in a general direction leading to her life's work.

 **Fact**

The famous British zoologist Jane Goodall (born 1934) became interested in animal life at a young age. By the time she was ten, she decided to travel to Africa to work with animals. Her studies of chimpanzees and their unexpected behaviors were groundbreaking, leading to a number of books and films about her work.

Be sure to have your daughter start early in mapping out a possible career trail. Have her take an introductory prep class for her high school SAT to ACTs. Seventh grade is a good time to start. Every time she masters a new scholastic skill and drill, her grades will rise and her career opportunities—no matter how far down her path—will look rosier.

Essential

Don't allow your daughter to get overscheduled. Check her school schedule to see that she has a few easier courses. No girl can be in a pressure-cooker atmosphere all the time without blowing her top. One or two afternoons must be totally her own. You don't want your girl to burn out by the time she is sixteen.

Whatever job your daughter will settle on eventually—whatever good she will do in this world—for the rest of your life, you can take pride in the fact that you were the candle lighter in her life. Whether she combines raising her family with a career, or works intermittently outside the home, or forges ahead with a great discovery or a cure for a dreadful disease, you got her started and well equipped for that wonderful path. It was you who got her interested in exploring the depths of her mind. You passed on to her whatever greatness was in you and watched her magnify it.

The quest and love for knowledge that you instilled in your daughter will have many increasing returns.

CHAPTER 9

Peer Problems

Y our daughter's peers are very important to her. She wants to have a sense of belonging and importance and to fit in with the rest of her classmates. To become an independent adult—in the not-too-distant future—she is supposed to transfer her allegiance from her parents to her peers, a process that can take years. That is the desired development in your daughter and you welcome it. But what if her peers are a bad influence on her and get in the way of her progress?

The Mean Chicks Phenomenon

Since the early 1980s, our country has seen a sharp rise in violence among boys that has not abated. While the nation's attention has been focused more on them—especially since the Columbine tragedy—more girls have recently shown a pattern of violence. This can be explained in several ways: by trying to close the gaps in their actions and achievement with boys, by society's changing expectations of girls, or because law enforcement is now taking acts of violence by girls more seriously. Meanwhile some segments of our population encourage girls to be mean, with comments such as "It's way overdue. Girls really should fight back."

 *Fact*

Psychologist Leonard Eron states that, in order to cut down on our violence, boys should be socialized—that means introduced to and taught how to fit into society—more like girls. However, the fact is that in recent years, girls have been socialized more like boys. As a result, girls are now more prone to be aggressive and violent.

No matter what the explanations are for the phenomenon of a larger number of girls acting like mean chicks, more of them are indeed showing their aggressive sides. That does not bode well for society. Instead of humans becoming more civilized, the trend may be the reverse. The worst is that your daughter may be on the receiving end of aggressive and violent behavior by other girls. Yet even if there is no outright violence directed toward her, there are many subtle ways her feelings can be hurt or she can be stymied by girls her age.

You cannot protect your girl from every instance of hurt feelings, and that is not your purpose. Being exposed to some peer meanness and overcoming it is emotionally healthy for her, just as is having her immune system—her body's defense department—strengthened by exposure to some germs. It is much better for your daughter to face unkindness from other girls and learn to overcome it, rather than be shielded from it entirely and never have a chance to develop the necessary tools to combat it successfully. Without experiencing that struggle, your daughter would be deprived of the confidence that is a by-product of overcoming acts of rudeness and hostility by her classmates.

Mean Chick Conduct

Although you cannot protect your daughter from every mean behavior of her peers, you can arm her with knowledge about what to expect from some not-so-nice girls in her world and how to be prepared for it. Then she can disarm and defuse any of her classmates or "friends" who might be inclined to mistreat her. This mistreatment can take the forms of other girls engaging in:

1. Stealing her friends
2. Excluding her from social events
3. Stabbing her in the back (figuratively)
4. Spreading lies and rumors about her

Alert!

Do not feel complacent if your daughter reports no outright physical abuse, such as pushing, punching, or shoving, from her female classmates. Girls usually express their anger toward other girls in more subtle ways, such as through mean-spirited notes, phone calls, instant messaging or text messaging, and other electronic communications in a powerful peer rumor mill that aims to inflict pain.

There are many other ways girls can be mean to one another, but if your daughter is aware of the most prevalent signs of hostility some girls in her circle may exhibit, she can easily dodge or deflect them in whatever forms they may appear. Also, realizing that it is not the girls themselves—only their unkind behaviors—that she should object to, your girl can watch out for any red flags shown by other girls and avoid the accompanying negatives.

So the first piece of information to give your daughter is to let her know what types of mean chicks, identified here by their behavior, she may run across in her school, neighborhood, or community. You want her to be able to do the following:

- Understand and recognize the kinds of unfriendly or aggressive girl behaviors that exist.
- Learn to deal with girls showing those characteristics but only on her terms and conditions.
- Help those girls to be nicer, and create a more accepting climate at her school, neighborhood, and community.
- Avoid them and help her friends to avoid them as well.

 **Fact**

Dr. Marian K. Underwood, a professor who studies anger, aggression, gender, and children's peer relationships, calls the way children and adolescents can express their anger and contempt toward their peers "social aggression." By resorting to it, kids intend to hurt their peers through lowering their self-esteem and standing in their groups and relationships.

Mean Chick Types

Parents must not forget that the unfriendly or hostile girls your daughter meets all have their reasons for the way they behave. Most often these reasons arise from their home life, from the way they were raised from babyhood on, or from what they have observed in their parents' dealing with relationships. For example, if they see their parents manipulate their friends, they will act similarly. Or if their parents live to gossip about their neighbors, their daughters will indulge in that as well.

Yet no matter how adept some girls become in their negative machinations of others, they rarely feel good about themselves. In truth, most of them feel miserable and—by lashing out at your daughter and her friends, most often verbally—they try to get other girls to feel miserable too. Based purely on their behavior, these mean chicks can be divided into the following categories:

1. **Snobs.** These girls judge the world, your daughter, and other girls only in terms of their "wealth" or their connection, if any, to famous people.
2. **Gossips.** These girls love to spread bits of information around, especially if it is negative, which they tend to embellish.
3. **Teasers.** These girls enjoy finding a weakness or sore spot in other girls, including your daughter, and needling them about it constantly in a mean way.
4. **Bullies.** These girls, though rarer than the others, threaten to, or physically hurt, other girls.
5. **Traitors.** These girls are the most dangerous in the long run. They will gain your daughter's complete confidence and then betray her by word or deed. Therefore, they can leave lasting scars.

It bears repeating: No girl is ever born mean. They are made that way. An unkind girl is the product of her environment, just as your daughter is the product of hers. Sad to say, but some girls come from homes where snobbishness, gossiping, sarcastic teasing, bullying, and betrayal go on every day. These patterns of behavior are shown to them not only by their parents but also by their siblings, while the parents stand by and condone the actions.

Alert!

Watch how you treat women. If you are nice to their faces but as soon as they leave, criticize them and make disparaging remarks about them to others, you are teaching your daughter to become a back-stabbing girl who will then become a backstabbing young woman.

For that reason, you want your daughter to understand that planned acts of unkindness from other girls are rooted in their personal background and she should pity girls whose character training has been neglected, but that does not excuse their behavior.

Mean Chick Tactics

Should some of the different types of mean girls target your daughter, she will need to know how to handle them and defend herself. It is always best to assume that at some point in her school career she will be exposed to rude remarks or other signs of brattiness by other girls. Therefore, a generic approach to run-of-the-mill bad behavior, such as contemptuous glares, expressions of disgust, or abrupt turning away, can come in handy. Here are a few tactics your daughter can use.

- Never take the meanness personally.
- Try to feel sorry for the girl who acts that way.
- Never revert to the same behavior herself.
- Try to take the upper hand by saying, tongue-in-cheek, "Sorry, I didn't realize you are having a bad day."

Also, practice with your daughter how to stand in a powerful way, with her spine straight, her head up, and facing her potential detractors. Tell her she can send any mean chicks scurrying by her stance, attitude, and confident signals. One thing to remember about mean-acting girls is that they usually look for the meekest and quietest girl in the crowd and leave stronger girls alone. To take charge in a negative situation means to be empowered. Empower your girl not to be a doormat. Instead, rehearse with her how to take a stand against unkind girls.

You also want to make sure your daughter has some classmates who will insulate her against being singled out and give her a network for support and for venting her frustrations.

Long-Term Advantages

What is so heartwarming when you teach your daughter about any mean chicks is that you are giving her another important life skill.

In the years to come, she may run into them in various mutations in college, on the job, in her neighborhood, her house of worship, or her workout place—as her superiors, coworkers, or subordinates—in short, wherever there are women who have not experienced the skillful and wise parenting you are dispensing. So there is always a good chance your girl will run across quite a few unhappy women who try to make others feel as bad as they do via their mean-spirited and cat-fighting tendencies.

Question?

My daughter who is going into seventh grade is neither outgoing nor tall. Will she get picked on by the bigger and tougher girls?
Do not let your fears spill over onto your girl and scare her unnecessarily. Be extra supportive to her during the first few days of school and expect that she will do fine. There are so many different girls in school that she will soon find a few who are friendly.

Counter Catfights

With her insight into mean girls, your daughter will know how to handle any catfights. She will recognize any spiteful females from a mile away. Actually she will welcome their presence because she will have a chance to help them improve their behavior, if possible. If not, she will deal with them to her best advantage, not theirs.

That does not mean your girl will not feel a twinge of hurt when confronted by female rudeness, but the twinge will be just another sign that she is making progress. Physical exercise can make her sore. Exercising her relationship muscles is no different. Your daughter will get better each time she triumphs over the disrespect from other girls. Plus, being empowered, she will be able to help other girls who contribute to her growth and make her life more fun.

Finding Positive Friends

One of the best protective strategies for your daughter is to surround herself with numerous positive friends. You cannot be with her in school, after school, and during her practices and meetings. You cannot cull through her classmates and kick the negative ones to the curb, but you can give your girl every opportunity to associate with positive friends who add to her well-being rather than subtract from it. Girls change in their stages of forming friendships as they go through their school years.

 **Fact**

As girls get older, they go through "transitory" friendships that change according to age. At age eight or nine, girls walk in loose clusters of three to six members, with all of them talking, as observed by school psychologist Dr. JoAnn Deak. By age ten or eleven, girls walk in sets of twos, a sign that the "best-friend era" has begun.

Typically, your daughter and her girlfriends graduate from an early stage of side-by-side playing to interacting as they play. Then they move to friendships in groups and the best-friend stage. After that girls reach the clique stage, the interest-based group stage, and finally—in their senior year—they develop an accepting spirit and openness to finding friends almost everywhere.

Friendship Variations

Not all girls follow the friendship stages exactly. Some linger at a certain stage while others skip one or two. No matter where your daughter finds herself in the development of friends as she gets older, she can benefit from having a wide range of girls to choose from. So should her friends move, for example, or should she change schools, she will be able to select new or more friends with ease and confidence.

Benefits of Girlfriends

According to Lyn Mikel Brown, a women's studies and education scholar, girls make use of their girlfriends as their "emotional and psychological safety nets." With their friends beside them, they will be braver, speak out more often on important topics, and show more courage as they stand up for others—and for themselves.

Essential

According to a KidsHealth poll, only 19 percent of boys who have been threatened or mistreated by their peers tell someone or ask an adult for help. In contrast, 32 percent of girls tell their friends, parents, teachers, or guidance counselors about peer problems and ask for help. Encourage your girl always to tell someone.

Therefore, having girlfriends is most important for your daughter. She needs them as her allies and to make her strong, feel respected, and more successful. Even though your daughter may already have one fabulous friend or best buddy, how can you make sure that her army of allies expands?

Types of Girlfriends

Explain to your daughter that girlfriends come in many different forms, from casual to close ones, and that it is best to have one or several in each group. Life for a growing girl is filled with enormous possibilities, so she should not limit herself to just one relationship with one girl. She should be sure her circle includes many different girls. Here are a few types of good friends:

- **Study buddies.** These girls are in her classes; they are motivated and, like your daughter, want to excel in scholastics.

- **Good friends.** These are girls your daughter is comfortable with; they make her life more fun. They can be old friends she re-connects with, or new friends she meets now.
- **Best buds.** This is usually one girl, or two, who is a close, reliable, and unwavering friend she can talk to about everything.
- **Soul pals.** These are girls with whom your daughter can form a forever friendship because they think and feel alike, almost like twins. Now matter how much they grow and change, their connection stays the same. A soul pal may even be the girl herself, to herself.

Assuming your daughter is ready to make more friends, point out where she can best find some.

Girlfriend Meeting Places

Where your daughter meets new friends is important because the places are often an indicator as to what kinds of friends she will find there. Although she might meet new girlfriends anywhere, she can increase her chances by looking around the school library, the computer lab, or where girls usually hang out to study. Also by being an active participant in clubs and extracurricular activities, or in youth groups in the community, she can scout out more potential friends.

Girlfriend Keeping

By watching you, your daughter has already learned the friendship basics. But it will not hurt for you to remind her of the most important friend-keeping strategies:

1. Being trustworthy and not telling her friends' secrets unless they are in danger or need help.
2. Not being envious or jealous, and remaining good friends even when the going gets tough.
3. Sharing some of her failures, as well as her successes, to bond better.

Alert!

The more you find fault with your daughter's friends, the more she might feel she has to defend them. The same goes with the groups you may find your daughter beginning to cultivate. Forbidding her to associate with certain peers may do the exact opposite of what you want: It may cause your daughter to find them more appealing.

You, the parent, have a lot of influence on your daughter's friend-making skills. You can make your house a place where your girl and her friends want to hang out by providing plenty of soft drinks, snacks, and appropriate movies. You can encourage her to bring her girlfriends home, but do not critique them harshly.

You can also be a good listener when your girl complains about her friends or about being excluded from something they do. Listen to her with all your attention and tell her that her friendship dilemmas will diminish the older she gets.

Tricky Cliques

The word *clique* means a close group of friends that is seen by outsiders as excluding them. It comes from the French *cliquer* and originally referred to clicking or clapping, as in applause. Cliques exist in most schools from middle school up and can be "iron cliques"—permanent ones—or more casual and last only a short time.

As girls move to more and more independence and individuation—the process of becoming a separate and distinct identity—they tend to miss the stability of the close-knit family unit that once was the center of their lives. As a result, they look for a family substitute and form groups or cliques.

Overall, group behavior is important because from middle school on it is the conduct of the group your girl associates with that has enormous impact on her. Surrounding herself with girls who look or act similar makes her separation from her mother and father easier. For that reason, joining a clique is a positive developmental step, but cliques can be tricky. They can be known by a name that brands them.

Essential

Discourage your girl from always affixing a judgmental label, such as "She is a "preppie," a "nerd," a "jock," a "goth," or a "loser" to every girl she sees, based only on superficial evidence. Encourage her to look beneath the surface. Too many girls write others off according to their clothes, hairstyles, weight, and accent.

Of course, some cliques can be very beneficial; but when a clique is toxic, trouble can start. How can you know? Ask yourself what the purpose of the particular clique is. Why are the members hanging out together? If it is for a school-connected or other positive purpose, such as a sports activity, that is one thing. But if the clique meets only to denigrate others, help your daughter to find a more positive group. You do not want her to be pulled into doing something hurtful by peer pressure, also known as the "clique squeeze." Not having a group to belong to is much better for your girl than to associate with a clique that could hurt her in some way.

Unsafe Friends

Countless proverbs warn of the strong influence your daughter's friends can have on her, such as "Show me your friends and I show you who you are." While you do not want to belittle your daughter's friends, you do want to have your eyes open and notice their appearance and the way they act, especially how they conduct themselves when they think you cannot see them.

As a parent you have one great weapon: your instinct. When a friend of your daughter gives you an uneasy feeling, examine the reason. Is this girl dressed strangely all the time? Does she wear outlandish makeup every day? From age twelve on, some girls consider adults the enemy and want to get back at them by exposing body parts, wearing underwear as outerwear, and getting lots of tattoos and body piercings. Also read what it says on their T-shirts or what they doodle on their notebooks.

 **Fact**

> Be aware that a *Lord of the Flies* effect has been observed among pre-adolescents and adolescents in which the lowest common denominator always prevails among a group of friends. Therefore, if your girl associates for a long time with girls who act much more mature or are engaged in destructive or unhealthy practices, she will be tempted to take part in them as well.

Friend Wise

Talk to your daughter about what you have observed about her friend. Perhaps she is feeling sorry for this particular girl because other kids make fun of her. Compliment your girl on her kindness and see what you can do to help this "weird" dresser fit in better. Or perhaps this is just an unconventional girl who is very creative and artistic. Help her shine in some way in front of the group. Whatever the situation may be, do not let your girl abandon her other friends and spend all her time with girls who give you a bad feeling.

Friend Choices

You do not want your daughter to gravitate only toward girls with problematic backgrounds that she cannot solve at this stage of her life. Instead, encourage her to make friends everywhere—at school, at athletic practices, in the neighborhood, and at her place of worship. Having friends from all social spectrums and ethnicities can be a big plus for your daughter. The more she widens her circle, the more she can learn from all kinds of talented girls.

Brand-Name Pressures

Sometimes girls are drawn into groups that espouse shallow values. To the members of this type of clique, only a girl's outer wrappings matter. Designer labels and complicated, expensive hair routines rule, not what is inside a girl. When you find your daughter suddenly trying to fit in with an extremely high-maintenance group, give her a wake-up call. Tell her that trying to fit in with girls who cherish designer purses more than persons may make her more popular, but that the word *popular* means average or ordinary. She should not strive so hard to just be ordinary. She should always strive to be extraordinary.

Question?

My daughter refuses to wear anything that does not have an expensive brand name. What can I do?
Ask her to use her own money to buy brand-name apparel. You will buy her what is attractive on her yet reasonable. If she still insists on the designer polo shirt, for example, point her in the direction of some part-time work opportunities where she can earn extra cash.

Bullying: Victim or Victimizer?

In recent years, bullying has received a lot of attention. In fact, about 5 percent of all students have been bullied in ways that go beyond the occasional teasing or name calling. While girl bullies are much rarer than boy bullies, they do exist. Usually they do not use their fists; instead, they use safety pins to "accidentally" stab other girls, trip or elbow them, or knock their books off the desk.

Watch for these classic red flags:

- She pretends to be sick when she is not.
- She loses her appetite and wakes up during the night.
- She is sad without a reason.
- She loses interest in doing well in school.

Any time you notice a marked change in your daughter's behavior, probe into the cause. If she is being bullied, sit down with her and map out some solutions to solve the problem.

Essential

Do not call the teachers, principal, the sheriff's department, the highway patrol, and anyone else you know in law enforcement the first time your daughter comes home and tells you she has been bullied. She will not tell you the next time if you don't stay rational and calmly help her with the problem.

Some good tactics for dealing with a bully include:

- Using humor. Tell your girl to have a funny line ready such as, "Are you trying out for a part in the movie *Mean Girls II*?"
- Role-playing. At home, have her act out the bully part and you be the strong girl.
- Documenting the bully's behavior with a notebook or a camera phone.

The best way to remove the threat of bullies from your girl's life is to tell her about the Greek alphabet. The first letter is alpha, a term researchers use to describe girls who are admired by their peers, as in "alpha girls." The second letter, beta, is used for girls who tag after the alpha girls as followers or would-be alphas, as in "beta girls." It is the beta girls who most often are the victims of bullies because they appear vulnerable. But there is another type of girl, one who is independent-minded and comfortable with herself. She makes the most of her talents and has goals in life. That is the gamma girl—an amazing and productive girl who forges ahead, sets an example for others, and enjoys just about every day.

Show your daughter how to bring out more of her gamma-girl qualities, and she will be all set. Bullies may try to cow a gamma girl, but they will back off when they realize they are outsmarted, outdone, and outclassed. But what if your daughter has bully tendencies herself? That is easy to stop. Do not snoop, but listen to how she talks to her classmates and watch how she treats younger girls. As you drive her and her friends to school, keep your ears tuned. Listen for unkind words about other girls and then take your daughter aside. Tell her it is completely uncool for any girl to add to the tribulations other girls may already be experiencing.

Constant Change

As your girl grows, parenting evolves from meeting her basic needs to teaching her skills to teaching her to let nothing get in her way. Just as an artist first sketches the outline of his masterpiece, so you begin with the ABCs of girl-raising. Then you fine-tune your efforts. During the first few years of her life, that meant making sure she wore a coat and hat in cold weather and sunscreen in the summer. Later it was how to protect herself from simpler to more insidious dangers.

As your daughter gets older still, it may seem that external forces would like to prey on her. But be confident; you can keep them at bay. Meanwhile your girl never stands still. She is constantly in the process of evolving, so there are always more stages and challenges—biological and emotional in nature—for which you want to be prepared.

CHAPTER 10

Understanding Your Tween

B eing a tween—the stage between childhood and the teenage years—can be difficult for a girl. On the one hand, she is trying to separate from her parents' influence and become an independent person. That means letting go of the comfortable and secure hands of her parents or caregivers. On the other hand, she is beginning to experience huge changes in her body, which means she needs her parents more than ever. So expect your daughter's tween years to be turbulent, tumultuous, and, with your guidance, terrific.

Puberty and Menstruation

The time in your girl's life when secondary sexual traits develop is called puberty. The word *puberty* has two different Latin origins. One is *pubertas*, meaning "like an adult." The other is *pubescere*, meaning "to grow hair." Going by these early definitions, we find puberty to denote a time of growing up and sprouting hair where none was before. It usually happens between the ages of ten and fifteen, and refers to the physical changes in your daughter that set the stage for the emotional changes of the next segment in her life, adolescence. Girls experience the start of puberty at different ages while the entire process can take up to four years.

Most girls begin to show noticeable changes in their bodies that include the growth of breasts, pubic and underarm hair, widening of the hips, enlargement of the

uterus, and the start of menstruation, at age ten to twelve. But even some third-graders can exhibit prepuberty signs.

The process of puberty is a miracle, so tell your daughter about it long before it happens. Certainly by the time she is eight or nine, talk to her about the wonderful physical changes that are ahead for her. Use side-by-side talk if you are watching TV together and a commercial pertaining to sanitary products comes on. Use over-the-shoulder talk if she is in the backseat while you are driving to the mall. Just make sure the topic is out in the open and on the table any time she has a question or concern about it. Get her excited about the wonders that will soon take place in her body and clue her in to the specifics.

Essential

While the average age of a girl starting her period is twelve and a half, it is normal for some girls to begin menstruating much earlier and others much later. Getting her first period can be traumatic for some girls, so be available with understanding, advice, and a few good books on the topic written just for her. The library offers many choices.

Plan ahead for a celebration just for you and her for when the big event occurs, discuss the details of the festivities with her, and ask her how she wants to kick off her entrance into the circle of biological womanhood.

Puberty Perks

Becoming more adult-like in her body, looks, and thought is the result of your daughter's puberty. This process is generally thought to be complete when she has regular periods that happen at predictable intervals.

Make sure your daughter keeps a record of when the following events happen: spotting, a light menstrual flow, a medium flow, and a heavy flow.

By keeping track of these events she can record the miraculous way her body works, predict her next period, and have plenty of supplies on hand. Go to the store and pick up several types of sanitary products—from liners to minis to wings to tampons—give them to her and let her pick through them. In other words, show your daughter that her puberty matters to you and that you will make it fun for her.

Alert!

The age at which menstruation begins has been decreasing for the past hundred years. This may be due to an overall improvement in nutrition and the standard of living. Heavier girls menstruate earlier while a girl's strenuous sports activity can delay the onset of her periods.

Get your daughter to vent what is on her mind about the changes she sees in herself. See beneath her "camouflaging," that is, her acting in a conforming manner that denies her individuality. Tell her everybody handles puberty differently. With your help, she will use this time as a stepping stone and not a stumbling block. Giggle with your girl over any embarrassing experiences during your puberty. Tell her a few decades ago people did not even discuss the topic of puberty, poor things.

Menstruation Mastery

If you are uncomfortable with the topic yourself, load up on pertinent pamphlets from the guidance department of your daughter's school. Scan them and hand them to your girl. To master her menstruation ABCs, she needs to know more than just the clinical definition of menstruation, which is the shedding of the endometrium, or lining, of the uterus. The usual monthly blood loss varies; about two fluid ounces in total is an approximate norm. But again, there is really no normal period.

Alert!

About 10 percent of girls experience cramping in their lower abdomen before their periods. That happens because the uterus spasms to release the period flow. Exercise such as walking, jogging, or biking can help. A warm bath or a heating pad can also ease the pain. If the cramps are severe, ask the doctor what medications she recommends for your girl.

Whatever periods your daughter experiences, they are normal for her, with the spacing between periods being, on the average, between twenty-four and thirty-five days. In the beginning, she will not be regular, but within a year or two, she will ovulate predictably. Should she, or you, feel something is out of kilter in that department, of course, see the doctor.

A New Daughter

The many changes your girl experiences, starting with her tweens, will affect all major aspects of her life. This time is an important prelude for her; she is on the verge of growing up. She can use this time as a starting block for a new emphasis on her academics or a change in her athletic involvement. As her body morphs from the shape of a rectangle to more rounded, her thoughts will change, too, from little girl ones to more mature ones. Her social connections and relationships will also undergo a huge upheaval. In short, your daughter is on the edge of blossoming into the inner and outer beauty she is meant to be. Congratulate her.

Blossoming Sexuality and Crushes

Your daughter's sexuality can be described as her behavior, emotions, and sensations connected with the use of her sex organs. In other words, it refers to what makes her female and implies being attracted and having control over expressing herself sexually. One problem you may encounter is that these days, sex is mentioned everywhere and often far too casually. So your girl may be more openly curious about her sexuality than girls were in the past.

 **Fact**

In a 1993 study conducted with several colleagues, feminist scholar and author Carol Gilligan noticed that girls are seriously impacted in their tween years, which she calls the "edge of adolescence," but that this time span is often ignored, partly because girls seem to "lose their voice" at this point of their lives.

The Power of Sex

Turn this fact to your advantage. Tell your daughter that while "everyone" now seems to talk casually about sexuality and sex, nothing has really changed. Sex still has major emotional, physical, and relationship importance. It has to be very powerful and is—after all, it can create a life!

Maturing sexually is a big part of your daughter's adolescence. So during her preadolescence, get prepared for it. Tell her she may already feel the first stirrings of her emerging sexuality and its amazing power. That is her chance to get control of what is happening to her. Instead of letting herself be pulled blindly by the biological forces forming her, she should grab the reins and choose the direction. This is a great time to talk to her about values, emotions, and attitudes.

Empowered Girl

Explain to your daughter what is happening to her. She should enjoy having sexual feelings, if she does. Like a rose bush sprouting new leaves in spring and creating buds, her sexual feelings are an indicator of more growth and beauty on the horizon. So she should revel in her more mature thoughts and feelings.

Now it is normal for her to:

- Pay much more attention to her hair
- Wear tighter-fitting clothes
- Start putting on makeup

Your daughter is just practicing and learning how to make herself more attractive. Compliment her on her efforts and give her frequent hugs.

 **Essential**

Experts call it "skin hunger" when the cuddling little girls experience by their parents suddenly stops as the girls get older. Skin hunger has to be fed just like regular hunger. Be sure to pat your daughter on the shoulder, rub her hand, and stroke the top of her head every so often, so she won't turn to boys prematurely to have them fill that void.

Set aside time to talk only about your daughter's new stage: becoming physically and emotionally mature enough to use the power of her sexuality. Tell her just as her regular periods started out little by little, so will her sexuality—and with it the associated emotions and feelings—grow little by little. This is the perfect time to discuss the various stages of love with her.

Crush Course

A crush is an early stage in a girl's development of her ability to eventually love deeply. It can be a sudden intense liking for someone, have minor proportions, and fade quickly. Or it can be a major experience that sets your daughter's heart racing and gives her a tingly feeling. A crush can be from afar, as on a movie star, or up close, as on the boy next door or the one who sits behind her in class. But no matter what kind it is, rejoice with your daughter over her crushes if she tells you about them. If not, just smile as you observe her "crushing" every time the interest of her admiration appears on the TV screen or walks past her at the mall. Just as you were happy to see her crawl for the first time as a baby, be glad she is moving in the right direction and get ready. Boy craziness may be about to start at your house.

Flirt Factors

For many girls your daughter's age, having a crush can segue into flirting. That means, acting out in some way on the excitement a crush can bring. By flirting, your girl is letting the other person know she is attracted. Holding hands, kissing, touching, and otherwise showing an emotional connection with someone are typical signs of flirting. Tell your girl that flirting is done best in small doses, with a glance, a brief touch, or a certain comment. But too much can be misinterpreted by society. At school her classmates might describe your daughter's overt flirting as "gross" or "desperate" because it is offensive to the observer. It resembles a baby who can barely walk trying to run a marathon. Everything has a time and place, especially in matters of romance.

While having a crush and being flirtatious are your girl's early attempts to get a grip on her feelings of attraction for another person, she could experience jealousy in the process. Warn her about it.

Besides the possibility of getting jealous, there is another danger for your girl. She may choose to flirt with the wrong boy. Being new at this, she might not even notice the signals she is sending out, but she should make a note of anyone who seems to fixate on her.

What your girl needs from you during her tweens is empowerment. She has control over herself and her life no matter what changes are occurring inside her. The stages of having a crush and flirting, and the emotional highs and lows they bring with them, are simply two more rungs up the ladder of her overall growth. With your help she can climb them easily, especially if you equip her with as much information as possible about her emotions.

Alert!

Tell your daughter to let you know if a boy at her school makes comments about her looks that make her feel uncomfortable. If he touches her, asks her to look at pornographic pictures, or send her photos of himself naked over the Internet, you must take action. Sexual harassment is not only wrong. It is against the law.

Emotional Turbulence

Recent cutting-edge research by the California neuropsychiatrist Luann Brizendine—as reported in *Newsweek* (July 31, 2006)—may explain how brain chemistry and genetic wiring can especially influence women's actions and feelings. Dr. Brizendine's work focuses on why girls act like girls, which by no means implies inferiority. Among the various brain parts this scientist has her eyes on is the hypothalamus, a region of the brain the size of a cherry that is responsible for hormonal control. In females it springs into action earlier than in males, causing girls to enter puberty sooner than boys, and making girls more sensitive to the fluctuations of their hormones. While this study is ongoing, it may shed light on why your girl experiences emotional turbulence and mood swings.

Hormones and Mood Swings

Because puberty starts with the pituitary gland producing hormones to stimulate the ovaries to secrete more estrogen, the resulting physical changes and the process can cause mood swings in your daughter. You can see them for yourself: One day she is her usual self, the next you feel as though a stranger has taken over her body. Suddenly she is sullen and uncommunicative and acts as if she doesn't know you. Nor does she appreciate all you have done for her. Be happy about this development, and grin and bear it. It shows that her body and brain are working as they are supposed to.

 **Fact**

The phrase *green-eyed monster*, meaning jealousy, was used by Shakespeare; he may have coined it. Throughout history, the color green was associated with sickness because people's skin can develop a greenish hue when they are very ill. Extreme jealousy, called morbid, appears more often in males than in females.

Moods Matter

Do allow your girl to blame her moodiness on raging hormones, but do not allow her to take her moods out on you or other people in your home. Be aware that, as a preadolescent, she is doing a most important job every day—growing and separating from you—and expect a pendulum effect in her emotions. But be sure to teach her to get a grip on her moodiness, and learn to apologize for any rude behavior resulting from it. Remind her to excuse herself politely from the rest of society when she feels a mood attack coming on. Soon she will be able to predict her cycle of sadness or irritability and be prepared.

PMS Stress

Some girls feel different before they get their periods, sometimes as early as two weeks before their periods start. They find themselves changing emotionally, crying easily, being grumpy, or really wanting to be left alone. They can also have sore breasts, feel puffy, or crave sweets. Yet this is just another diagnosis for your daughter, if needed, not an alibi. Tell her to look at the calendar and predict when she might experience another episode of premenstrual syndrome, and you might cut her a little slack.

Ventilation Time

What can help your girl most is letting her tell you how she feels without rushing her. Or letting her write it all down in her journal, or venting her feelings by chatting with her friends. Tell her to think of emotions as ocean waves. Sometimes all you can do is just stand still and let them wash over you. Allow your daughter some time and space to find her own way back to being the sweet, kind, and caring girl she usually is. Even the loveliest rose has a thorn or two.

Your girl can also elevate her mood by:

- Reading her favorite book or listening to her music
- Taking a nap with her pet
- Being by herself and doing absolutely nothing for as long as she wants

In short, your daughter needs to acquire her own set of tools for dealing with potential mood swings that can plague women for decades. Embracing the fact that girls are more influenced by hormones than boys can make your daughter feel special—and it will, with your support.

Rebellion and Secrets

Picture a pet trying to get off its leash. Wanting to get away from you, it will yank in the opposite direction from where you are going. The same process occurs with your tween, and it should. More and more she wants to be her own distinct person and have her own personality, so naturally she pulls away from you. She does this physically, by spending more time with her friends, and psychologically, by rebelling against you. This is a welcome development that can go overboard.

Defiance

A good way to honor your tween daughter's desire to defy you now and then is to let her have her say in matters that are not important in the long run. Consider her choice of hairstyle, clothing, purses, and nail polish among them. As long as her options are not offensive and against the school dress code, she can have fun with them.

Essential

Be sure your preadolescent daughter has some rules and regulations to rebel against. If there are none in place, she will take her instinct to rebel to school and to the community. For a tween, the urge to break rules can be confined to a minimum if it has room to play itself out on the home front.

Do not cave in on matters of safety, health, and important values, however. Make it clear to your girl that you will not bend when it comes to her physical, mental, and psychological well-being. But you can do a few important things:

1. **Compromise.** Let your daughter explain to you why she has to stay up until midnight—to attend a concert by a teen idol you approve of, for example. Then have her take a long nap before the concert, and another one the day after the concert.

2. **Let her individualize her meals.** She can have dinner foods for breakfast and breakfast foods for dinner, for example; but she must eat three meals a day.

3. **Let her set her own weekly schedule,** as far as after-school activities are concerned, as long as she schedules some free "me-time"—time for chilling out—on a regular basis.

Give your girl as long a "leash" as you can and only tug her back when you see her approaching a ravine.

Secrecy

Keeping secrets is another trait of girls in their tween stage. Suddenly you find your daughter whispering to her best friend and being whispered to by her. This is a normal stage among girls that age. Some researchers say it is the precursor of later intimacy, a close warm relationship with the "absence of fences." Use a common-sense approach when dealing with your girl's sudden tendency to keep things from you. In the past, she probably came to you with every little concern. Now you find her discussing all sorts of topics with her friends. Be glad. Do you really care about who had to go to the bathroom twice during social studies?

 **Question?**

My daughter talks to her friends on the cell phone a lot, but whenever I enter the room, she hangs up. Do I need to worry?
No, if you notice her overall progress in school and at home continuing along the same lines as in the past. Girls like secrets. But yes, if you find your daughter suddenly neglecting her studies, changing her habits, and refusing to look you in the eye when you ask her if anything is wrong.

If your daughter's secrecy worries you, it is time to find out why. You do that best by getting her to open up about it.

Getting Your Daughter to Talk

Talk therapy is very popular, not only on TV but also in the offices of people trained for it. You are also trained for it. Since your girl was little, you have been talking to her regularly, and not just about her chores and grades, but also about her wishes and hopes. Instead of talking to, and with, her less as she gets older, talk to her more. It is therapeutic for both of you.

She and you can reveal what is bothering you. So up the ongoing talk time with your daughter and never stop. If she is close-mouthed, find an unthreatening topic to chat about, such as a silly TV reality show. Have fun talking with her about your history. Share the story of when you first liked a girl or a boy. Mention your quirky behavior when you were her age.

One Time My Sister . . .

If you cannot talk about yourself, tell your girl about your brother or sister or childhood friends, and how they tried to get a girl or boy interested in them way back when. Exaggerate! The more hilarious the stories are, the better she'll like them. When your girl laughs with you, she momentarily forgets that she has decided not to talk to you anymore. So get her grinning and keep at it. Talk about the end result of the important growth stage she is going through. It will all be worth it before long. The successful mastery of one stage of development leads to more success in the future. Chit-chat with your girl, or have serious conversations with her. Another time communicate by phone, through texting, and via notes that end with a question, such as "What do you think of . . . ?"

Terrific Tweens

Without a doubt, you are the most important factor in the equation. Your example, attitude, and determination to make the tween years ten times better for your girl than they were for you are what matters. You are an involved parent, so dig into the topic of preadolescence, research how other parents handle this time, and start an e-mail conversation with other moms and dads. Make sure the tween stage is not a time when your daughter slips through the cracks, but rather that she gets as much attention as possible.

Jesse Jackson once said, "Your children need your presence more than presents." He was right. Your girl always needs you more than any gifts you can buy her, no matter how extravagant. But she needs you especially during her preadolescence as she is trying to enter her teenage years that bring with them even more exciting changes, challenges, and conquests.

CHAPTER 11

The World of the Teenage Girl

As the old saying goes, it is much easier to build a girl than to repair her. You have done a great job in building your daughter up to her teenage years. Now in her teen years, do not allow anything to undo your good work and damage her in some way. After all, her adolescence, which runs from age thirteen to nineteen, is the last stage before her adulthood. So be especially thoughtful in your parenting during this crucial part of her growth and development.

Teaching Her Media Smarts

As a teenager, your daughter has important work to do, in addition to going to school and doing everything else she does. Being an adolescent is a learning process that revolves around becoming an adult. Your girl will pass this period with flying colors if—at the end of her teens—she can joyfully answer the question, "Who am I?" to her satisfaction and to yours.

However before your daughter can do that with any certainty, she—like all the other girls her age—may find herself unclear about her identity. She may go through a few years of floundering during which she may engage in the following activities:

- Experiment with various pretend personas, even negative or delinquent ones.
- Try these personas out to see if any of them are a good fit for her.
- Find one that is most suited for her and relish in it.

During this key trial-and-error process your teenage daughter truly needs you more than ever. She wants and seeks your leadership and guidance to become a successful teen.

Media Mis-messages

What gets in the way of your daughter building her positive identity is that the media have an entirely different goal. They give teens a bad rap because it makes for better news. You know their motto, "If it bleeds, it leads." When it comes to teenage girls, their motto is, "We want salacious, not gracious." So every time a kind and productive teen does some good for her community, her story is relegated to the backburner. But every time a girl gets involved in something seedy, the paparazzi are all over it.

 **Fact**

American psychoanalyst Erik Erikson (1902–1994) contributed greatly to the field of child development and identity establishment. He coined labels for the various stages of growth and called the adolescent years a "psychological moratorium"—a time when girls can take time to acquire self-certainty and to overcome self-consciousness and self-doubt.

The "Mess" Media

The mass media—consisting of newspapers, magazines, TV, radio, movies, and blogs—have become very powerful during the last few decades. In fact, these days, television, advertising, and the latest technology permeate every corner of life. For example, most homes have more than one TV set and radio, as well as computers, video games, digital recording devices, and the latest requisite accoutrements. Thus, the mass media influence every facet of our existence.

Alert!

Girls nowadays are seen as a huge potential market by advertisers. Why? Because they have more money than in the past and because today's busy parents tend to substitute things for the time and attention they used to devote to their children. Parents want to make their daughters happy, so they give them what they want.

Whether you want it or not, your daughter will become ensnared in whatever fabric the mass media weave when they portray teens. In regard to girls, that fabric is often messy or just plain flawed. The media often portray girls as rebellious, disrespectful, self-centered, and superficial. Worse, they show girls as precocious or "slutty."

From middle school on, most girls do tend to live in a world preoccupied with:

- Friends
- Clothes
- Popularity
- Grades

Girls want to be pointed in the right direction, but the mass media are not the place for that. Powered by a profit-making mentality, at all costs, they zoom in on your girl as a fresh new consumer with deep pockets and plenty of ditziness. They could not be more wrong.

Mass Media Mastery

You do not take your responsibility as a parent lightly. You know that forewarned is forearmed, and forearmed is unharmed. Therefore, you want your daughter to be prepared for the onslaught of deceptive advertising that she experiences each day via the mass media. In our culture, there is not only an ever-growing expectation and belief that teenage girls are flighty, but there are also marketing gurus at work that decree that it is to our economy's advantage that adolescent girls should be more concerned with their appearance, their relationships with others, and approval from men than about their own ideas, their own expectations, and their own achievements.

 **Fact**

A study, reported in 1993, found that the average magazine read by teenage girls contains between eight to twelve beauty and fashion articles, which can take up to two-thirds of the magazine's content. These magazines also focus heavily on profiles and opinions of men. Usually these magazines have only two or three stories that are not on beauty or beauty products.

With every teen magazine that girls read, they are bombarded with the message that their minds are unimportant. It is their looks, their bodies, and their emerging "sex appeal" that matters most. In short, the mass media are devaluing teenage girls as persons and value them as purchasers. Use this fact as a great tool for smartening up your daughter. Tell her that as far as she is concerned, it is a buyer's market. She is a hot commodity. The advertisers—whether on TV, on the radio, in print, or on the Internet—are desperately trying to market their products, services, and a certain lifestyle to her. While the commercials and ads can be considered a form of free expression, the methods they are using can be very misleading. With your help, your daughter can begin to examine closely the types of ads and commercials aimed at her, the overt messages behind them, and the hidden implications.

You will both laugh as you channel surf and check out a lot of commercials. Flip through the ad sections of your newspaper and scan the glossy portions meant for girls. "Buy me, buy me, buy me," all the advertisements scream. Soon your daughter will discover that there is a big imbalance, with her, an informed teenager, holding all the power. She is the one who can pick and choose; the marketers can only lose.

Essential

Teach your daughter to tear out any keepers—the valuable stories—from her magazines and yours, but let her select which ones. Any article that deals with political issues, the environment, teenage health, sexual harassment, or her hobbies may be what she wants to hang onto. Libraries call a collection of "miscellaneous resource materials" stored separately from books a "vertical file." Let her start her own.

Laugh with her at deceptive sales practices she notices and keep some note cards handy to record them. Before long, she will have a stack with almost every lame advertising technique listed. Your teenage girl and her friends will have a ball. As you will see, ad-smart adolescents can be great activists: They can write the companies, complain, and make themselves heard.

Besides making your girl savvy about the mass media, counter the wrong messages they send by starting a mother/daughter or father/daughter book club that focuses on writings about girls who face real challenges and do heroic things. Let her start an e-mail correspondence with girls from countries besieged by famine or other tragedies. But before you do, make sure she is thoroughly up on her computer ABCs.

Computer Safety Basics

The most important computer basic is the skill to use it successfully. While tests show that kids who have TVs in their bedroom score lower on exams, those who have access to computers score higher. So without a doubt, computers and the Internet can open a door to a vast arena of information and entertainment for your teenage girl but only with your involvement. Without close supervision, the Internet can do much more harm than good.

 **Fact**

> Research shows that in general girls are equally as comfortable on the Internet as boys. But girls show a tendency to use the Internet in a more productive form: They use it for homework assignments, e-mail, and chatrooms. In contrast, boys use it more for entertainment and games.

Therefore, welcome all the positives the Internet offers, but be alert to its potential for enormous negatives. Most parents do not realize that the Internet can be considered a gate to and from your home, with the door always wide open. No matter how many safety features and parental controls you install, and upgrade regularly, someone somewhere will always be able to get around any walls or other protective measures you add to your computer, come right in, and visit your daughter—and that someone often has predatory intentions. So unless you are sure, which you can never be 100 percent, do not set the computer up in your girl's bedroom. Set it up in the den or the kitchen. Or do you want to leave your daughter alone with a pedophile?

Alert!

Tell your daughter never to hand out any personal information, phone numbers, addresses, credit card numbers, or the name or details of her school to anyone online. Quite a few sites enable a user to find a street address by entering a phone number or a school by entering the size of its student population and state.

Too many criminals consider the Internet their personal trawling grounds for prey, and often girls are their favorite game. Make sure your daughter is not among them, and do not be lulled into a false sense of security because she is school smart. Too many girls can be gullible when it comes to Net connections and end up in harm's way. Even if nothing more serious than being exposed to some porn site happens to your girl, avoid the slightest chance it could.

Computer Rules

Instruct your daughter on how to avoid all Internet dangers. She should never open an e-mail or attachment from people she does not know. Do not allow her to visit sites you do not approve of; if she is in doubt, she must get your permission first. Post a running list of acceptable Web sites and your computer rules. Show her the "history" feature on your computer and tell her you will check it sporadically. Tell her you trust her, but you do not trust the millions of strangers in cyberspace.

Computer Consequences

If your daughter breaks your computer rules, ask for an explanation. She may have clicked on something accidentally. If she continues to visit dangerous sites, however, you will have to do what you would if—when the times comes—she drives unsafely. You would take away her driving privileges then. So, restrict her computer use to only homework, with you looking over her shoulder. In all likelihood, it will not come to that.

Lifetime Cyber Risks

It is not only the potentially dangerous access via the Net to your daughter by questionable characters you want to warn her about. It is also the risk of her sharing something about herself with the cyber universe that can have bad consequences. That is the reason *Newsweek* (August 2006) calls the Internet a "web of risks." Naïve kids can indeed risk their future as potential college students or employees if they are careless in what they post online.

 **Fact**

In 2003 Harvard student Marc Zuckerberg and some of his classmates created Facebook to make the contact among students easier. When he launched the service a year later, it spread quickly at his university and before long to all 2,100 four-year schools. Last year the service, which now has 100 employees, started admitting high school students.

There are several ad-supported services that are very popular with young people. While your daughter may not be old enough to participate in a social networking site such as MySpace, she and her friends will have heard about them from older students. So before she is tempted to reveal anything about herself on that type of network, warn her about the illusion of privacy. Whatever she may post about herself may come back to haunt her. These days, companies planning to hire her may enter her name not only into a search engine but also research her on the various social networks.

For that reason, have your girl learn to draw the line between the benefits of the Internet and its bugaboos. Make her as computer-cognizant as possible, and who knows, maybe she can teach you a thing or two as well. Just be sure to remember this: The dangers from the Net are constantly changing, so keep the warnings coming. You do not want to let your guard down.

Essential

Laurie Sybel, a director of career development at Vermont Technical College, advises students to think of their page at Facebook and similar services as a job application or resumé. She knows from experience that a student can get rejected from an internship because of a picture of him "partying" that was posted on a social-network page.

Music Mania and Hollywood

Two more areas to be wary of, in regard to your teen girl and her healthy development, are popular music and Hollywood. Both can present false images. While you cannot understand why your girl loves a certain song, you must keep in mind that this situation is centuries old. Think of the type of music you adored when you were an adolescent and how it shocked your elders. They shook their heads in disgust at what they called "that awful noise," as in, "Turn that awful noise off—now!" As a teenager, you thought your parents did not understand "good music." Now it is your turn to be baffled by your daughter's selections on the radio or what she uploads on her portable media player.

Do not—like a broken record—repeat your parents' mantra about the "awful noise." They did their best, but you are the new type of parent. Listen to your girl's music first. Maybe then you can get an inkling of what makes it so "hot," in her opinion. Perhaps it is the beat or the background sounds, but pay attention to the lyrics and get ready to be shocked. These days, the b-word and the f-word are the favorites of rappers and other musicians. A "hoe" used to mean an implement for gardening, not anymore. Now a "ho" is a demeaning term for a girl doing demeaning things.

Nix Name-Calling

Do you allow your daughter to be called ugly names? Of course not. So do not let your girl listen to the verbal degradation of women or the description of violence toward them, no matter how enticing the melody or rhythm. Simply give each song with an f-word the grade F—it failed. Tell your girl that listening to women being called bad words is condoning it. Besides, you do not allow her to curse. Why then would you allow anyone in the music world to curse at her?

 *Question?*

Isn't downloading music from the Internet illegal?
Before you allow your daughter to download music, ask her to research the various options—from free to small-fee sites. Get her to find out from her friends what the best and most price-worthy sites are and discuss with her the realities and legalities. Make sure that you and your daughter make an informed decision together.

Hollywood

Hollywood also is of a mindset that the grosser the language and the depicted scenes are, the higher the gross income. Plus, the movie industry often uses women only as décor, and makes a huge profit from hyper-sexualizing young girls. That means it features barely adolescent girls as femme fatales with a deep décolleté. Of course like any commercial venture, Hollywood is profit-based. Ask your girl to read the movie critiques carefully. Allow her to flex her discerning muscles as to what films she might like to see.

Enjoy some chick flicks with her and especially enjoy discussing with her afterward what in the movie was factual or based on reality. In those discussions, it will become obvious that, slowly but surely, your girl is getting better at judging what is real and what is just "reel."

Real Life versus Reel Life

Watch any movie or fashion show on TV, and you can see at a glance that these days incredibly thin actresses and emaciated models dominate the screen. Most of them really are thinner than what you would think is healthy for them, but perhaps they are under the guidance of their nutritionists. What you should worry about is the negative impact all that skinniness has on your daughter.

 **Fact**

When Harvard professor Carol Gilligan did a study on the psychological development of adolescent girls, she found that they experience a big drop in self-esteem as they become teens. Only 29 percent of girls that age said they felt "happy the way I am." In contrast, 60 percent felt that way at age nine.

According to a 1998 report by Exeter University in the United Kingdom, 90 percent of teenage girls think frequently about the shape of their bodies. When nearly 50,000 girls were asked what their biggest concern was, their answer was "appearance." Make sure that your daughter is able to separate what she sees via a movie reel from what is real. She is a real girl with many fascinating activities on her plate, many great concepts to learn, and a fabulous future ahead. While appearance does not have to be the last item on her list, it should definitely not be her first and only one.

Encouraging Healthy Relationships

Worshiping underweight actresses and starving models is unhealthy for your girl. Make sure her life is filled with people she can adore who present a healthy image for her. Introduce her to young business-women, artists, and coaches. Teach her to be proud of the way she looks, be it in sneakers or heels. Tell her—over and over—that she is the daughter you always wanted and how proud of her you are.

What is of the utmost importance for your girl is to develop a healthy relationship with reality and with herself. She needs to understand both the pull of independence and her need to remain grounded in her parents' domain.

Understanding Independence

To assert her ever-increasing independence, your daughter must put a measure of distance between herself and you. That is a good development that you should welcome. On days when your daughter is easy to guide and when she listens to every word you have to offer with appreciation, you feel gratified. On other days when she seems to develop strange tastes and goes for idol worshiping that is foreign to you, you may feel that whatever you tell her falls on deaf ears. Yet never retreat and pout when your daughter impatiently says to you, "I know, I know. You've told me about this a million times." Just smile and say, "Sorry, I guess I was having a teenage moment." You are of course referring to the many times you told her to put her jacket away only to have to tell her again the next day.

Culture Change

Each generation of parents has faced the turning world of the next generation. Technology, culture and fashions change constantly, so smile at the latest trifling trends and share your most important values with your daughter. Ask her to make a list of her own emerging values—whatever she treasures as she advances through her teen years.

Encourage her to categorize them under topics such as activities, things, people, ideas, and beliefs. Share with her your own list, and ask her to tack hers up on her bulletin board as a point of reference. She can add to it as she continues to emerge as the successful girl she is in the process of becoming. That means she is getting more and more able to circumvent any trouble spots and to take on more and more responsibility.

Culture Cornerstone

Every day your daughter is growing and learning to earn trust, keep trust, and if need be, re-earn trust—with you always close enough to help her. Instill in your daughter the unwavering certainty that amid whatever changes she goes through emotionally and physically as a teenager, you are her permanent haven of encouragement and safety. You are her hand-rail and her first and best support system—always available and never closed.

CHAPTER 12

Daddy's Little Girl

The relationship between a girl and her father is crucial and deserves to be treated as such. It is most often the first male-female relationship in a girl's life and can form the foundation for how your daughter approaches her future relationships with men. Many men feel awkward dealing with their growing daughters, but your interactions with her are pivotal in her life. From this relationship, your daughter develops a sense of acceptance of herself. Since a child tends to regard herself as others regard her, her father's view of her is very important. But the father-daughter bond has many more beneficial aspects. If it is strong and healthy, it sends your daughter into the world with clear and healthy expectations for men.

One-on-One Time with Dad

One benefit a daughter gets from relating to her father is a healthy concept of self. According to family therapist Dr. Jane R. Rosen-Grandon, a little girl's self-concept is "largely shaped by this early relationship." Your daughter learns to feel good about being a female child by her interactions with you, as her father. The result is that she feels secure in that role. She reasons that if you respect her as what she is, she must be worthy of that respect and acts accordingly.

Your role as father can only play out if it is allowed to express itself. Therefore, your daughter needs to get as much meaningful time with you as she can from early on. Make it a definite and specific part of her everyday experiences. Dad time does not always just happen. It must be scheduled, just like other important things. How do you accomplish this?

- Set aside a special few minutes every day for your daughter to spend with you and you alone.
- Make sure your daughter has a chance to eat at least one meal with you.
- Be sure to take part in your daughter's bedtime ritual.
- Encourage your daughter to come to you for advice.

 **Fact**

Research funded by the National Institute of Mental Health and the National Institute of Child Health and Human Development describes the part fathers play in their daughters' development as "an important role," an understatement that indeed emphasizes a father's pivotal role.

If you are not your daughter's biological father, honor her connection to him. As her "second" or "real" father—in the sense that you are raising her—do not overlook the original bond between your girl and her birth father. Thus, it is even more important to plan ahead for those occasions when your daughter and her biological dad can spend time together. While that time may be limited, there are other ways to make the connection between her and her original father strong. The same goes for you if you are divorced and your daughter lives with a stepfather, maybe even far away. Insist on seeing her as much as possible.

Thus, whether your daughter is being raised primarily by another man, whether you are the girl's stepfather and part of her everyday life, or whether you are raising your biological daughter, remember the importance of the father-daughter bond and do all you can to make it strong and vibrant. The best tactics go beyond any "hurt-feelings" game playing between adults and focus solely on what's best for the girl. Some examples of helpful strategies include:

- Informing the biological father regularly of your custodial daughter's progress and insisting the same is done for you, should you be the noncustodial dad.
- Having her develop a strong phone or e-mail relationship with you and with her biological dad.
- Planning a weekend ritual with her, you, or her "other" father that will not be deviated from unless absolutely necessary.
- Setting up vacation and holiday plans that include specific times for your daughter to spend more time with you, whether you are her biological dad or her custodial dad.

If both a biological father and a stepfather are in the picture, the scheduling can be tricky, but you must prevail. You, as the girl's father—no matter how you came to assume this role—must put yourself in your daughter's shoes and always think of what is best for her. So split up the vacations and holidays, or alternate the destinations. Be flexible and have your girl spend some time with you, and some time with her other father.

Surrogate Fathers

If you have a sister, other female relative, or friend, who finds herself in a position where neither a biological nor a custodial father is present, help her find a substitute male to fill in for her daughter's dad. Take that role on with a generous—in regard to time—attitude. Or help your sister, other female relative, or friend choose a substitute father figure for her daughter, but be very careful in your selection and realize the importance of finding the right man.

Discuss the fine qualities your brother, cousin, or neighbor possesses with the mother of the girl. Encourage her to include that exemplary male to become a closer part of her life. That means this "chosen" father can come along on outings with your niece or your friend's daughter. Or you can spend time with this family and fill in as a father substitute. As you parent your own girl, share some of your parenting wisdom and attention with your sister's, cousin's, or female friend's daughter. Maybe you already have two daughters, so why not extend your girl-raising circle to include three or four girls. You are a good dad, are a great dad, an extraordinary dad; therefore, be an inclusive dad as well. The world needs more men like you.

Alert!

Statistics prove that the risk of physical and sexual abuse goes up when unrelated adults move into a home with children. Your sister's or friend's daughter needs safety and trust much more than having a bad father figure in her life. Therefore, discuss these dangers with your sister or your female friend before she has a new partner moving in with her.

Grandfather Time

Think of your own father and how you can make use of his strengths in raising your girl. Remember what he excelled in as your dad and be sure to allow his parenting excellence to move down to the next generation in the form of your girl. If a grandfather is not an option, inviting several appropriately aged men to play a role in the life of your girl can be a solution. She definitely needs to see a grandfather figure—her biological one or an alternate one—in her life on a regular basis.

Reconfigured Father Figure

Only through a father figure can a daughter learn what it means to be female in relationship to a male. But don't feel defeated if you cannot be present in your daughter's life on a daily basis. Modern life has made our existence much more complex. You want to be a strong father to your daughter and spend much time with her, but if that's not possible, just remember: Your girl's father time can be a composite, made up of several regular periods spent with several different men who all have something positive to contribute to her growth. If you can't attend all her volleyball games, swim meets, and play rehearsals, maybe her uncle or your male cousin can step in. Be resourceful in including a male role model in her experiences.

 *Question?*

What can I do to get closer to my girl and be less emotionally distant?

Many men have been brought up in an environment that suppressed their flow of emotions. That does not mean they don't feel. It only means that they fear to reveal their inner selves. By making sure you are a part of as many events and stages of your daughter's life as possible, you can get closer to her. Also, you will know in the future that you did all you could.

Just as your girl benefits from time with you, so do you benefit from time with her. Little girls help their fathers consider the world through the eyes of a girl. Legendary Duke University basketball coach Mike Krzyzewski says that his three daughters make him talk about things guys usually do not talk about. "That is a strength," he adds. Indeed, every girl is Daddy's little girl after all, and if you are truly present in her life, she will tell you exactly what occupies her mind, thereby widening your horizons. You in turn, will be enriched by her presence. Your conversations with her will become very special to her. Whatever you say to her has a deep meaning in her life.

By choosing what messages to send to your daughter, you can greatly influence her self-esteem. She looks to you as her first and most important source of validation.

Self-Esteem Building via Dad

It is crucial that you help build your daughter's self-esteem. Low self-esteem can undermine your daughter's desire to achieve and affect her negatively throughout life and may lead to depression. (That topic is addressed more fully in Chapter 16.) Even if she turns out to become a high achiever, the question is how much more she could have achieved with her self-esteem at the highest level.

 **Fact**

American suffragist and social reformer Elizabeth Cady Stanton (1815–1902) said her father hurt her by his lack of pride in her. In contrast, Rev. William V. Guy, father of actress Jasmine Guy, and Fred Turner, father of Miss America Debbye Turner, are outspokenly proud of their daughters.

Fortunately, these days the number of fathers trying to do their best by their daughters is increasing even though they may have trouble with the issues of personal relationships. In the book *Raising Cain: Protecting the Emotional Life of Boys*, psychologist Michael Thompson refers to the challenging gender gap between mothers and sons that can translate later on into a man's problematic emotional existence.

A Father's Challenge

Fathers of girls, however, face an even more challenging gender gap when trying to connect with their daughters, according to school psychologist Dr. JoAnn Deak. In her book, *Girls Will Be Girls*, she points out that mothers, being women, are generally better prepared in relationship skills for their parenting jobs. In contrast, men as fathers do not have the best emotional equipment for their task of raising a girl and may have to struggle with it. But what a great payoff they reap by making an effort.

A Father's Choice

By making a deliberate effort, you can overcome your own parents' child-rearing shortcomings and construct a loving and lasting relationship with your daughter. The decision to commit to making a connection with your daughter is all you need to get started. Your presence and uniqueness will guide you in the right direction. All you have to do is be yourself and be willing to share a part of yourself.

 **Essential**

You should never tell your daughter that she is eating too much or getting fat, even if you are trying to be helpful. You should not focus on her good looks and refer to her physical characteristics. Instead, you should focus on her achievements and praise her for them.

Your strengths can show themselves in many ways, such as:

- If you are inclined to be funny, you can be goofy with your daughter, play silly games with her, and make her laugh.
- If you like to tell stories, you can start telling her a tale of adventure—or read one to her—that has many installments, one of which you can narrate to her daily over the course of weeks or months.
- If you are the quiet type, you can ask your daughter to tell you the names of all her stuffed toys and to fill you in on the background of each one.
- If you like to sing, you can ask her to teach you the songs she learns at school and sing them with her.

Whatever your personality, you can use it to strengthen your bond with your daughter. She will appreciate all your attempts, especially if you establish a pattern in your interactions with her and are reliable and trustworthy, so that she can learn to be reliable and trustworthy too.

Even if you are a very busy man, you must make time for your daughter. If you have little free time, you can include your girl whenever you do your chores at home. She can splash in the lawn sprinkler while you do yard work, ride in the wheelbarrow when you transport the raked leaves to the curb, or go to the post office with you.

The more time you devote to spending with your girl, the more her confidence rises. The most important man in her life prefers her company. That makes her feel important not only in your eyes—and the world's—but also in her own. Yet besides raising your daughter's self-esteem, you play another crucial role in the development of your daughter.

 **Fact**

A study by Vanderbilt University researchers involving 173 girls found that the quality of the fathers' involvement with their daughters was the most important feature in relation to the onset of the girls' puberty. Girls raised in father-absent homes experienced puberty earlier than those in father-present homes.

Even when your daughter becomes a preteen and teen, she needs to spend time with you on a regular basis. You should never take "Leave me alone!" as a signal that you're no longer needed by your daughter. You should take it for what it is—a temporary breather in your girl's dependence on you.

Role Modeling: Your Daughter's Boyfriends

You are the role model for the various types of boys your daughter may become attracted to. Through your behavior and actions, she will learn two important things that may affect her happiness for the rest of her life.

1. Which male characteristics to rate highly, treasure, and try to find in a potential boyfriend.
2. Which male characteristics to rate poorly, trounce, and be sure to avoid in a potential boyfriend.

Besides getting firsthand knowledge about a man's good and not-so-good qualities, your girl will also get her first introductory lesson in the possibilities of romantic love between a man and a woman by watching how you treat her mother.

Therefore, you should not only exhibit your best side in front of your daughter but also in front of your mate. When you treat the mother of your girl like a queen, your daughter feels like a princess. When you compliment the mother, you compliment the daughter. When you praise the mother, you extol the daughter.

The same goes for how you treat your own mother. If you make it a point to be loving around her and your wife, your daughter learns that a man is supposed to be loving, how he shows that love appropriately, and what she needs to expect from a future mate.

 **Essential**

You and your mate should spend as much time in your roles of husband and wife, or as a couple, as feasible. Making your relationship as solid and as permanent as you can helps your daughter realize that a good and lasting relationship is possible. This will become a top goal for her future.

Whenever possible, you should show your love to the mother of your girl by expressing your fond feelings through cards, flowers, and notes left around the house. Flowing from that might be a special surprise for your daughter (such as tucking her favorite snack into her lunch box), your compliments to her about her abilities (such as remarking about her keeping her room neat), and your recognition of her talents (such as displaying her artwork in your office).

Practicing Daughter

When a girl begins to relate to her father as a male-gendered adult, she needs him to be her guinea pig. Therefore you should let her show her daughter-dad love by letting her brush your hair, "criticize" your clothes, and bring you your favorite newspaper when you get home from work. She needs to practice how to make a connection to the future males in her life.

Role-Modeling Mother

The mother should do her part as well in building a good father-daughter relationship by praising your outstanding qualities, by showing the daughter a photo of herself and you when you two met, and by telling your girl what makes you special and what attracted her to you in the first place. Thus, the father-daughter relationship—realized in its rich potential—can offer great benefits to every member of the family.

Alert!

In families where there are both girls and boys, you must make sure you do not invest more time and energy in the relationship with your sons than in the relationship with your daughters. If daughters are relegated to a second-class status, they will never forget it, and the sons will grow up to perpetuate the unfairness.

Through your daily actions and your attempt to understand your daughter you will show her that you love her unconditionally. Plus, you will instruct her in how a fine man acts. Your example of masculinity is something she will use as a measuring stick in her future relationships with other males. If she has been taught well, she will do her best to find a good mate. You can help her in this by encouraging her early boyfriends to come to the house. As she gets older, you can instill in her the fact that she should expect chivalry from the boys, the same kind of chivalry you always show her mother. You also must make certain that she will always know when she is not treated well.

Sharing Your Daughter's Passions

Society tends to define young girls by their activities, such as: She is an equestrian, a softball player, or a gymnast. You should make sure your daughter has something positive in her life by which her friends and community can define her. Ask her what her passion is and then help her explore it more deeply. Often that passion revolves around a sport she is drawn to. You can use this activity to teach her more self-control and patience.

 **Fact**

> A study of 140 eighth-grade students, published in 2006 by *USA Weekend Magazine*, found that self-disciplined kids outperformed their less-disciplined peers not only in their grades but also on their standardized achievement test scores. Self-discipline is best taught by your example.

You model self-discipline by the way you act, and you foster your daughter's self-discipline and control by her involvement in something that demands:

- Practicing a skill for a long time, such as playing golf or tennis
- Working on a long-range project, such as building a piece of furniture
- Investing much of her time and money in something, such as starting a collection

You can also watch to see what natural athletic talent your daughter may have and build on the passion she feels for the sport. You can coach her, or by following your own passion, guide your girl into rooting for your preferred teams, or get her to imitate your own sports prowess. She may end up loving something you excelled in or take the sport to a whole new level. You should always include both your boys and girls in the sports training you provide and the sports equipment you install in your backyard. In fact, you should make no distinction between how much time you devote to your son's little league games and your daughter's track meets. You should also give your daughter more "masculine" presents, such as a baseball mitt or a chemistry set.

 **Fact**

> When Michelle Wie was four years old, her father, a professor at the University of Hawaii, first took her to the driving range. She took her first swings with a baseball grip and almost toppled over, but her father had her practice in the backyard until she straightened out her technique. Michelle, at seventeen years old, is one of the top professional women golfers.

You can teach your daughter many valuable life lessons connected with sports. For example, how not to take tryouts too seriously, how to be a good winner and a good loser, and how to throw herself into a pursuit she loves just for the sake of it. Hobbies can also bind fathers and daughters.

Sharing Hobbies
Most of all, share an interest that allows you and your daughter to keep up with each other and with the developments in your lives over time. There is always an occasion to talk during a fishing trip— at least during the drive to the lake and back home—or a camping

excursion. Traveling together, by bike, boat, car, or on foot, can also nurture your father-daughter connection. During those travels, you and your girl will have many chances to solve problems. You can teach your daughter how to create something out of nothing, or how to make the best out of any situation. One example is calling a flat tire an opportunity for adventure. Documenting your travels and rehashing your trips or your visits to the zoo or the planetarium will give her many precious memories.

Sharing Hopes

Spending an evening with you looking at the stars will nurture your girl's sense of awe. As you explain your view of the universe, and your hopes and dreams for her, she will feel free to tell you of her hopes and dreams while developing an allegiance to something greater: humankind's universal striving to be the best. Things worth doing and realizing dreams can take a lot of time and work, but each step along the way, you can help your daughter soar.

Inspiring Her to Aim Higher

You play a pivotal role in your daughter's academic achievement and ambitions. If you introduce her to brain teasers and strategic games like chess from early on, she can learn to use her head and be proud of it. Together, you and your daughter can do crossword puzzles or sudoku.

Essential

Encourage your daughter to spend time with other curious kids who are eager to think on their own. Many communities have science museums and libraries that sponsor activities for kids wanting to explore new fields. Take her to the meetings and watch her get involved in experiments or activities that require thought.

The more your daughter has a chance to think, the more her capacity for thought will increase. This capacity underlies all learning and has a long shelf life. In fact, clear thinking is the firm foundation on which all schoolwork builds, and your actions can be a great impetus in furthering this ability.

Way above Average

There are several ways you can inspire your daughter to grow mentally and not be content with being average. You can encourage her to be a top achiever in school, which may lead to her becoming a high achiever in life. You can explore several possible career paths with her, long before she enters high school, by taking her to visit places where those careers are practiced. You can show her how to research several topics of interest on the Internet. You can send her postcards and e-mail from your business trips, bring her back maps from where you were, and take her to work to show her how you spend your time away from home.

Encourage Her Curiosity

Most important, you should encourage your daughter's curiosity and avoid squelching it. When she asks you something, you can tell her where to find the answer, if you do not know it. You should also take your daughter to hear inspiring lecturers—male or female—who can thrill girls with motivational pep talks that make them eager to acquire more knowledge. Be sure to let her overhear you in discussions with other people and ask her opinions.

Of course, either a father or a mother can use many of these strategies, but the fact that you, a dad, use them makes them so special. It is your male point of view, your male interests, and your male approach to life that infuses your girl-raising actions with extra power in her eyes.

Q & A

You can showcase your daughter's growing fascination with a new topic by posting the results of her Internet research on the refrigerator. You can ask her to write to an agency or corporation and share her joy when she gets a letter back. You can cheer her on as she dashes off a question to a girl living on another continent via e-mail. You can guide her in the selection of books and other materials, such as articles, movies, and artifacts, about her latest fascination.

No Limit

You can take your daughter on a stroll across the campus of the nearest university, walk with her to the philosophy department, and show her where college students spend their time inquiring into the nature of things. You can tell her that many powerful ideas are still waiting to be conceptualized and that you hope that she will not only have such ideas but will be willing to express them to others. Introduce her to some famous women in history, so that she will feel the power of the strong women who have gone before her.

 **Fact**

Two famous philosophers are Hypatia of Alexandria (370–415), an Egyptian woman with a passion for astronomy and astrology who became a well-known orator, and Simone de Beauvoir (1908–1986), a French writer and the author of *The Second Sex*, who worked to eliminate the oppression of women.

If your connection to your daughter is strong, you can expect her to flourish under your tutelage. Your inspiration will produce great results. She will stand on tiptoes mentally, constantly reaching for new ideas or some new understanding. The more often she does that, the more she will enjoy the process. Trust that you can stimulate your daughter's thoughts and the visions of her future success more than anyone else in the world. To realize as much of that success as possible, she needs to be determined, have an independent mind, and be strong willed.

Making Girls Strong Willed

Besides helping your daughter think for herself, you should make sure she has a strong will. By giving her many avenues to express herself in word and deed, and by not stifling her, you can increase her determination. Teaching your girl that obstacles are only opportunities for increasing her resourcefulness is important. Overall, the crucial thing for you to remember is that the lessons you teach her when she is little need to last and to help her long after you are gone. So your goal is to make your daughter so strong and powerful that she can apply your lessons as the years pass and tackle the problems of the world someday, if she chooses to.

For that she needs to learn to use the phrase *I think* often and express what she thinks. She also needs to be strong enough to put her ideas into actions.

- She needs to accept the responsibility of the task at hand and see it through.
- She needs to be able to disagree with others, even her superiors in the future, without being unpleasant or becoming aggressive.
- She needs to be able to realize that because she is smart and strong willed, she is obligated to put her talents to the best possible use and give back to her community when she is an adult.

You have a tremendous influence on your daughter. You are the guardian of her future. You inspire her to aim higher and to set the course of her life. In return, she will certainly give you her best efforts and something even more precious. Through your involvement in her life, she will grow into an independent, self-confident adult who can easily relate to males and will gravitate toward men who respect her and treat her as an equal. But don't feel too much pressure to be the world's perfect father; just having you in her daily life will make your daughter stronger as a woman and better able to handle life.

CHAPTER 13

Mother-Daughter Relationships

T he mother-daughter relationship can be one of the most amazing and magical relationships in the world. If it works well, it is exponentially better than any other relationship because it interconnects two people who have a similar talent—the ability to share their emotions and feelings—and yet are a generation apart. Therefore, one of them has the wisdom of experience and years, and the other has the dewy freshness of youth and yearning. Bonded together, a mother and her daughter may find that there is no problem they cannot overcome.

Clashes and Challenges

The special relationship between a mother and daughter is primal, the first one the daughter experiences. As she matures, the daughter starts focusing more on her friends and later perhaps on men, but her original love connection is always with her mother. After all, she receives so much from her mom—food, shelter, and nurturing, to name just a few things. From babyhood on, a girl also consciously or subconsciously patterns herself after her mother in speech, mannerisms, and other means of expression. Of course that can cause clashes and challenges.

One of the most common problems between mothers and daughters is the fight over control. The daughter feels that the mother is always trying to control her, and the mother has trouble accepting her little girl as

an independent adult. Also many mothers are not sure of who they are and how they feel about who they are as people, so they focus all their energies on the person their daughter is turning out to be. A mother who is secure and comfortable as a person will be a better role model for a daughter than a mother who is constantly badgering a daughter to improve herself.

 **Fact**

In recent years the term *matrophobia* has cropped up frequently in literature. It denotes the quite common fear of a young woman of growing up to be just like her mother. Often this is the flip side of a little girl thinking of her mom as a diva until she gets older and starts thinking of her mom as a disaster.

But two headstrong women who are only one generation apart can come to many disagreements and end up in a battle based on control and rebellion. What worked for you does not always work for your daughter, but you must set a pattern early on of quickly settling any disagreements with your daughter. This pattern should include compromising, laying out the pros and cons of a decision she has to make, and admitting you were wrong.

Resolve Clashes

The more often the process of conflict resolution between you and your daughter occurs, the smoother the relationship. But even then difficulties can arise. One major stumbling block is the silent treatment. So, dash it at all costs. Silence does nothing but erect a wall, or an abyss, between you and your girl. Keep communicating even if your daughter turns mum. If you are afraid of opening your mouth for fear of saying something to her you will regret later, turn to a note pad or your computer.

By writing down what is on your mind, you have a chance to examine the words before you show them to your daughter. When you speak, the thought process is often minimal because the words can fly out of your mouth like fall leaves tossed by the wind. But the simple act of committing your thoughts to a sheet of paper or a computer screen slows down the flow of verbiage. So the message you send will be reduced in harshness.

Keeping Communication Open

Whether your daughter is thrilled about finding herself saddled with some of your quirks or not, never take it personally. If she does not accept everything she inherited from your side, it shows she is thinking and talking about it. In fact, it is good for a girl to reject anything in you that you have not yet resolved. But usually a girl looks at life as a wonderful smorgasbord of opportunities if her mother feels that way at least partially and communicates these feelings.

Alert!

Dr. Lee Starkey, who directs the Women's Studies program at the University of Maine at Farmington, advises, "Women grow up and our energy is largely turned toward men, but the original love relationship is with a mother. If we as daughters don't acknowledge that, we're closing ourselves off from a great source of power and fulfillment and understanding of ourselves." Don't let your daughter close off this avenue of understanding.

It is your job to initiate the flow of communication after your daughter has cut it off. If you do not make the effort, both of you will feel helpless and hopeless. Give your daughter power by showing her that you are not afraid to tackle a touchy subject that stands between you. It is always a sign of strength to broach a difficult topic. But verbalizing hurt feelings can be tricky for both mother and daughter.

Remember when communicating with your daughter that not only do the words you choose carry weight, but also your tone of voice and the facial demeanor you use while expressing them can make them come across as overly critical. The written word, thought out beforehand, is much more neutral. The sharpest thorns in the hearts of grown women are the unkind words said to them at one time or another by their own mothers. Make sure you do not pierce your daughter's core with careless or unkind remarks.

Light Touches

Whenever you two have a differing opinion, take a deep breath and rehearse something nice to say before launching into what upsets you about your daughter.

If you cannot find the right words, you can always:

- Dash off an e-mail to your daughter or send her a joke.
- Chat online with her about a book that has nothing to do with your current conflict and everything to do with your determination to keep communicating with her.
- Write her a long explanation about why you feel the way you do. Give reasons from your life. Or draw a picture of yourself looking dejected with the caption, "Please help me understand."

Do whatever you can to get your daughter to open up to you. You know that you and she speak the same language even though she may not know it yet.

Note to Mom

Encourage your daughter to communicate with you in various ways whether she is upset with you or not. She can scribble you a note when she is mad or sad. This can be her "pass," similar to a bathroom pass her teacher hands out. Use the note over and over as a quick reminder that it is time for both of you to talk. Vary the talk stations. Talk to your girl at a place and time of her choosing. Sometimes while doing the dinner preparations or before a ticklish situation develops works best.

A Friend or a Mother?

"A daughter is a little girl who grows up to be a friend," an unknown author once wrote. That is correct, but a mother is already grown up, so she should take precedence. Besides, the relationship between a mother and a daughter should never be an either/or situation, as in "Is my mother my friend or my mother?" You are both. As such, you realize that from the beginning of time, girls have told their mothers when they disagreed with them, "You just don't understand me."

 **Essential**

Because mothers and daughters are on a different path due to their changing times and the span of years between their ages, they cannot always be best friends, according to Laura Tracy, a family therapist who counsels mother-daughter pairs. Therefore, expect at least a few disagreements to pop up between yourself and your daughter, just as a matter of course.

Mothers always try to be as understanding and supportive as their daughters' best friends. That is, however, not quite possible because a mother's wisdom and experience overarches the friendly feelings, thereby giving her the ability to sense or see obstacles on the horizon long before her daughter can discern them. But every woman who has given birth to a daughter has the potential to be both a motherly friend and a friendly mother. Tempered with patience and a willingness to see your daughter's side, you can be a great mom if you just hang in there steadfastly during your daughter's ups and downs, and offer encouragement whenever needed.

Why Nothing Moms Do Is Right

Sometimes it seems as if nothing you do is right, from your daughter's point of view. In this case, just be confident that those days will pass too. What can help is having a good relationship with yourself, so you do not rise or fall with the emotional roller-coaster ride your daughter will have to take—sooner or later—to grown into the fine girl she will eventually become.

 **Fact**

According to the New York–based therapist Juanita Johnson, the best gift a mother can give her daughter as she develops and becomes an adult is permission to be herself. As a result, a daughter can be who she wants to be because the mother is who she wants to be.

If you are a mother of a girl who suddenly is very critical of you, realize that she is maturing. While examining some characteristics in you—some of which she may see emerging in herself—she may be surprised. Criticism of a mother is a girl's attempt to find traits to adore and adopt. In a way, it is a flattering development. If she did not care, she would simply overlook you.

Being Dethroned

Do you remember the day your mother fell off her pedestal? Suddenly one day you saw her as the most out-of-touch frump in the world. Even her best shoes made you shudder. Yet a few years later, you changed your opinion of her again drastically. As you hit your twenties, you saw her again the way you did at age eight or nine—as the best mom in the whole world.

Essential

Mark Twain said that when he was a boy of fourteen, his father was so ignorant that he could hardly stand to be around him. But when he became twenty-one years old, he was astonished at how much his father had learned in seven years.

It is only natural in the creation of a strong mother-daughter bond that tension will occur to test the threads that make up the bond. That tension helps your connection with your girl prevail over any temporary kinks or knots that creep in. Now as a mother, you may find it difficult to see yourself dethroned overnight but feel relieved. You can be a real person now, not someone so elevated in your daughter's eyes that you fear making a mistake.

Being Human

Trust that you will make mistakes, and not only as a mother. You are human, and as your daughter changes, so do you. Get out your old yearbooks and prove it. Show her pictures of yourself with bad hair and geeky outfits. Laugh with her over your first dance dress and your first date. Do not be surprised if your daughter acts like a chameleon. One day she giggles with you and sees your point; the next she gives you that look that says, "Mom!" Just remember that you have years of experience as a parent, and it is your job to keep your eyes on the big picture. Often the more volatile your relationship with your daughter is at times, the better it will turn out to be when she is older.

Give her a little extra TLC whenever she makes you feel you cannot please her:

- Put a surprise present—small and just right—on her pillow.
- Mail her a funny card with a five-dollar bill for a tiny treat.
- Leave a special message on her cell phone.

- Give her a diary with a big lock and key and tell her to use it to "spill her guts."

Count on this: Confrontations, accusations, and emotional outbursts from your daughter show that you are on the right track with her. Often it all depends on your and her personality types. Some mothers and daughters show little friction in their relationship overall. Others have a run-in every other week, but how can you expand your parenting skills if you are not confronted with new challenges?

Question?

My daughter keeps telling me she hates me. What should I do?
Tell her, enough! She does not have to repeat herself. You heard her the first time. When she has calmed down, ask her why she hates you, acknowledge her feelings, and do what you can to mitigate the conflict, if possible. Most of all, tell her you love her enough for both of you.

Think of raising your girl as a wonderful adventure. Certainly there will be a few nerve-racking moments. Otherwise it would not be an adventure. So assume that the generations will clash now and then at your house, and be ready for it. Call it the pangs of your daughter becoming herself.

Being Cool with Your Daughter

One of the hardest things for mothers is to accept their daughters as they truly are because—it seems—that many times the universe is in a joking mood. Many former tomboy moms get girly girls, and vice versa. Many social-butterfly mothers get daughters who are shy and like to bury their noses in books. This appears to be the result of a generational pendulum that is invisible. A majority of mothers indeed end up with daughters who are their opposites in personality, preferences, and pastimes.

Nature's Balance

Obviously nature uses this phenomenon as a way of balancing things. Otherwise an outdoorsy type of mother would have an even more outdoorsy type of girl, and a girly mom would have an even more girly daughter. In the end, we would have nothing but ultra extremes of daughters, and these developments would be too pre-dictable. Just be thrilled about the girl you are lucky you have. She is just right for you.

Essential

If you make your life a little happier, you will make your daughter's life a little happier too. You cannot be a good mother unless you are first good to yourself. You know that as a mother you can easily get overextended, so you have to be sure to make room in your life for some free and fun times for yourself—and your girl.

A Special Relationship

The more your daughter tests your parenting limits, the more she makes you expand your abilities. You will feel special because you have a special girl. Should there be a moment when you feel like throwing your hands up in frustration because you may see in your daughter the precursors of mistakes you made in your youth, enjoy the moment.

How? By focusing not on the negatives from which your frustration sprang, but by enjoying your daughter more. Remember a mother is as positively affected by her daughter as the daughter is by her mother. Raising a girl is an important task and benefits you by giving you the chance to experience the following:

- Grow and become a better person because you realize how important setting a good example is.
- Repeat and relive the highlights of your life because you can share your daughter's gala occasions, graduations, and award ceremonies.
- Stay young in outlook and often even physically because you can experience firsthand the younger generation.
- See a part of yourself immortalized before you pass on because some trait—big or small—will emerge in your daughter and send ripples on to the next generation.

For these reasons, make sure your relationship with your daughter is strong. That requires a back-and-forth connection that is vibrant. Discussing the benefits for both parties involved is important.

Bonding Activities

Mothers and daughters can have more fun than any other twosomes because they have a common history, tend to think alike, and may have many similar passions. Find out what your girl gets excited about and share in her excitement. There are so many opportunities for you two to do that. You can go shopping together at the grocery store, the antique shops, the flea markets. You can stretch, work out, run, or walk the dog together. Afterward you can eat out, or search through the cookbooks and try cooking the most mouthwatering dishes. You can splurge and head for a day spa for mother-daughter manicures and pedicures, or do housework together until you are ready to drop. You could treat each other to a sauna and sweat buckets like marathon runners, dip into the ice-cold dunking pool together, or have a relaxing massage.

Just ask your daughter what would make her happy and incorporate her wishes into your week, month, or vacation time as much as you can. Zero in on her interests and yours. If they are not compatible, follow your heart's desires as individuals, then meet up and talk about what each of you did, saw, and experienced. Every day work on that wonderful bond you have with your girl. It takes a little work, but how nice that you have the chance to do it. Therefore, fashion the bond with your best intentions, efforts, and the sweat of your brow and your soul. Give your girl all the goodness in you that you can muster.

Essential

Keep in mind that the happiest times for you and your daughter come from being active or going through a process together. "One of the biggest stumbling blocks for women is thinking happiness is something you can reach out and grab," advises Angie Speranza, who works as a life coach and is based in New York City.

Skills for Connecting with Your Daughter

A daughter's bond with her mother is one of the deepest, most enduring relationships she will experience in her lifetime. It should also be one of the healthiest and most supportive. Here are some suggestions for building a strong, loving connection with your girl:

- **Listen and observe.** Good mothers are willing to spend time just listening and watching. Ask "what" and "how" questions to draw your daughter out; let her finish her thoughts before offering suggestions or advice.
- **Spend time just being together.** Relationships require time. You must be willing to hang out, to play, and to do things face-to-face with your daughter. Have at least fifteen minutes a day that belong just to your daughter.
- **Respond to your daughter's cues.** When she says, "I can do it myself, Mom!" teach the necessary skills, be sure she's safe, and then allow her to try. Skills and experience build self-esteem.

- **Be curious about her interests.** If your daughter loves an activity, sharing her enthusiasm is a wonderful way to build connection. Watch her favorite sport with her; admire the new pair of jeans she bought or the new painting she made. Understanding your daughter's world will keep you connected.
- **Know her friends.** There is no better way to learn about your daughter than to watch her at play with her friends. As your daughter grows, welcome her friends into your home. If she can bring her life to you, she is less likely to feel the need to hide it from you.
- **Respect her privacy.** Even little girls need time to themselves. Your daughter may choose to play alone in her room from time to time, or to disappear into her computer or stereo headphones. You can show her that you care and still respect her need for private space.
- **Provide kind, firm discipline and don't be afraid to follow through.** "Wait till your father gets home" doesn't work. Learn effective discipline skills; then be willing to set limits and follow through.
- **Be sensitive about touch, especially in public.** Hugs are wonderful, but sometimes public affection may make your daughter uncomfortable, especially in the later tween years when her friends may tease her if they see her being openly affectionate toward you. Respecting her needs will keep the connection between you relaxed and open.

Girls need connection with their mothers. Your knowledge of your daughter will help you know when she welcomes a hug and when she does not. It is a delicate balancing act, but time and love will teach you how to stay connected to your daughter at the same time that you encourage her to exercise her independence.

Mom as a Foundation

Think far ahead as you parent your daughter. Consider her in the years to come and how—in all likelihood—she may experience some pain, some tragedy, and some heartbreak.

Alert!

Do not agonize too much or too long over the current terrorist situation or the possibility of theft or some other crime occurring to your daughter. Concentrate on the now. Teach her how to be strong and smart and self-sufficient and able to bounce back from mishaps should they come her way.

In life, it is inevitable that she will face her share of losses. Even you may not be able to prevent them from happening to your daughter at some point in her life. But you can ease her disappointments and dim, divert, or alert her about many of them. Be sure to give your girl the certainty that whatever will happen, the two of you can deal with it.

You want your girl to be daring, determined, and devoted to doing good things in this world. You want her days sunny and her nights lit up by the brightest of stars. You want her to have everything you never could have, and so much more. Be strong and solid for your daughter, and help alleviate her worst times by being her support. In return, you will feel empowered that you were able to pass on to her the gist of your strength. You want so much for your daughter to grow up to be independent, strong willed, and kind. You want her to find herself and unfold herself fully, with you as her base. Help her on her way with empowerment, energy, and endless love.

CHAPTER 14

It's All about
Self-Esteem

One of the most overused phrases these days is *self-esteem*. Countless problems with girls are attributed to the lack of self-esteem, from low achievement to depression and other ailments, to a rise in teen pregnancy, drug use, and crime involvement. Unfortunately parents cannot give their daughters self-esteem. Its roots already lie within her. But armed with proper knowledge and unyielding determination, they can create a home climate conducive to boosting it in their girl—and how.

 **Fact**

In years past, the term *self-image* was more popular than the term *self-esteem*. Self-image was thought to be a person's view of her personality. Some psychologists believed that a disorder could arise from the disconnect between a girl's self-image and how others saw her.

Images of Women and the Media

The main reason for a girl's low self-esteem is the reflections of women she sees all around her in the media, the malls, and the movies. Wherever she glances, she sees images of females that are completely unrealistic. They are presented to her as ideals to emulate while being out of her reach. No matter how much your daughter strives to be just like them, she cannot achieve the extreme thinness, height, and photogenic facial structures. For that reason, the constant barrage of what your daughter feels she ought to look like can erode her confidence and lower her self-esteem.

But do not worry. The false images that flood your daughter's field of vision cannot stand up to the real images of females you present to your daughter. You can get a handle on this issue. You can make sure she meets real women who do great things, and that she knows real women come in all sizes.

Fact

One popular definition of *self-esteem* is self-worth. Psychologically speaking, this is a human being's self-image at an emotional level and has nothing to do with logical thinking or reasoning. Some experts define *self-esteem* as self-respect or a feeling of confidence in one's own merit.

Master Myths

You know how detrimental it would be if someone told your girl every day that she does not measure up and never will. So you are not about to permit her to receive similar negative messages without first teaching her to separate fact from fantasy. It is time for her to master the myths about female appearance that millions of girls still buy into.

Most women shown by the media are fantasy creations. There is very little reality to them. Explain the airbrushing techniques used in photo shoots and layouts to your girl. If she is interested, take her for a glamour photo session and let her experience all the lengthy preparations it takes to get ready for just one picture, like the hassle of the hairdo, the stiff and aching muscles that result from hours of staying in one position, the uncomfortable feeling of having layers of heavy makeup put on her face.

It is important that you take every opportunity to teach your daughter the following quick facts:

- Everybody is born with a different body and all types are great.
- Models and many movie stars have genes that make them tall and thin.
- That fact encourages them to be dependent on their looks to make a living.
- Since looks last a short time, models and movie stars only have a short prime period and often end up looking for other work.

 **Fact**

In medical circles the expression *inferiority complex* denotes a neurotic state of mind that can arise as a result of hurt feelings and frequent failures. This feeling of inferiority can arise when there is a conflict between a person's wish to be recognized for something valuable and the fear of being seen as worthless. As a result, a girl may try to compensate by becoming aggressive or violent.

Your daughter does not have to feel sorry for girls who—for their own reasons—sacrifice so much to become famous or frequently featured in magazines, unless she wants to, but she should feel empathy for them. She should also know that even the thinnest, tallest, and best-photographed young women may have low self-esteem because every year there is another huge crop of newcomers in their field. Models and actresses are constantly in danger of being replaced; for them, fame is fleeting.

Once you have added some reality to today's fabricated media images of women, you want to use some sure-fire self-esteem builders with your daughter. Begin with yourself. Be comfortable and happy with your looks. Do not compare your daughter to the screen versions. Know you are the most influential person in the growth of your daughter's self-confidence.

Toy Test

Take a look at your girl's toys and games to make sure they are not detrimental to her self-worth. Many playthings marketed to girls these days, besides the obvious Barbie dolls, contain secret esteem-damaging messages. One of them is that your daughter is only valuable as a beauty-conscious and fashion-aware consumer.

Alert!

In a 1997 survey by the Renfrew Center, a facility for girls with eating disorders, researchers found that 90 percent of the toys meant for girls that were examined dealt with beauty and beauty products, shopping, and dating. The stores featured in one game were a beauty salon, a bridal shop, a store for ball gowns, and one for ballerinas.

Do not buy a product from a company that runs ads that make girls feel bad about themselves. Also, do not let your daughter buy magazines that make her feel less confident than she is, unless it has other redeeming features. Why should you, or she, support any business that makes her feel worse about herself?

What you want to do is make your daughter more critical of the girl messages she receives. Teach her to critique what she sees and be proud of her body and her self. She is no one's object to be manipulated, duped, or used. No one can make her feel inferior, according to Eleanor Roosevelt, without her consent.

Your daughter must know how wonderful she is. She is your most precious possession—a special young person with many options, talents, and important tasks ahead. Although it is true that nationally the self-esteem of girls reaches a peak when they are nine years old and plummets from then on, you can be the parent and leader to reverse that alarming trend by making your girl extra-confident, which will rub off on her girlfriends.

Question?

What can I do about my daughter who spends every free moment reading magazines that feature super-thin girls?

Tell your girl that sometimes magazines can be like upscale clothing stores for her to browse through and to enjoy; they can give her some idea of what styles and outfits might be flattering on her, now and later. Ask her to tear out a few pages to keep and to toss the rest. Also make sure she has plenty of other reading materials on hand, including her textbooks.

Am I Pretty?

With so many false images crowding in on her, is it any wonder that your daughter asks, "Am I pretty?" Of course she is, but she needs to hear it from you over and over. Tell her in specifics how pretty she is. Recite what is so special about her: her shiny hair, her lively bright eyes, and her warm smile. Besides her pretty outer package, her inner qualities are pretty too. Tell her so, and mention her intelligence, character, and kindness.

See to it that your daughter does not obsess over her looks and allow her body to become her pet project by which she measures herself from then on. The problem is that most girls have an "ugly duckling" imprint on their minds because when they first start peering at themselves in the mirror—at age nine, ten, or eleven— they may have been at their most awkward stages in their lives, as far as their looks are concerned.

 **Essential**

Roughly 60 percent of girls—from grades five to twelve—reported being dissatisfied with their bodies. For that reason, make sure your daughter is happy with hers. Skip any empty, overused words and find plenty to compliment her about her body and all the good things she gets accomplished with her body, such as helping you around the house and excelling on the track team.

Worst Moment

Just like an image imprints itself on fresh film, too many girls take a mental snapshot of themselves at a time when their bodies are still child-like and their teeth are misaligned, or when they have gangly arms and legs and have not yet grown into their proper height and shape. Then they cling to that snapshot like a road map to a hidden treasure and never let go of it. This mistaken imprint sets them up for a life of body discontent.

Instill in your daughter that women, like men, are so much more than their appearance. People are measured by what they accomplish, not by what they look like. It is your girl's brains and bravery that will take her far. Encourage her friendship with girls and boys who possess these traits and have the qualities of drive and determination in common with your daughter.

Best Move

Of course your daughter's self-esteem will ebb and flow, like the tides. One day she will be supremely confident because she just made an A in algebra. The next day she will feel less sure of herself because she was not prepared for a Spanish pop quiz. Tell her to accept the fluctuations of her self-esteem. Show her you always esteem her unwaveringly. Prove to her that you like her company and include her friends if you can, but do not coddle her. Let her experience failure sometimes. Redoubling her efforts the next time will make her stronger. Most important, have many meaningful talks with her, and ask her a lot of questions, such as:

- What do you like?
- What do you think?
- What do you feel?
- What would you change if you could?

Alert!

In a famous and often-cited scientific study, young geese tended to attach themselves to the first moving object they saw after birth, no matter if that object was animate or inanimate. As a mother, make sure you do not still carry within you the false imprint of yourself from decades ago and project your long-standing dissatisfaction with your own looks onto your daughter.

Treat your daughter's answers with respect. Value her ideas and encourage her to have many wild, wacky, and wonderful ones. They will be the basis of more thought for her. Then make a list of your daughter's favorite sayings and yours, and post them. Make your daughter feel important, so that she will not feel the need to constantly seek the approval of others.

Popularity

Some people call popularity "glory's small change." By this, they mean that when it comes to making a difference for others, big accomplishments can have lasting and glorious effects, while just going for popularity may bring in nothing more than a few cents, if that much. However, girls from middle school on can become concerned with popularity. They notice a girl being admired by her clique for her looks, the way she acts, or her material possessions, and are impressed.

Miss Popularity

Dig a little deeper and you will find that your daughter actually finds little to admire about the Miss Popularity at her school. Perhaps she spends too much time in front of the bathroom mirror fixing her bangs and talks mainly about "he said, she said" issues. In contrast, your girl likes to do more than repeat hearsay and has her own ideas. But even if she is intrigued by the most admired girl in her grade, the fascination will probably not last for long. Popularity at school ends with graduation, at which even the most gushed-over girl goes off to college—where she may become a small fish in a big pond and often is never heard from again.

Missing Purpose

Most girls who are swept away by the allure of popularity and become preoccupied with the approval of their peers are missing an important concept that can stabilize them even during uncertain times. The therapist and writer Dr. Mary Pipher calls this a girl's North Star; other experts call it anchor, focus, or center. Whatever name is attached to this concept that guides a girl is unimportant. What is important is that your daughter has a core interest, a passion, a love for something that truly clicks with her. It may be her involvement with sculling or the Girl Scouts. It may be studying the effects of global warming in her backyard or starting a paperback give-away program with her English class.

Mission Accomplished

Whatever your daughter has settled on as her centering activity, stand behind her and support her in a loving way. The drawing power of popularity and the urge to fit in with the popular crowd at her school will wane quickly when your daughter has something in her life that is much more important to her. Trust her not to be blinded for long by girls who are still searching for a purpose in their teenage lives and by that clique swarming around them. She will eventually understand that these girls are attempting to feel good about themselves by finding safety in numbers.

Fads and Trends

Fads and trends can be fun for your daughter when they are not overdone. By definition, fads enjoy a brief popularity. In other words, they come and go, and sometimes they come again, as in retro-fads and retro-trends. They can add spice to your girl if she knows how to handle them and put them into their proper perspective. Fads and trends generally express themselves in the areas:

- Fashions
- Collectibles
- Activities
- Events

Fads can be harmless, adding color to her otherwise blah days, should she have any. Or they can be harmful, have repercussions, and leave lasting scars. In talking to your daughter, point out some of the foolish trends of the past decades. Each had one major "craze," or several.

Fabulous Fads

When we think back to the last century, several fads come to mind immediately. Here are a few you probably read about, heard about, or even participated in:

- Stamp collecting in the 1930s
- Hula-Hoops in the 1950s

- Tie-dyed T-shirts in the 1960s
- Video arcades in the 1980s

Each time young people took up the latest fad, their parents probably shook their heads, wondering, "What will they think of next?" Besides that, however, not much that was negative came from those fads. They were diversions not perversions.

Bad Fads

But other decades showed us that humans can be fascinated by odder activities. In fact, certain time spans in history offered several quite questionable pursuits as the latest things to do. Here are a few that may not have been insane, but they were definitely inane:

- Goldfish swallowing in the 1940s
- Streaking naked across a sporting field in the 1970s
- Getting many tattoos in the 1990s
- Body piercing in the 2000s

Chuckle with your daughter over some of the zany fads of the past and make sure she can tell the difference between a benign fad and a not-so-benign one. Try to be less judgmental as you might like to be when you discuss fads with her—reality TV shows, for example. Why not let her have her fill and fun with *American Idol* or the many talent, cooking, dancing, and fright contests/reality shows that have overtaken TV.

Clothing, Style, and Makeup

What makes raising a girl so wonderful is that she can have the whole world at her fingertips, in her choice of clothing, style, and makeup, long before she really has the whole world at her fingertips, in her choice of colleges, careers, and lifestyles. Unlike with boys' clothing, girls have a huge menu of modes to explore. They can gravitate to the preppie look, the boho (bohemian) style, sports apparel, classic clothes—whatever they think expresses their personalities best. And they do not have to get stuck with one designer look or line.

Essential

Watch out for any sudden changes in your daughter's outfits or posture. If she usually wears fitted clothes and has her shoulders back but overnight starts wearing oversized shirts and slouches, find out what caused the change. Promptly address the reason for the change. She may have been the victim of hurtful remarks about her body or have been harassed sexually.

Fashion Vane

Your daughter can change as frequently in her preferences of clothes, purses, and shoes as a weather vane. She can dabble in makeup and hair ornaments. While boys' gear usually sticks to the same colors and styles and varies little from year to year, girls have at their disposal a whole gamut of hues, haute fashions, and haberdashery items. No other segments of society have more apparel options than your daughter and her girlfriends. Use this fact as an opportunity for your girl to engage in the following:

- Explore the designs she likes.
- Develop new fashion interests.
- Celebrate her creativity and sense of color.
- Be daring in trying new looks.

In this way, the world of style is just a forerunner to the real world. At the makeup counter, the sales shelves, and the shoe racks, she can practice making good, informed choices. This quality will serve her very well for the rest of her life. So by all means, if your girl's budget allows it and you approve, let her get the latest hot sunglasses or the glittery eye shadow.

What you want your daughter to develop over the years is her own style. Do not overlook passing on to your daughter the real secrets of timeless style: posture, poise, speech and voice, and etiquette.

She can learn, refine, and experiment with these aspects of style. They will always be her best assets and cost nothing.

Alert!

Tell your daughter that shoplifting is theft. Some girls try out lip glosses and perfume sprays at a makeup counter, and then "accidentally" slip an eyeliner pencil into their pocket. If your daughter has friends like these, she might follow suit and could get into serious trouble over an item worth just a couple of dollars.

When it comes to your girl's emerging style, just relax. Letting her have her own way of being and doing things is a universal issue. Do not let it interfere with your relationship. There is never a need to push and pressure your daughter about her outfits, as long as they are not offensive. Some girls simply do not give a flip about Lacoste labels and Prada purses. Good for you, if your daughter is one of them. It saves you money, plus it shows that she is ahead of other girls who act as though they cannot go to school unless they are wearing the latest style, which looks a lot like what you or your sister wore when you were her age. There are only so many styles, so of course a lot of them are recycled—and more than once.

Current Culture

Ever since the early 1960s, the term *popular culture*, or *pop culture*, has been on many people's lips. It refers to the modern lifestyle that finds its expression in fashion, music, sports, movies, and the media. For your daughter to get a grip on it, inform her that she and her generation are the engine that drives the latest current culture, not the other way around.

For that reason, imitating current culture or keeping up with it is beneficial when it adds something positive to her day. But when it detracts from her healthy development and growth, she should avoid it. Current culture has tried unsuccessfully to pigeonhole women. Your daughter's beauty is not related to her shape, size, and style. Those vary from one girl to the next and matter little, overall.

Girl Power

Young women are wonderful persons who should make waves, work on fulfilling their wishes, widen their scope as much as possible, and try to right wrongs, if they can. They are not mindless things, walking clothes racks, sales inducements, objects, or adornments. Make sure your daughter understands this and does not allow other girls, or pop culture, to define who she is.

 **Fact**

Mary Pipher, who wrote *Reviving Ophelia: Saving the Selves of Adolescent Girls*, a long-term *New York Times* bestseller, coined the term *girl-poisoning culture* and explained the damage it can do. She offers parents strategies for overcoming the negative effects that might show up in their daughters.

Every day the way parents look at their daughter and talk to her helps her become stronger and more capable. When you greet her with joy and encouragement in your eyes, and a few well-chosen warm words, you add to her outer and inner armor. Make it powerful so it can withstand any onslaught from whatever cultural currents might come rushing her way.

A Parent's Legacy

Concentrate first on leaving your girl strength and buoyancy. Financial downtimes may wipe out the portfolio you plan to leave her, but they cannot wipe out the power within that she is developing. Sometimes the poorest man leaves his children the richest inheritance, according to Ruth E. Renkel. Make sure the empire you build for your girl is made up of the sturdy walls of her self-esteem, self-respect, and self-determination.

CHAPTER 15

Dangers and Warning Signs

I n addition to the miasma of girl-demeaning messages that permeate society, many other dangers can lurk in the wings for your daughter. These dangers may be posed by her environment, peer group, the opposite sex, or they may be of her own making. But take heart. All these dangers send up red flags. Therefore, all you have to do is be on the lookout for them, and then deal with any potentially perilous situation.

Drinking, Smoking, and Drugs

The most obvious dangers your girl can face may come from drinking, smoking, and drugs. All three of these activities are in evidence everywhere she goes. From sixth grade on or earlier, some of her classmates will probably experiment with them.

Daughter Dangers

While the overall illicit drug use among adolescents has declined by 19 percent since 2001, and while teenage boys used to try alcohol, cigarettes, and drugs at a higher rate than girls, the reverse is now true. This puts your daughter into a precarious situation because most people believe girls are at a lesser risk. Therefore, they concentrate on helping boys refrain from using harmful substances.

By focusing mostly on boys, people neglect the girls who need our attention as well. Unfortunately you cannot rid your girl's middle school or high school, or her community, of these dangers, although do what you can. But rest assured that you are powerful in this regard. You definitely play the most important part in enabling your girl to resist any drug- or alcohol-related temptations she may come across.

 **Fact**

In 2006 John Walters, director of the White House Office of National Drug Control Policy, released a survey stating that 1.5 million girls, ages twelve to seventeen, started drinking alcohol in 2004, in comparison to 1.28 million boys. Similar findings were reported for smoking cigarettes and using marijuana.

Safe Daughter

According to Dr. Ralph Lopez, an associate professor at Cornell University's Weill Medical Center, girls are more at risk for drug and alcohol abuse than boys because they are under more stress—the stress of succeeding academically and of looking perfect. In contrast, boys do not face that double pressure.

Know that with your parenting skills ratcheted up in high gear, you can tackle anything that threatens your girl. You belong to the types of parents who would—to quote family psychologist John Rosemond—without a moment's hesitation give their lives to save their children. Therefore, you are tough—good for you. As a result, you welcome the chance to educate yourself about how best to protect your girl from the scourge of illegal drug use.

This is especially important because not only are girls more vulnerable to the lures of drinking, smoking, and drugs than boys, they can also suffer worse consequences than boys. Research findings, reported by BBC News in 2002, prove that girls and boys react to drugs quite differently.

- Girls may become addicted to nicotine more quickly than boys.
- Girls' normal growth pattern can be interrupted by even moderate drinking.
- Drugs may also interfere with the development of female reproductive systems.

Fortunately, you have been talking to your daughter about the dangers of cigarettes, drinking, and drugs from first grade on. If not, now is the time to start having a serious conversation—parent to daughter—about these topics and to keep the conversation going. Tell your girl about the high expectations you have for her. You expect her to say no to any temptations, loud and clear.

Essential

When it comes to nicotine, drugs, and alcohol, parents should never try to be popular with their daughter and her friends and allow them to drink a beer, a glass of wine, or smoke a cigarette at home. Parents may think they are doing the teenagers a favor. In reality they are teaching them to break the law.

The sooner you let your girl know exactly where you stand—in regard to the use of alcohol and drugs—the better. This begins with you serving as her role model. Your personal conduct vis-à-vis these substances will reinforce your heart-to-heart talks. One without the other will ring hollow. If parents cannot control their conduct with nicotine, booze, and illegal drugs, how can they expect their daughter to control hers? Also, arm yourself with knowledge so that you can recognize the warning signs of your daughter's dabbling with these dangerous substances.

Girls Drinking

To get overly suspicious about your girl's every move and gesture is unwarranted. Too often just plain growing pains are the reason that your daughter's behavior is a little worrisome now and then. But when you notice the same type of conduct that is so different from the way she acted in the past over and over, and when you have a sinking feeling about it, you should investigate if she and her friends have started drinking. Thus, be on the lookout for the following signs that may indicate your daughter is beginning to experiment with alcohol including:

- Suddenly switching to a new group of friends and not wanting you to meet them.
- A "who-cares" attitude coupled with neglecting her former interests and her appearance.
- Finding alcohol in her room or smelling it on her breath.
- Bloodshot eyes, slurred speech, and the lack of coordination.

If your daughter exhibits any of these signs, she is calling out for help. This is when you have to put everything else aside, sit down with her, and find out what is going on.

 **Fact**

According to a 2005 edition of *60 Minutes* by CBS, 10 to 20 percent of the alcohol sold in the United States is consumed by drinkers who are underage. Even worse, nearly 90 percent of the drinking done by teenagers is binge drinking. That means drinking to intoxication and beyond.

Do not sweep your uneasy feelings about what you think you have observed in your daughter under the rug. Since alcohol is forbidden until age twenty-one in the United States, it is seen as more enticing by teenagers than in countries where the age limit is lower. Therefore, most parties that your daughter and her friends attend will probably have opportunities to imbibe. Talk to your girl before she heads out to one of those parties. Tell her you are concerned about her welfare and safety. Warn her about the possibility of the punch being spiked or someone offering her something alcoholic. It is much easier to root out the beginnings of a teenage drinking problem before it sets in. The same is true for your girl's attraction to smoking.

Girls Smoking

To many parents, cigarette smoking seems the much lesser of the other evils: drinking and drugs. They know that about a quarter of all adolescents smoke, or have tried it, so they are not too worried. Besides, some parents smoke themselves.

Essential

Girls whose parents smoke are much more likely to start smoking than girls whose parents do not smoke. Not only are these girls more used to the sights and smells of smokers, they also are able to help themselves to their parents' pack of cigarettes without any trouble and without having to pay for them.

But what some parents tend to overlook is the fact that nicotine is addictive. Once your daughter picks up the habit, it may be hard for her to quit. Smoking cigarettes may also be the first step to smoking marijuana, so watch out for these warning signs in your girl including:

- Using air freshener or perfume to minimize the smell of tobacco.
- Hanging out with a crowd of known smokers.

- Always needing money, yet having nothing to show for it, such as a new purchase.
- Your own cigarettes disappearing at a faster rate than usual.

Make it very clear to your daughter that you do not want her to smoke. Tell her that about one-third of all smokers will develop a serious smoke-related disease such as emphysema or lung cancer. She may not seem to pay attention to your lecture, but some of it will stick with her—count on it. That may mean you have to stop smoking in front of her, if you do. You do not want your girl to look at you with pity every time you light up, or think you are not as strong as she thought you were.

Girls Doing Drugs

Just as some teens your daughter befriends will start drinking and smoking long before it is legal, some of them will be enticed by the drug world. Especially in high school, your girl may become exposed to adolescents who use the whole campus as their drug-dealing domain. Warn her to be wary of any teenager who possesses huge amounts of cash. Also ask her to stay away from adolescents who find the drug culture "cool." Yet even if you could patrol the halls of your girl's school personally, some of her classmates would still manage to offer her an illegal substance. Not all adolescents have parents who supervise them properly; therefore, a few teenagers may start dealing drugs even in the best schools, or start producing them in a lab somewhere. "Meth is almost like a body snatcher. It reaches out and grabs these kids almost overnight," warns Dr. Jim Lewis, a school district superintendent. Therefore, be on the alert for these warning signs that may indicate that your daughter could be experimenting with drugs. Watch out for:

- Exhibiting secretive conduct and frequent irritability
- Seeming to be dizzy, staying up late, and losing weight
- Being unusually silly and giggling for no reason

- Having red, bloodshot eyes and acting differently than before

Some of the signs relate to using marijuana; others are red flags for additional drugs. In any case, it pays to be aware of any abrupt changes in your daughter and also to notice other symptoms of drug use in her, such as unusual tiredness, listlessness and depression, and a worsening relationship with long-time friends and close family members, and—of course—the appearance of drug paraphernalia.

 **Question?**

I'm afraid that one day my daughter will ask me if I ever smoked marijuana. Should I lie to her?
Don't wait until she asks. During your next serious talk, depending on your daughter's age, tell her about some of the mistakes you made when you were young and how you have regretted them. Tell her little was known about the bad effects of pot when you were younger, but they are known now. Stress that overlooking the latest research is not the thing for a smart modern girl like your daughter to do.

Besides identifying and worrying about your daughter's alcohol, cigarette, and illegal drug use, parents of girls in particular have another headache these days. They have to be less concerned with traditional drugs and more with drugs that are very easy to obtain and hide. What is worse, most girls do not even consider them drugs because these are legally prescribed medications.

"Pharm" Parties

The latest rage among kids is holding "pharm" parties, or get-togethers where pharmaceuticals are passed around like potato chips. Girls are especially susceptible to participation in these parties because they require—as admission tickets—nothing more than a handful of their parents' medicines that the parent will surely never miss. There is no dealing with any shady characters in a pharm party so they seem to have a more innocent feel to the girls involved. The girls who attend are all from nice homes and similar neighborhoods, so there is a false sense of safety. Therefore your daughter may think, "What's wrong with popping a pink or purple pill, or two?"

Alert!

Boys are more likely than girls to be enticed by, and to try, harder drugs, such as heroin, cocaine, ecstasy, and methamphetamine. Not only do they feel more invincible than girls, they are also more intrigued by the behind-the-scenes buying, dealing in, and delivery of many of the harder drugs than girls.

What the girls who go to pharm parties do not realize is that many drugs are incompatible. Besides, taking drugs meant for an ailment can make a healthy girl sick. Plus, there is always the chance of overdosing, which can lead to death. Therefore, you must be on the lookout for these warning signs that may indicate your daughter in engaged in pharming:

- Your old medicines are disappearing.
- Your current medicines are running out faster than they should.
- It looks as if someone has gone through your medicine cabinet.
- Your daughter is suddenly very curious about all your prescriptions.
- Your daughter has someone else's medicine in her purse or pockets.

In regard to your daughter and her friends getting into your medications and maybe even passing them out to other teens, you cannot stick your head in the sand. You need to talk frankly with your girl about the dangers of legal and illegal drug and nicotine use. Your number-one goal is prevention. Your girl's health is precious and she must not compromise it. Furthermore, her reputation is fragile. It will follow her wherever she goes. So she must make it a point of staying away from kids who have the mindset of "I'll try anything once." What can make kids like these so dangerous is that your daughter may be attracted to some of them because she thinks they are "cute."

Abusive Boys

Your daughter may dream of holding hands with a cute boy her age, but instead she may end up with a bruise. Why? Because some boys—having no positive role models at home—may grow up to be controlling and abusive in their relationships.

 **Fact**

A 1999 survey released by the *Journal of the American Medical Association* suggests that one in five teenage girls who participated in the survey admitted that she had experienced physical abuse from her boyfriend. Yet, just like some adults, the abused girls found it difficult to get out of the negative relationship because they were afraid to lose social status.

Frequently your daughter's friendship with a boy does not start out being violent. It may begin with a little jealousy and escalate to threats and physical blows. You want to warn your daughter about that possibility and clue her in to the types of bad boys she may meet, including:

- A boy who is insecure, immature, and uninterested in school, clubs, and sports
- A boy who is unreliable, sleazy, dishonest, and egotistical
- A belittler who always criticizes your girl
- A control freak who tries to run her life
- An angry guy who hates the whole world and may turn delinquent

Fortunately in most middle and high schools, the undesirable boys make up only 25 percent or less. The rest of the male population in your daughter's world is nice, goal oriented, and definitely worthy of her attention.

Safe Strategies for Temptations

Besides cluing your daughter in to the dangers associated with alcohol, smoking, drugs, and bad boyfriends, give her some strategies to deal with the dangers. She will not always be able to contact you on the spot and ask you for advice, although these days, cell phones can be of great help. Being knowledgeable to such a degree that it is almost second nature to do the right thing will help your daughter even more.

 **Essential**

Remember that not every girl learns important information that will stick with her the same way. Some girls can learn better from a lecture. Others learn better from graphs and charts. A third group does best with flashcards, and still another group learns best through repeated discussions.

Young girls can get easily distracted, so going over the ways your daughter can extricate herself from all kinds of tricky situations many times is vital. Here are those crucial strategies you want to give her verbally, but also in written form for her to post. Your daughter should be sure to do the following:

- If she feels uneasy about being with a group of kids, it is best to leave.
- Choose the name of her dog, or some other word, as a code to text to you. As soon as you get the message, you will call her immediately with a good excuse to come home—now.
- Never get in the car with someone who has been drinking, smoking pot, or popping pills.
- Never accept an open drink from someone she cannot trust.

Besides making sure your girl has several exit strategies imprinted on her mind when it comes to perilous situations, you want to be absolutely certain that you use the following prevention tactics yourself:

- Network with other parents to present a united front when it comes to your children's drinking and drug use.
- Keep an eye on your medications and dispense of all old pills, especially painkillers.
- Attend workshops and read up on materials about how to address specific alcohol- and drug-related problems in your area.
- Get to know your daughter's friends and the guidance counselor at her school.

Keep in mind that the use of booze, cigarettes, and pot in teen girls often opens the door to more inappropriate conduct, even serious criminal behavior. So it is best to direct your girl's attention to more suitable pursuits. Encourage what she loves to do while keeping your eyes peeled. These days new dangers for girls crop up every day.

Even the most enticing temptations for your daughter are simply opportunities for you to flex your parenting muscles. There really are no parenting concerns that you cannot deal with successfully if you make up your mind to do so.

Alert!

When you read in the paper that somewhere in this country teenagers have gotten into trouble with the latest version of detrimental conduct, do not ignore this early indicator. Assume that this type of behavior will spread to your daughter's school shortly, educate yourself about it, and be prepared.

Your Girl's Privacy versus Her Safety

Your daughter considers her room her castle, with herself being the princess. She is right. Naturally you want her to have a cozy haven at home where she can fling off her school clothes, plop down, and relax. She needs a private space where she can play her favorite music, chill out, and regroup. Therefore, in many ways, her room is similar to her diary—for her to have as her own, and for you to be admitted to—maybe now and then—but only if you ask her permission.

Home Rules

Your daughter will have no trouble telling you what she considers an invasion of her privacy. Find out from her what she wants you to do in regard to entering her room by asking her to fill you in. Most girls and their parents can—after discussion—come to the following understanding, or a similar one:

- When the door is open, the parent should feel free to walk in.

- When the door is closed, the parent should knock and wait for an answer.
- When the parent enters, he or she should not snoop.

Since it takes time to build trust, do not break it by disregarding her rules. There are some parents who cannot wait for their daughter to leave for school so that they can rifle through her dresser drawers and closet, pry into her journal, read her e-mail, and poke through her purses. Do not join that group.

Rewrite the Rules

As long as you feel you can count on your girl, abide by her privacy rules and respect her wishes. But when she refuses to talk to you about behavior that worries you and after you have tried several times in a calm and respectful way to discuss her conduct, you may be forced to invade her privacy. You really may have to take a closer look at her possessions. If you find something that concerns you, talk to your girl about it. Admit what you did, tell her why you did it, and assure her that together you can find a solution to the problem. Assure your daughter that she can tell you anything—the fewer secrets the better. Never forget: She depends on you to be safe, to become the best she can be, and to progress rather than become waylaid by problems.

Failing Grades and Cutting School

A quick and easy way to check on how much progress your daughter is making is to measure her interest in school. Apathy toward academics is a red flag. Her role as a student is paramount. Therefore, look closely at her most recent report card. If her grades have been sliding, do not wait until the next nine-week grading period is over. Instead, put an interim report system in place.

Be sure to give your cell phone number to your girl's teacher and guidance counselor. Be your girl's academic coach, someone who wants to help her solve her academic dilemmas. In other words, always be a problem-solving pro in her corner, and not a punisher who is opposed to her.

Early in the school year, identify at least one member of your daughter's school staff who is accessible to parents. This does not have to be one of her teachers although that would help. Build a friendship with this educator and benefit from his or her inside knowledge of the school culture and customs.

Favorite Subject

Make sure there is at least one subject on your daughter's school schedule that speaks to her. Quiz her about her classes and find out which one she likes best, either because of the material taught, the teacher presenting it, or her favorite classmates. Work on enhancing your daughter's achievement in that particular class. Often doing supremely well in one subject rubs off on her efforts in others.

Alert!

When your daughter does not do well in a class, evaluate her capabilities, the effort and time put into the subject, and her teacher's instructional methods. Some girls develop a dislike for a subject that may have nothing to do with the topic and everything to do with factors that can be changed, such as the room location or the quirks of the class or the instructor.

Just as you work on forming a strong and unbreakable bond between yourself and your girl, get busy and fashion one between her and her scholastics.

Good Attendance

Besides keeping a close eye on your daughter's school progress, zoom in on her attendance as well. Not every girl can have perfect attendance. Some suffer from allergies. Others twist their ankle playing softball. But it is their attitude toward missing school that matters. If your daughter misses a day now and then but does her best to make up her work, you can breathe easily. If she frequently seems to seek an excuse to stay home, investigate why.

Fact

School phobia—a fear of school or refusing to go—can occur in as many as 5 percent of students. It is usually seen in elementary school kids but can develop during the upper grades. Signs include creating excuses and numerous complaints about not feeling well enough to go to school but having no specific symptoms to report.

In middle and high school, skipping a class is often seen as a rite of passage. While boys usually leave the campus, more girls hide out in the bathroom. Make certain that your daughter is not lured into a ditching-class habit that rears its head every time she has a tough test or a term paper due. By teaching her to take a baby-step approach—doing a little schoolwork at a time—a few days before a major exam or project looms, your daughter will be ready for it and feel no need to cut school.

Parent School

The best antidote for your daughter's lack of interest in school and her poor attendance is to increase your own interest and attendance. Do not just attend the mandatory conferences; set some up before your girl begins to slide. Sign up for a school committee or two, and get immersed in the SAT study program your girl's school offers. Help the teacher who runs the program with added practice sessions or proctoring. Ask the office where you might be able to do some good. Rest assured that your daughter's school can use your help in many ways. The more school-focused you are, the more your girl will be.

If she still makes grades lower than she should and exceeds the absences her school policy allows, check to see how well she sleeps. Some girls suffer from bouts of insomnia. After the onset of menstruation, some girls may in fact sleep less well. Other girls consume too much caffeine in their sodas before bedtime. And still another group of girls stays up after their parents' bedtime to get on the Internet—without supervision.

Internet Red Flags

When your daughter prefers to get on the computer late at night and spends hours on it, you want to remember that getting online means she is out in public—unprotected. The people she meets in cyberspace are often not who they pretend to be. So take time to go over, and update, your Internet ground rules with your daughter. Be sure to discuss the following:

- Setting a time she can use the Internet and for what purposes.
- The possibility of her being bullied, harassed, or "hit on" by others, even her classmates, while in a chat room. She must tell you when it happens, so you can notify her school.
- Exchanging mean or "flirty" e-messages with her friends, which she should not do, even as a joke. She can never take back what she sends out into cyberspace.

Whether we live in a more dangerous world than other generations or not is hotly debated these days. Some people say we do. Others claim that the dangers have not increased but the opportunities to hear about them have—a thousand-fold. One thing is certain, however: Never before has such a vast arena as cyberspace existed as a meeting place for people who want to take your money, irk you with unwanted advertising, and show you disturbing pictures.

The Worst Risk

The most serious risk your daughter can face deals with the possibility of a stranger hurting her because of some information she posts online or because of whom she meets online. While the number of teenage girls who are molested, kidnapped, or induced to run away from home is relatively small, when it does happen, the end result can be disastrous.

Alert!

In 1984 the National Center for Missing and Exploited Children was established as a private nonprofit organization. It serves as a centralized clearinghouse of information dealing with missing and exploited children. It has a twenty-four-hour toll-free hotline, plus a CyberTipline for anyone with information about missing or exploited children.

Tell your daughter that some Web sites are first-class, while others are blatantly false, racist, sexist, and violent. Should she encounter one of them, she must shut down the computer immediately and tell you about it.

Computer Credit

The best use of the Internet is as a family tool: to plan vacations, check on prices of items to purchase, print out coupons and credit card information, get the scoop on upcoming movies, and keep up with current events. Also use it to access the latest government suggestions to prepare a family emergency kit. Have your daughter pitch in. Ask her to mark household items and personal possessions of utmost importance with a red sticker—to be saved in case of a natural disaster, or terrorist attack. Decide where to meet outside your home, and where to meet up outside the immediate area. In short, use the best of the Internet and forget the rest.

Choice Parents

In regard to your own use of alcohol, nicotine, illegal drugs, and legal drugs—those prescribed by your doctor—and the Internet, examine your lifestyle. You always want to be the best role model you can be, someone your daughter can be proud of, and someone she wants to play a robust role in her life.

 **Fact**

Study after study shows that children of parents who are deeply involved in their lives, hold ongoing conversations with them, attend school events, are active in the parent-teacher organizations, and truly listen to them are less likely to drink, smoke, do drugs, or get into trouble via the Internet.

Your daughter wants you in every phase of her existence, but the older she gets, the more she observes. Girls, even more so than boys, hate hypocrisy with a passion. Therefore, there is no way you can be a closet drinker, smoker, drug-user, or a visitor to questionable Web sites without them finding out about it.

Greatest Expectations

As you have the highest expectations of your daughter, she has the highest expectations of you. Do not let her down and she will not let you down. Don't worry that children never listen to you; worry that they are always watching you, according to author Robert Fulghum. Just keep in mind that raising a girl can transform you and always for the better. How fortunate you are to have this opportunity to be the best parent and the best person you can be. Raising a girl means you are instilling and reinforcing what is best for her. At the same time, you are bringing out what is best in you.

CHAPTER 16

Health and Well-Being

B esides protecting your daughter from dangerous influences and clearing a path of obstacles for her, you must not overlook the routine maintenance her health and well-being require. Of course, she needs her usual periodic dental and vision checkups, her annual visit to the pediatrician, and the required physicals for her sports involvement, but she also requires something more. After all, she is a potential giver of new life and therefore needs extra attention and care in that respect.

Her First Visit to the Gynecologist

The American College of Obstetricians and Gynecologists recommends that you schedule your daughter for her first visit to a gynecologist when she is between thirteen and fifteen years of age. The exact age depends on the individual girl, but you should make this an exciting time for your daughter because this visit shows that she has successfully completed puberty and is now—biologically speaking—a young woman.

As a result, your girl is now ready for an appropriate physical examination, one that only young women get to have. Point out to her how lucky she is to be one. "It's the men who are discriminated against. They cannot bear children. And no one's likely to do anything about that," according to Golda Meir. Still, some girls freak out when they find out they are scheduled for their first

gynecological exam, which does not have to include a pelvic exam but often does. That is the reason you want to mention the topic ahead of time and discuss with your girl how important all aspects of her health are.

 **Fact**

The prefix *gyno-* means "woman" or "female," as in *gynecocracy*, the government by women. The rest of the word *-cology* means the medical science of health issues. Therefore, a gynecologist is a doctor specializing in working with female health concerns, including menstruation and the various choices of contraception.

Preparing for the Exam

Tell your daughter that getting ready for a GYN exam is like getting ready for any other medical checkup, except she should not be having her period at that time. Even better, let her choose with whom she wants to have her first one. She has the following choices:

- Her pediatrician, with whom she is familiar. Many pediatricians perform pelvic and breast exams for teenage girls.
- A gynecologist, either her mother's, a new one, or the one her girlfriends like.
- A nurse practitioner. This medical professional has advanced training in women's reproductive health.

Your daughter can discuss the gynecologist options with her girlfriends who can put her at ease and most likely tell her that there is nothing to it. Some girls even ask their best friend along to wait in the waiting room—as a support system, the more the merrier.

Reasons for an Exam

No one likes to see a doctor for no reason, so it is best to inform your girl that her GYN exam has three main purposes:

1. A routine examination, to make sure she is developing normally.
2. A preventive measure before she has sex, and to discuss birth control and sexually transmitted diseases (STDs) long before the fact, not afterward.
3. A fix-it doctor visit, in case she should have problems with her periods, pain, or an infection.

Once your daughter realizes what a great opportunity this is to ask a medical expert whatever questions about her development may have been on her mind, she may have lots of queries. Teach her to write them down before the visit, so she will not forget them. If she doesn't want you in the examination room, by all means comply with her wishes. You want your girl to feel as comfortable as possible and to speak as freely as she wants to. Therefore, go over the names of several of her reproductive body parts with her at home before the checkup, so she will not stumble over the words or have to ask the doctor what they mean. Lack of familiarity with the various terms can make her feel embarrassed, but familiarity with them will empower her.

Gynecological Terms

Talk to your daughter in depth about the anatomy and function of her body. Or if you want to, pick up an illustrated pamphlet from the doctor's office, give it to her in advance to read, and ask if she has any questions. Some daughters are very curious. They want to know all the details: the location and description of every body facet that makes them so special. Others just want to have their checkup over with and get on to other things. You know your daughter best, so you know how to handle the situation.

Fast GYN Exam Facts

Your daughter's first GYN exam will start with a breast exam, during which the doctor will press lightly on the various parts of your daughter's breasts and show her how to examine her own breasts. As a result, she will know which lumps are normal for her in the future. After that comes the pelvic exam during which the doctor makes sure everything looks okay outside the vagina. Then with the help of a speculum—a thin piece of plastic or metal—the doctor will investigate to make sure everything inside is okay as well. Sometimes the doctor will do a pap smear, which includes picking up some cells from the cervix, the opening of the uterus; other times, this will come at a later visit. None of these procedures takes very long, so you and your daughter will have plenty of time left to schedule a special outing afterward.

After the GYN Exam

Your daughter will feel glad to get her first pelvic checkup behind her. She might tell you about some of the questions she remembered to ask, or not. But having her first female medical exam over with will make her feel more grown-up, and the next one will be a piece of cake. You, the parent, will be happy that you can mark this important event off your to-do list. Getting your girl over any awkwardness in dealing with the health of her girl parts and making her smarter about every ounce of her wonderful body and its upkeep is a great step. Rejoice with her over it. Should she be quiet or lost in thought; that is all right, too. As mentioned previously, every girl reacts differently to this female checkup. Maybe up to now she had not given the intricacies of her physical being much thought. Suddenly it is dawning on her just how miraculous the workings of her body are. But if your daughter's apparent down mood seems to linger, be sure you find out why.

Girls and Depression

At any time as many as 20 percent of kids can experience bouts of depression—temporary time spans when they seem to feel sadder or unhappier than usual. Some experts call this a case of having a touch of emotional "unhealth." By that they mean the youngster is experiencing a passing phase of not feeling as cheerful as usual. This is similar to how a cold might affect your daughter physically, except that this type of "cold" affects her emotionally.

Alert!

What makes depression in girls so difficult to recognize is that it can creep in slowly. In families with more than one child, kids are often stereotyped, such as "Johnny is the outgoing one, and Mary is the quiet type." Labeling children according to their personality types can be mislabeling and hurting them. The "quiet" girl may simply be quiet because she is sinking deeper and deeper into depression.

A temporary case of depression may be just part of your daughter's aches and pains as she grows up. It is to be expected in kids; they can get depressed like adults. But not having developed the few coping mechanisms many of their elders have, they show their depressed feelings more openly, and maybe even for longer periods. But should the sad feelings in your girl last and last, you'll want to know what to do.

The Reasons for Girls' Depression

Approximately 4 to 5 percent of all teens suffer from depression that is long-standing. Unfortunately, girls suffer from it at double the rate of boys. Therefore, if you notice a serious and lasting—that is, stretching for a week or two consecutively—change in your daughter's mood, pay attention.

In your busy everyday lifestyle, you have to keep your mind on so many things. But when you observe major changes in your girl's mood, jot down what specifically disturbs you. Does she "mope" all the time? Does she constantly have a somber expression on her face? Does she seem to find absolutely no joy in her life? Chronicle what you see—if you do not write it down you might forget!—then educate yourself about the symptoms of teenage depression.

 **Fact**

Several theories exist on why girls suffer from depression more than boys. They include the onset of puberty in girls and the accompanying hormonal changes, the gossiping and disrespect by their peers, the usual peer pressures, and their worries about their looks, personal problems, and romantic relationships.

The Symptoms of Depression

It can be difficult for you to know if your daughter is just going through a rough time emotionally or if she really is depressed. Asking her outright is usually not helpful because most girls do not know if they are depressed—they just are. So, take no chances when you notice the following in your girl:

- A big change in eating and sleeping habits
- Declining school performance and attendance
- Withdrawing from previously liked people and activities
- Persistent anxiety and unhappiness
- Constant irritability or marked silence

Then look into the situation. What can be difficult in determining if your daughter suffers from depression or not is another type of behavior that she might exhibit—bipolar disorder. This is a mental disorder that varies between the opposite extremes of mania (overactivity and elation) and depression (withdrawal from activity and sadness). It used to be called manic depression before the term *bipolar disorder* was coined.

 *Essential*

Parents of girls with bipolar disorder frequently report that their daughters' periods are problematic. Either the girls have long absences of menstruation or much longer cycles, or they experience heavy bleeding and extreme cramping. Therefore, visit the gynecologist to discuss this particular problem any time your girl's periods are very irregular or associated with a lot of pain.

Equipping yourself with knowledge about bipolar disorder is helpful because some girls may have an episode of it during some stage of their lives. These temporary bipolar behaviors can be the result of trauma or just a fleeting occurrence. In girls, the basic signs of bipolar disorder can resemble what is fairly normal in teen behavior. But it is the persistence and duration of these signs you want to watch out for, not the one-time occurrence of them.

The Signs of Bipolar Disorders

If you are worried your daughter is suffering from bipolar disorder, take on the role of record keeper. Make a note if you observe the following conduct in your girl:

- Severe difficulty in sleeping
- Nonstop and fast talking, and racing thoughts
- Frequent mood changes—up and down, down and up
- Risky behavior and seemingly unlimited energy

There can be still more characteristics depending on the individual girl. None of these behaviors alone, or if they only occur for a short time, are extremely worrisome, but in combination and long-term, they should be of concern to you. So what should you do, should you notice them?

Parental Wisdom

Remember those times when your little girl used to come to you crying because she stumbled and hurt herself, or the wheel of her tricycle fell off, or her favorite teddy bear lost a leg? Remember how you told her then you would make it all better? You picked her up, kissed her, put a bandage on her knee, fixed the tricycle, and sewed on the stuffed animal limb. You proved to her that you were powerful in making her feel better.

Now do the same thing; really make it all better. That starts with putting your arm around your daughter's shoulder and telling her that you will fix this, too—whatever her problem may be. Whether it is depression, bipolar disorder, or any of the serious health concerns detailed in the following pages, the very first thing you always want to do is reassure your daughter that you have, or will find, the answer to her issues no matter what. She is not alone and can always count on you. You will indeed do everything you can to make things better for her and will not rest until the issues are resolved.

Sit down with her and repeat these statements, and then tell her that in some cases the best any parent can do is to reach beyond their expertise and enlist the help of experts in the medical field. That is because you do not want to try several halfhearted approaches on your own only to waste time before you finally find one that might work in the end. No, in serious matters like her emotional and physical health and well-being, you are starting at once and are going straight to the top.

Top Parent Plan

In cases of serious health matters—mental or otherwise—that concern your daughter you have to spring into action immediately. Therefore you want to waste no time before taking these steps:

1. Make an appointment with a medical or mental health professional as soon as possible and get your girl some help.
2. Be more supportive of her than ever, listen to her, and don't criticize.
3. Become the most informed parent you can be via the library, local support groups, and the Internet.

Thus, you are using the full power of your love and care for your daughter in combination with all the knowledge of the health experts. Then working together, fiercely attack the problem. Using all your resources and theirs, keep at it until you make some headway. After all, this is your chance to show what a truly remarkable parent you are.

Suicide Warning Signs

Today's movies, music, video games, and other media can lead many young girls to believe that suicide is a glorious experience. Added to that are easy access to weapons, pills galore in the medicine cabinet at home, and the glamorization of a drug overdose. Some girls go so far as to mention their suicidal leanings to their friends but swear them to secrecy. Please warn your daughter about that possibility and tell her that the consequences of keeping quiet could be tragic. Should her friend commit suicide, your daughter would feel a horrible burden of guilt for the rest of her life. Therefore, tell her to let you know immediately when a girl in her circle mentions suicide more than once, even in a joking manner.

A phrase such as "I'll kill myself if I don't get asked to the prom" may just be part of a teen girl's everyday verbal chit-chat. But when this statement is repeated over and over with a somber expression and with tears cascading down her face, the girl's friends need to listen up. Maybe there is more to it. Teach your daughter to do the following:

- Keep an eye out for any friend who seems to be sad for an unusually long time.
- Encourage her friend to look for help and go with her to the guidance counselor.
- Discuss what worries her about her friend with you or another trusted adult.

Besides listening to your daughter and her friends' conversation for any hints of a possible suicide, a parent needs to be familiar with the associated risk factors.

Alert!

The reason that girls in trouble—real or imagined—can often think of suicide as a first step—not a last—is that their short lives have not equipped them to come up with other and better solutions. Adolescents don't think like adults and react with gut instinct when they process emotion, according to Deborah Yurgelun-Todd, M.D.

Suicide Risk Factors

Once you know the risk factors for suicide in girls, you can be especially watchful not only in regard to your daughter but also the girls in her group. Plus, you can pass this information on to other parents and make them aware as well. Who knows, you might even save a young life.

Here are the risk factors for teenage suicide:

- Previous suicide attempts or having a close family member who committed suicide.
- Recent tragic losses, such as the death of a loved one, or divorce, or a breakup with a boyfriend.
- Social aloneness—no friends or activities to engage in.

- Drug or alcohol abuse. They can decrease the impulse control, making impulsive suicide more apt to occur.
- Loaded weapons in the home.
- The presence of depression, eating disorders, and other medical conditions.

However the good news is that most suicidal girls send up plenty of red flags about their intentions. Of course, they do; they want someone to notice. So in addition to paying attention to any suicidal talk among your daughter and her friends, watch out for other crucial signs.

 **Fact**

Some researchers believe there are two groups of suicidal teens. One is the long-term chronically or severely depressed group. The suicide attempts of this group are carefully planned. The other group may not be as severely depressed and acts more impulsively and on the spur of the moment, using whatever method is handy.

There are other signs of impending suicide in a girl. Some can be quite noticeable and should be eye-opening. For example, teenage girls usually "love" their favorite clothes, shoes, purses, CDs, and movies. So when they suddenly start giving them all away, investigate why. Also watch out for any girl preoccupied with death and dying, taking excessive risks, being extremely depressed, and acting so differently from the way she used to be.

Best Health News

The excellent good news is that the mental health field has made enormous strides. Depressed girls can now be treated early, before they go too far. You and your daughter have all kinds of treatment options available these days, should she need them. There is talk therapy, a vast array of new antidepressant medicines, and—most often recommended—a combination of both. Know that you are surrounded by a regiment of the best doctors, psychiatrists, and psychologists in the world. All you have to do is summon that regiment. You really have to do that, should your girl experience any of the next disorders that are impossible to overcome if you should try to go it alone.

Anorexia, Bulimia, and Other Eating Disorders

Eating disorders—anorexia nervosa, bulimia, binge eating, and other types of eating disorders—can be among the most difficult problems your daughter could develop. Because these disorders deal with what girls should have a good relationship with—daily nourishment—and can appear in so many different and scary forms, parents are often in denial. By the time parents wake up, the problems their girls have can be deeply ingrained and even harder to eradicate.

 **Essential**

The two most frequent eating disorders are anorexia, meaning loss of appetite, and bulimia, meaning having the appetite of an ox. Anorexia was once called the "slimming disease." Bulimia was part of the ancient Roman orgies in which people binged on food, and then purged themselves to make room for more food.

No Blame Game

Parents are hardly to blame. Some come from an era when food was less abundant than it is now, so they grew up wanting more food, not less. Others have never heard of these disorders whose exact and precise diagnoses and cures are relatively new.

Most girls with eating disorders cloak themselves in secrecy—at least at the beginning. Furthermore, some girls who are perfectly normal can suddenly develop one of these disorders and leave their families dumbfounded. All these diseases are thought to occur because of a teenage girl's problem with her body image. But the answers are not as clear-cut as they may seem. There are now boys with eating disorders, and older adults have come out of the closet, admitting they have had them for years.

Eating Disorder Prevention

Preventing eating disorders sounds easy but is hard. By the time your daughter is an adolescent, you do not have much control over her body, exercise, or eating. Of course you should criticize her little, avoid counting her calories, encourage her to exercise appropriately, serve healthful foods, and not compare her to other girls. But there is also a strong hereditary component involved that you can do nothing about. Do not ignore these warning signs:

- Losing weight at an alarming rate
- Losing and gaining weight like a yo-yo
- Talking a lot about being fat
- Barely eating anything or eating secretly
- Exercising to excess
- Spending much time in the bathroom after meals

This is only a partial list. Should you have any concerns about your daughter's weight—either being too little or too much—talk to her doctor at once. When dealing with eating disorders, every hour counts. So do not wait until the following occurs:

- Your girl eats only crumbs, develops a vomiting habit, chews laxatives like candy, and spins out of control with overactivity.
- Your girl is tired and weak all the time, stops having periods, develops baby hair all over her body and thinning hair on her head.

- Your girl ends up in the emergency room with heart problems, looking like a baby stork with nothing but skin and bones, and barely clinging to life.

You are too strong and too smart a parent to let that happen to your daughter. A recent report states that the average bulimic waits five and a half years before seeking help. The girls are often too ashamed to tell their doctors. But that is not going to happen at your house. You will put an end to whatever derailment in relationship to eating your daughter has developed and you will be watchful in other areas of her growth as well.

Self-Mutilation and Intervention

Self-mutilation is the general term for a girl hurting herself without hoping to die. The most common behavior is cutting herself with a razor, but it can also include biting herself, bruising herself, burning herself with a cigarette, or amputating parts of her body.

 **Fact**

Since the early 1990s, the incidence of self-mutilation seems to have risen. Less than one percent of the general population is thought to practice self-mutilation, but the incidence is highest among teenage girls. Self-mutilation, however, should never be confused with getting tattoos and body piercings.

Many researchers think self-mutilation is the result of a girl's feeling of shame or her wish to relieve unbearable tension within her. It can also represent anger at someone else that is instead directed against the girl herself. What makes it worse is that "cutters" always try to hide their scars from the public, so you have to wonder what is going on if your daughter always walks around covered from head to toe all year—even in mid-July.

Hair-Pulling Disorder

The disorder of hair-pulling (trichotillomania) is present when a girl repeatedly and nonstop pulls out her hair and maybe even her eyelashes and eyebrows. It often begins in childhood or adolescence. The cause is not crystal clear, but as with all self-harming conditions in their daughter, the parent should seek help immediately. Overall, the majority of self-mutilators have experienced some sort of trauma in the past that set them off. It is your duty to find out what happened—now.

Causes

When you find your daughter in pain, you hurt. The more she suffers, the more you do. So end the suffering for both of you. Girls who self-mutilate in whatever form are in an agony worse than you can imagine. Most of them have experienced something truly awful, such as:

- An overwhelming trauma
- Sexual abuse as a child or tween
- Severe physical abuse
- Emotional neglect, starvation, or imprisonment

For your girl to want to hurt herself is a sign that she may feel dead and yet wants to be alive so bad that the sensation of pain gives her that momentary feeling of existing.

Intervention

Should you sense or see any signs of self-mutilation in your daughter or her friends, take charge immediately. Probe into the past. Find out what happened and when. See to it that the guilty person or persons are dealt with. Even more important, see to it that your lovely daughter can start healing—from this moment on.

Runaway Signals

Sometimes a girl has been hurt so badly that she sees no other solution than to run away from home. Her natural instinct is to escape from something she feels she cannot go through again. Or maybe she has done something her parents told her not to do and she feels she will never be forgiven, so she packs a few things into her book bag and starts hitchhiking—not knowing that she could end up in incredibly tragic circumstances. Most runaway girls give signs that they are thinking about leaving home. These signs can include the following:

- Your girl acts completely unsociable.
- Your girl hangs out with kids who drink, use drugs, and have run away.
- Your girl steals money from you, which she then hoards.
- Your girl starts staying out all night.

If your daughter seems to seriously withdraw from the family, make secretive plans, and talks about running away, call in the cavalry—all those professionals ready and waiting to help you: the guidance counselors, the school psychologists, the social workers, the psychiatrists, the medical doctors. There are a huge number of specialists poised to help you. To think you have to solve your problem by yourself is a huge mistake. When you have a problem with your house, you call someone in to fix it right away. When you have a problem with the core of your life, your darling daughter, set everything aside and go to battle for her. Trust that the caring cavalry will fight side-by-side with you until victory is near.

Do you remember how your daughter was as a little girl? How she came to you then. Now come to her, help her, and help heal her. Forget about your heavy heart. Forget feeling you have let her down. Now you have another chance. As the old saying goes, a daughter may outgrow your lap, but she will never outgrow your heart. As soon as you send your daughter on the road to recovery, your heart will be light again.

CHAPTER 17

Your Daughter and Sexuality

Nothing can scare parents more than their daughter's sexuality. This term encompasses her behavior, impulses, and feelings connected to her as a sexual being. Mention *sexuality* in connection with their girl, and many parents immediately worry about STDs, pregnancy, and her life being ruined forever. But not you because you are the type of thoughtful parent who realizes that this wonderful aspect of your daughter is a chance for you to inform her, guide her, and make sure she can fully rejoice in her sexuality, but only when the time is right.

Teaching Your Daughter about Sex

If you don't teach your daughter about her body, sex, and sexuality, her friends will be more than happy to do so, and they are far less likely to have the correct information. Many parents think there is only one major talk about sexuality and sex they should have with their daughter. In actuality, there are three discussions you should have with your daughter:

1. What's happening with her body?
2. What's happening with boys' bodies?
3. What is intercourse and when is it appropriate?

The reason most parents feel awkward about even one of the three talks—let alone all of them—is that their parents did not talk with them about sex. These days, however, sex is exerting its influence in every aspect of our lives, and especially the lives of our young. Your daughter will be curious about her body and how it functions early on.

 **Fact**

The reality is that we live in a sexual culture. Society places few limits on adolescent sexual conduct and assumes that girls are, or would like to be, sexually active, like adults. That makes sex a key event in the lives of teenagers. How well it is handled can strongly affect a girl's future.

Some parents also feel embarrassed when discussing sex with their daughter because they cannot picture their baby having grown into a sexual being. Or perhaps they made mistakes when they were young, still regret them, and want to make sure their girl does not do likewise. So their conversation on sex may not be their smoothest delivery. But remember, your own attitude about sex is important. Educate yourself as much as possible so you are informed and not easily shocked. Your daughter should understand that you are willing to talk to her about sex and are relaxed and approachable.

The Talk

You certainly want to collect your thoughts and feel comfortable with the subject matter before you launch into your sex talk with your daughter. To gain a sense of comfort, educate yourself about common changes in puberty for both males and females. Remember if you are uncomfortable, your child will sense it and will adopt that uneasy behavior. There are three common approaches to speaking to your daughter about sex, and not all of them are good choices:

1. Handing your daughter a book and avoiding the topic completely.
2. Using scare tactics and telling your daughter she will make a big mistake if she becomes sexually active.
3. Discussing openly and honestly with your daughter the pros and cons of sexual activity at this stage of her life.

You want to choose the third approach. If you feel uncomfortable with it, go with the first approach—the book—and then follow up with a long talk during which you point out what a healthy relationship with a boy entails, what your family's values are, and how your girl should handle sexual matters. Using scare tactics shows a lack of communication and trust that will make her uncomfortable speaking with you about sex and may force her to explore her sexuality in secret.

 *Question?*

Should I put my daughter on birth control pills as soon as she turns fourteen?
Unless prescribed for medical reasons, you should not just put your daughter on birth control when she reaches a certain age. Randomly putting your daughter on birth control pills shows her that you do not trust her to be an intelligent, independent-thinking girl who has good values and can make smart choices. Instead, sit down and talk with her.

Also, do not just have just one sex talk with your child and then never say another word about it. Sexuality is in the forefront of the lives of teenagers, so it should become part of your favorite things to discuss with your daughter. Keep the lines of communication open. Tell her stories about how you found out about sex when you were young, and show your girl that today's openness in sex talks is so much better than the silence and ignorance of the past. During the "talk," you may want to lay some ground rules.

When the Time Is Right

Don't feel as though you have to give your daughter all the information on every possible situation all at once. You should give your daughter age-appropriate information throughout her life.

- **Birth to two years old:** Use the correct names for parts of the body.
- **Three to four years old:** Answer truthfully your child's questions about the differences between boy's and girl's bodies. Discuss what it is to be female or male. Remember children at this age can only retain about one fact per conversation.
- **Five to eight years old:** Children this age are curious about how babies are born and what pregnant women go through; answer their questions honestly. They may also have questions on breast development, menstruation, and growth of body hair. Reassure your daughter that the changes in her body are normal and may happen at different times for different girls.
- **Nine to twelve years old:** At this stage you might want to talk to your daughter about intercourse and its consequences. Also talk about pregnancy and disease prevention. Encourage your daughter to come to you with any questions regarding her body or things she may hear other kids saying. Support her talking to you about things she hears from her friends. Remember to be open and willing to talk about any concerns, no matter what they may be.
- **Thirteen to eighteen years old:** Continue to communicate with your daughter and give clear messages about your concerns and values. Encourage your daughter to think independently and with self-confidence about sex because as she grows older she will be making these sexual decisions on her own.

While you may be concerned with answering your young girl's sexual questions honestly, be aware that being knowledgeable can help protect her from molestation and coercion from older children and adults. Knowing that she can discuss sexual matters with you will make her less likely to keep any inappropriate talking or touching a secret.

Essential

Be sure to inform your daughter that many sexual myths exist, but they are all wrong. For example, she *can* get pregnant the first time she has sex, she *can* get pregnant when she has her period, she *can* get an infection from oral sex, and boys *can* relieve themselves of sexual tension without her help.

Sex Information

You encourage your girl to unburden herself with her friends and listen to them. When it comes to sex, however, your daughter should continue to talk to her friends about what she has on her mind but should be cautious about what her friends say. Tell your girl that in sexual matters:

1. Her girlfriends have little, if any, correct information.
2. Her boyfriends may be worse off; they may know even fewer actual facts.
3. Society and advertising are confused about their sexual messages.
4. You, her parents, are a reliable source.

Encourage your daughter to share with you any concerns or questions she may have about what she has heard her peers discussing. Be ready for the majority of information your daughter has been told to be incorrect and be prepared to be comfortable enough to explain to your daughter the actual facts. Promise to give her the latest and best knowledge there is, and then—and only then—should she even think about considering having sex.

Also teach your daughter a few great comebacks that she can use when being pressured into having sex. When a boy says, "Why not? Everybody's doing it," she can reply, "I've got news for you. I'm not everybody." Or when her girlfriends prod her with, "If you love him, you have to do it with him," she can say, "If he loves me, he can wait."

No More Rush

Nowadays girls prepare themselves for college, get a degree, start their careers, and after a few years, they might get married but not in haste—and, you hope, to their perfect mate. Today there is no more rushing to the altar right out of high school. Women are taking time to explore their career possibilities and who they are as individuals before entering a lifelong relationship.

 **Fact**

The median age of marriage for first-time brides has gone up steadily ever since the 1960s. In that decade it was twenty years of age and has increased ever since. By the 1990s it was twenty-four. A recent survey of the *New York Times* wedding announcements showed that many first-time brides are now in their early thirties.

In fact, nowadays girls have at least ten glorious years, which girls of the past did not have, to make a mark in their chosen profession. These ten independent years are wonderful times for girls to forge a path with meaningful work, to travel and see the world, and to meet a wide array of possible life partners. Why should modern girls throw these ten years away by becoming "old ladies" sexually long before their time, by getting embroiled in physical relationships with boys who still have a long way to go before they are grown up?

No Random Romance

Allow your daughter to think about what you have told her and then ask her to map out a long-range plan for herself. Just as she has a scholastic plan, she should have a sexual plan. She should decide when it will be appropriate for her to become intimate, most likely not for many years. Then help your daughter stick to her plan. Warn her about heavy petting, going to sleepovers where boys will show up, and wearing clothes that are too low-cut. Let her know that she can enjoy her sexuality without having sex. Tell her no girl—to your knowledge—has ever regretted not having had sex as a teenager.

Girls who feel they have strong supportive parents with whom they can have many conversations about sex and values appear to be more resilient to the sexual messages and pressures of our culture. Parents should acknowledge that their daughter's decision is not simple. They should not say all sex is bad but discuss the topic. In the end, parental expectations have a great effect on girls.

Promiscuity

Not enough parents talk to their daughters about promiscuity, a pattern of behavior that is characterized by casual sex with many partners. Yet they hope that their daughter is not promiscuous. Hope alone does not suffice. So make sure that you find the topic easy to broach. Just ask your daughter why she wears a certain pair of shoes with her jeans, for instance, or why she carries a certain purse with another outfit. Of course, it is because she is discriminating. She chooses her belongings carefully, so she does not wear just any old rag.

Talk to her about the dangers of promiscuity, which include the following:

- Ending up with emotional baggage, which can result from disappointing one's parents and the fear of pregnancy.
- Having bad sexual experiences, the chances of which increase with the number of partners a girl has.

- Not being able to develop a relationship. Boys do not feel an emotional attachment to a girl after sex the way girls do.

Count on this: Your daughter will weigh your words. She knows you cannot follow her around wherever she goes and prevent her from not sticking to her plan to delay having sex until after high school, until she has found her true love, or until she is married. But when you make talking about this topic comfortable long before she gets close to thinking about having sex, she will remember what you said. She will make the right choice. But even before she has her first boyfriend, she really should think about all the issues involved.

"Hooking Up" versus a Relationship

Let your daughter know that there are distinct differences between entering into a meaningful relationship versus a casual "hookup." The hookup, a now-common phenomenon, is an impulse action that does not lead to a serious loving relationship and often is a sign of poor self-esteem and lack of confidence. A relationship, however, is a meaningful venture in which both parties feel valued and cared for.

Hooking Up

These days hooking up (a quick sexual involvement that may only last one night and is between strangers or mere acquaintances) gets much attention on college campuses. Since whatever scenes play out at the universities can filter down to high schools, your daughter may already have seen some examples of kids in her grade hooking up. They have definitely been talking about it. So do not be surprised when your girl mentions the phenomenon. Tell her that is nothing new. Similar happenings used to be called a one-night stand, and it is an extremely unwise practice. Not only does a girl who hooks up not know anything about her partner—and his sexual history—but she also proves her lack of intelligence by assuming sex is nothing more than a snap of her fingers. That assumption could not be more wrong.

By buying into the notion that sex in high school is no more than a passing whim, a girl demeans herself by becoming depersonalized. Her ambitions will certainly take a hit: She cannot be ruled by teenage sexual gratification and by her wish to give her best in what should matter most to her at this stage of her development, such as grades, sports and hobbies, and friends.

 **Fact**

According to a report by Planned Parenthood, about 10 percent of all teenage girls—one in every ten—become pregnant before age twenty. Furthermore, the U.S. Attorney General reports that 38 percent of all date-rape victims are girls between the ages of fourteen and seventeen.

In short, hooking up is the exact opposite of what your daughter wants and needs. She needs to build relationships. To do that with a boy, she needs time to get to know him. A slow pace in warming up to a boy is her best course of action.

Your daughter may feel a sudden spark for a guy, but a good relationship needs more than that. Your daughter needs to get to know as much as possible about him, all his likes and dislikes, and what makes him tick.

Relationship How-To's

After your girl has met a boy she is interested in, maybe through a mutual friend, at a sports event, her volunteer work, or at her place of worship, she needs to start building a solid foundation with him to see if they have more in common that just the initial connection. Here are a few ideas:

- Learn about each other's favorite things and activities, and do them together.

- Talk about their future plans—colleges they might like to attend and jobs they might like to have someday, and the good deeds they would like to do.
- Discuss their dreams—their dream vacations, dream cars, dream homes, and dream future families of their own.
- Meet each other's families and spend time with each other's friends and siblings.
- Debate heatedly or coolly any topic that may come up—from school issues to politics.

As a parent, invite your daughter's boyfriend to family events. As a mother, teach her not to squash any of his chivalrous attempts. As a father, show her, by your example, how a man treats a woman well, so your girl will expect to be treated well by a boy. Tell her she is always in charge in a relationship, so she will be empowered to set the necessary limits.

Teach Your Girl to Say No

To grow up as well as possible and to explore all her potential as a teenager, your daughter needs to be empowered to be strong and to soldier on. If you teach her how to say no to sex—loud and clear—she will be especially powerful. She is too young to put her intellectual and physical growth on hold. Premature intimate entanglements, however, can do just that. So keep giving your girl all the tools you can to help her stave off society's and the teenage world's pressures in regards to sex.

Girl Courage

As with all parenting situations, give the sexual part of your daughter's development your best shot. Tell her it is in her very best interest to concentrate on her number-one job: being a great student and participating in extracurricular activities. Sex can come later; academic achievement should not. Once she finishes high school successfully, she can have a lot more freedom. For now, she should have as much fun as possible as a teenager and not burden herself with worries about birth control, sexually transmitted diseases, and the feelings of disappointment in herself because she was not strong enough to say, "No! I mean it!"

Your Girl Is Attracted to Other Girls

When you observe your daughter having crushes on other girls, realize this is a normal stage of her sexual development. Often girls begin in elementary school to idolize a pretty young female teacher, and then they admire an older girl from afar. Later they develop an extremely close relationship with one of their girlfriends and focus primarily on her. At age twelve or thirteen, some girls even start role-playing games with a group of curious girls where one is chosen to play the part of the boy, and the other girls practice their kissing skills on "him." They may take turns being the pretend-male, or they may ask for volunteers.

 *Essential*

Many girls start to experiment with same-sex relationships and bisexuality as they grow up. This is a normal passing phase for them. Only time will indicate your daughter's true sexuality. No matter what you may think, you cannot choose it for her as you would her prom dress.

Growing up, your daughter can take a circuitous path. So be ready for most anything and enjoy watching your girl make the journey from her early to her late teens. Let her be herself as she unfolds and accept whatever sexual orientation she turns out to develop. No matter how strong the beliefs of some groups, research tells us that girls neither choose to be homosexual nor heterosexual. They are what they are. In fact, according to the experts, about 5 percent of all teenage girls consider themselves to be gay or lesbian. What if your girl comes to you and tells you she thinks she belongs to that group?

Brave Girl

Give your daughter a big hug and tell her you are proud of her should she reveal she is gay. It takes courage for a girl to be honest about her sexual preference to her parents while still in high school. But also hug yourself—in spirit. You are to be commended for having done such a good job as a parent that your daughter could come to you. Tell her she was created as an answer to your prayers, and you are so proud of her—just the way she is.

Feel very special because you have been chosen to have a daughter who is extraordinary. Any mom and dad can raise a girl who only presents average challenges. You were chosen to have a girl who presents above-average challenges to you. This gives you even more chances to expand your parenting skills and to surpass what you have done so far.

Your Ultimate Goal

You expect your daughter—in regard to sex—to handle herself with the same intelligence and thoughtfulness she uses in all other aspects of her life. Always hold her to the highest standards. But should she make a slip, let her know that she can always come to you and tell you the truth—she must never forget that. Although you may not condone whatever she did, you will carry her emotionally through her troubled moments.

CHAPTER 18

Dating

R aising a girl is truly an adventure. Every year brings a new stage accompanied by excitement. One of the most exciting times in your daughter's life is the dating stage. It is when she starts to experiment with the social scene and tries to find out what types of boys she might like. She also has a chance to learn some solid dating techniques, build her self-confidence, and go through a rehearsal for perhaps finding a long-term partner. With plenty of information and encouragement from you, your daughter can travel through the dating landscape without too much trouble.

Dating 101

The time when your daughter starts dating can be the most wonderful stage in her life yet, and it will be once you get her on a great footing. She will have good experiences because she has you to launch her on the path to realizing her dating dreams. Indeed it is you who makes all the difference here. Being too harsh and forbidding, or too lenient or lax, are recipes for disaster.

So you need to think about teenage dating not with dread but with joy and get some clarity on the topic first. Discuss it with a suitable person—the other parent, a relative with older girls, or other parents of girls. You cannot skip getting ready for your daughter's dating when she is getting ready to start. Begin early in your girl's life

to spell out to her what dating is, what the rules at your house are, and what exactly you expect from her in this regard.

Dating Groundwork

Dating for your girl is like a great rehearsal that lasts a few years. She gets to practice having a boyfriend and going through all the excitement this stage of development brings with it: the joy, the excitement, the heart beating faster, hers and yours. Before she starts dating, you'll want her to learn three basic lessons:

1. How to respect herself and the person she is dating.
2. How to date—and know what the parameters of dating are.
3. How to protect herself and keep from getting hurt.

The groundwork for these lessons has to be laid before your daughter goes on her very first date. If you allow her to sally forth without a plan and without having prepared yourself and her, you are sending her into the dating wilderness, so to speak, without a road map. So do not even wait until the topic comes up; work on some dating guidelines ahead of time. Some guidelines for you might include:

- Be clear about your values and communicate them to your daughter.
- Answer her questions directly and honestly.
- Make sure that you don't stop talking when she says, "I know." Ask her what she knows and go from there.
- Be persistent. Without your messages, your daughter will have no direction and may flounder in the dating scene.

A good way to start is to ask your daughter what her definition of dating is. No matter what she says, be sure to point out to her that dating is not sex. There is a big difference. Dating is going out with someone, having a good time, and learning more and more about the person. Some people call it a character-building experience, during which teenagers learn how to deal with various situations together.

Essential

Parents should never "fall in love" with their daughter's boyfriends and invest too much attention, time, and care into building a friendship with them. Also they should not judge a boy by his looks, nor should they not push their daughter into a relationship just to be popular.

For your daughter to reap all the benefits of dating, you'll want to avoid overreacting when she mentions for the first time that a boy asked her out. Also put the following questions completely out of your mind:

- Is this boy right for her?
- Are they going to get married at age seventeen?
- Is my daughter going to mess up her life?

There is really no need to panic when your daughter mentions dating because you have done your homework, with the help of all the resources that are available to you.

Teaching How to Know When

Some people read about girls going on dates in sixth and seventh grade, and freak out. Of course, girls mature more quickly than boys and may want to start dating earlier than boys. Plus, they are usually not interested in a boy their age, but in one who is two or three years older. So your fear is that the older boys will be a bad influence on your little girl. "A father knows exactly what those boys at the mall have on their depraved little minds because he once owned such a depraved little mind himself," says Bill Cosby.

To put an end to your fears, do not allow any dating before you feel your daughter can maturely handle the situation, perhaps around age fourteen or fifteen. Of course, the appropriate dating age depends on her maturity and what experiences you may have had with an older child—or in your own past. Remember that some girls do not even start dating until they are sixteen or seventeen. Then set a few rules that can solve many of the adolescent dating dilemmas for your girl. For example, you could ask her to:

- Not date a boy she has seen only a few times and does not know well.
- Trust her instincts. Have a plan in mind ahead of time to be safe in a dangerous situation.
- Realize that alcohol and drugs decrease her ability to think straight, so don't use them.
- Tell a friend whenever she is leaving a party with someone she does not know well, and have that friend make sure she arrives home okay by checking on her.
- Know the exact plans for the evening and make sure her parents know them, too.

Most important is to teach your daughter to be strong in her communications with her date. If your daughter says, "I'm not sure," to her date, he might assume that she just wants to be pushed or pressured more until she says yes. Your girl should practice saying no loudly and repeatedly until her voice is strong, confident, and convincing.

Of the utmost importance is remembering that your daughter watches you carefully in your relationship with your spouse and other people. When she sees you model behaviors such as sticking up for yourself, disagreeing with someone in a firm but kind way, and giving and expecting respect, she learns these valuable qualities and will use them in her dating experiments and relationship rehearsals.

Curfew

There is no right time for your daughter to be home. Sit down with her when both of you are calm and talk about her plans and your expectations. How old is your daughter? Is there a legal curfew for adolescents in your community? How well do you know her friends? Cell phones have made it simple for teens to disguise their actual location; like it or not, there is no way you can have absolute control of your daughter's whereabouts. Instead, let her know your concerns and agree together on a reasonable curfew. You should also decide in advance what will happen if she fails to come home on time. Be sure that you are willing to follow through before finalizing your agreement.

Question?

My daughter wants to start dating. What kind of curfew is reasonable?
Be conservative with setting her curfew. Ask some of the parents in the PTA or members of other parent organizations what they think is appropriate—depending on the occasion. Be sure to put a suitable consequence in place if your daughter does not return on time.

Self-Respect

During preadolescence, girls undergo a mysterious transformation that is often a concern for parents. Even very saucy, self-confident girls are apt to shrivel into shy, insecure shadows of themselves. Preadolescent girls have a disturbingly predictable pattern of scaling back their far-flung aspirations. They soon convince themselves that they are not as bright or as capable as they previously assumed. The intense social pressures girls experience are probably largely responsible for this crisis of confidence. In fact, many girls define their self-worth almost exclusively in terms of what their peers think of them, or in terms of what they *think* their peers think of them.

It is critical to your girl's self-esteem to have other interests and receive constant infusions of emotional support from her family. These extra doses of encouragement will support your daughter and allow her to be more proactive in claiming her individuality and self-respect. Her belief in her own worth and dignity will help her tremendously when she tests and navigates the social waters. Just as you value her, she has to value herself. As with anything she esteems, she holds the object of her estimation in high regard and does not let others besmirch it. Teach your daughter that she is is so valuable that she must not let anything tarnish her, especially not a date.

She needs to be on the alert for these warning signs in a boy before she goes on a date with him:

- **Jealousy:** Love is trust and jealousy is distrust.
- **Anger:** Against other guys, in the way he drives, or slams his locker door.
- **Bad language:** Cursing other people is a sign of bad temper and lack of control.
- **Cruelty to animals or small children:** She could be next.
- **Blaming others for his mistakes and trying to make her feel guilty.**
- **Physical roughness—She could get hurt—and pushing her to do sexual things she is not ready for.**
- **Criminal tendencies:** Cheating, stealing, or using drugs.

If your girl does go out with a guy who exhibits these behaviors, she must make sure this is their last date. Help your daughter prepare an excuse for turning the boy down next time he asks her out. One good excuse is, "We are too different to go out again."

You cannot rip the mask off every boy who is interested in your daughter and reveal his true character, but you can make her more inquisitive and observant. Ask her to pay close attention to what other girls say about a boy. If he goes to her school, his reputation will precede him. If it is negative, she should wonder why and consider giving him the cold shoulder. It is a matter of her self-respect that she does not date a boy who has not managed to earn anyone's respect; not of his classmates, of his teachers, or of his coaches.

Alert!

Sometimes teenage girls do not know if what they have observed in a boy is really a warning sign or just a sign the boy likes her so much he cannot help himself. Tell your daughter that potentially dangerous boys can be accomplished liars, and she is too smart to be fooled by any of them.

Group Dating

Most girls start in middle school to hang out with a group of friends that may include both girls and boys. Certainly by the time your daughter is old enough to join a club at school or get into athletics, there will be quite a few occasions when she is going to an event—a movie, a college game, a banquet, an awards ceremony—with a large crew. Encourage her go out with a group and ask the whole bunch over for a cookout afterward, or to watch the video of the latest athletic meet they were in, while you have popcorn and soda waiting for them.

Provide transportation for the group when they go to a theme park with their club advisors. Your best move really is to encourage group dating. As long as your daughter and her teenage friends travel in a pack, they can have fun but rarely get into a sticky situation. The sheer number of people along on the date usually prevents that from happening.

Finding a Good Boyfriend

The teenage world is filled with all kinds of boys; some are frogs, but the majority of them—around 75 percent—are perfect princes. These princes do not ride up to your daughter's door in a coach and whisk her off to a ball in a castle, but they are special boys, just as your girl is a special girl. They are usually the boys she knows from school, her neighborhood, or her house of worship. However if your daughter seems to be more intrigued by a boy who comes out of the blue and has no connection to her in his background, sit up and pay attention.

 *Essential*

> Be sure to avoid the typical conversation stoppers with your daughter. Do not say, "You're too young!" or "Because I said so!" or "That's a bad bunch; stay away from them!" Have your daughter tell you something about each girl and boy in her dating group, and find something to like about them.

Boyfriends to Avoid

Your daughter may be frustrated by not landing a great boyfriend overnight, so she may tend to overlook the boys in her backyard. Way too tame, she may think. But she may be treading on thin ice when she branches out daringly and looks to meet some brand-new boys in questionable arenas. Make sure that she does not:

- Accept a ride from a boy or man she does not know very well.
- Develop a liking for boys who experiment with drugs and alcohol.
- Go alone to a boy's home—ever—or to the apartment of an older guy.

- Meet someone alone and in person she met on the Internet.

The best way for your girl to find a good boyfriend is to give all the boys she associates with already a closer look. Furthermore, all these boys have friends, so there should be quite a large number of young males she can concentrate on, if she wants to. If she is having a hard time finding a boy she likes, encourage her to get involved in other pursuits so that the pressure of teen dating will be lessened. She'll have many more—and better—opportunities after high school to find the right boyfriend.

If your daughter is not asked out, tell her that her time will come, if she wants it to. In the meantime, how great for her to be able to concentrate on what's really important—to grow into the finest young person she can be.

Boyfriends to Attract

Your daughter can tell if she has found a good and suitable boyfriend if she wants to introduce him to her family, if he understands her need for privacy, if he is thoughtful and respectful to his parents and teachers, and if she feels as if she can talk to him about things that matter to her. In short, she wants to choose a boy who is worthy of her attention, and not waste her precious time on the frogs; that is, the boys who eventually might turn out to be good boyfriend material but are not in their present shape. Don't worry, though. There are many successful boys your daughter can meet in her everyday life. Some stand out immediately, and others need a closer look. Some good qualities your daughter can look for in a boy could include:

- He cares about his future; he plans for college or beyond.
- He is optimistic.
- He is a good student or at least puts effort into his schoolwork.
- He is fairly mature and has a strong character.
- He is trustworthy and reliable.

From early on, you want her to develop the ability to look beneath the good looks and the charming smile of a boy and see what is there.

Boys as Friends

If your daughter has no brothers or close male cousins, she needs some boys as friends. Even if she has many male relatives, she can still benefit from having boys in her life who she is not interested in romantically. There are so many things she can learn from them— from the ways boys are different from girls to the way some of them can clam up rather than discuss their emotions to having a different outlook than girls.

Boy Buds

In high school, some girls manage to find good "boy buds" not only as their study buddies, but also for the years to come, as male confidants. To them, their male friends are like beloved brothers, only a family or a house removed. Male friends can often tell your daughter the truth better than her girlfriends and her boyfriend would, because there are no strings attached. Besides, they may get your girl into more outdoorsy activities and help build her confidence even more. Therefore, welcome your daughter's boy friends, as well as her boyfriends.

Alert!

Sometimes the most innocent boy-girl outings can cross the line. Do not let your daughter and her friends have a boy-girl slumber party at your house. Even though your girl may stay in her sleeping bag by herself, another girl and boy may not be as strong, and you do not want to allow them to act on their feelings for each other at your house.

Your Girl's Broken Heart

A good reason for girls to get involved in sports, besides honing their physical talents and learning teamwork, is that they learn how to accept losses. Sooner or later, even the best female athlete or the best girls' team in the world can get defeated. Yet the season, or the competition, goes on. It is a sign of good sportsmanship to accept victory and defeat graciously. Having a relationship with a boy is not a sport, but the end of a relationship can be compared to losing an important game. Naturally your daughter will be hurt when it happens, even if she is the one who calls it quits.

 **Fact**

Doctors report finding "stress cardiomyopathy," also called the broken-heart syndrome, in some patients. This is a condition of intense emotional stress that can cause rapid heartbeat and severe heart-muscle weakness. It can occur because of surprise, grief, or the death of a loved one.

Be sure to warn your girl about the potential of a "broken heart" before she starts a serious boy friendship. It is a normal risk that comes with any deep or long-standing relationship, even one with her best girlfriend. When your daughter has a breakup, she needs to know that she is not alone in what she is feeling: sadness, anger, confusion, and maybe a lack of confidence and a measure of jealousy.

Therefore give her these heartbreak-healing hints before she needs them so she has them handy. The best heart-pain relievers include:

- Sharing your feelings with someone you trust, and that includes crying.
- Doing something that is fun and taking care of yourself.
- Keeping busy helping others who are worse off.

- Counting the days. It can take from two days to weeks and months for a teen girl to get over a breakup.

If your daughter initiated the end of the relationship, she should be nice about it, not "tell all" and spread rumors. This boy may turn into a friend after a while, become her girlfriend's boyfriend, or become close again later, so it is best not to burn her bridges. In the meantime, you can be certain that your girl will get over her heartache, if you make sure her hurt does not turn into lingering anger. Tell her not to waste time blaming the boy or herself. Some relationships are for practice and some are for longer term.

Overall Goal

As mentioned before, dating is your daughter's time to rehearse her role as a potential girlfriend—mate—for an individual someday. At this point in her life, she should hold auditions for boys to convince her to spend some time with them. It is also her time to rehearse who she is. Secretly you are in awe of how well she is progressing through her vital growth stages. Smile at her and tell her you are proud of her.

Take a close look at your girl and remember your main goal: to make her the strongest, smartest, and most capable teenager she is able to be. Should she encounter some trouble spots in befriending boys, be available as a listening board, an advisor, and a person who knows how to fix what is broken—and to leave alone what is not.

CHAPTER 19

Family Challenges

R aising a girl brings excitement and complications to a family, even if her family is uncomplicated. But a family does not have to be the traditional family with a mother, father, and kids to be a loving and productive situation for a girl. It can be an arrangement in which a stepparent or grandparent plays a major role. Or it can consist of a solo parent, or be a shared situation where the girl spends a few days a week with each parent. As long as the established family pattern is solid and on even keel, your daughter will be fine. But what if your family is in turmoil?

Family Discord and Divorce

These days, parental arrangements can be endless: from the old-fashioned ones where both parents raise their girl to the new-fashioned ones that add various sorts of parent substitutes into the mix. These parental subs can be guardians, live-in boyfriends or girlfriends of the parents, or their partners, but difficulties can arise when serious disagreements crop up between the parents or parent figures. The most frequent difficulty in a traditional family is divorce.

Not only is divorce a major change for the parent, it can also be a trying time for the children involved—but only if you, the parent, are not prepared. You may not be able to lift the pain your daughter may feel over the divorce, but you can give her the following:

- The tools to deal with the big change in the family structure.
- The certainty that her life—after her parents' divorce—will go on.
- A chance to observe adults working out a serious problem to everyone's satisfaction as much as is possible.
- The assuredness that she, too, will be able someday to face the biggest challenges life may throw at her and handle them with confidence, class, and character.

 **Fact**

Approximately half of all marriages end in divorce, although the statistics vary from year to year. For second and third marriages, the divorce rate is even higher. As a result, more than half of children end up living in a single-parent home, but not necessarily for long, since the majority of divorced parents remarry.

If you consider the implications of divorce, take the steps leading to it carefully, and go through the whole process by taking the high road, you can actually impart a difficult but valuable lesson to your daughter that will serve her well for the rest of her life. Too many parents, however, are wounded by the breakup of their marriages and, like a hurt animal, withdraw into a dark corner to lick their wounds, forgetting all about their daughter.

Divorce Benefits

You are a proactive parent. You are the type of mother or father who studies the pros and cons of divorce long before the fact and is willing to do what it takes to make this experience as enhancing for your girl as possible. This exploration begins long before the actual separation because you read about what you are going through and get advice from people you can trust.

Sadly, too often predivorce couples try to minimize their difficulties with the use of alcohol or drugs. Or they turn to emotional and physical abuse of each other. Witnessing these signs of parental dysfunction can be more harmful to your daughter than the actual breakup. In fact, the actual breakup can be a relief for her. When you sink to behaviors that are not only unacceptable but also harmful to yourself, your girl can lose respect for you. A screaming parent embarrasses a girl. An hour-long mother and father fight makes a girl feel it is all her fault. Staying up all night hearing accusations flung at each other by the adults she loves most will definitely not stand your daughter in good stead when she has to take a history test in first period the next day.

Alert!

Parental discord can play a major role in their children's well-being. It can turn out to be more disruptive than the absence of a mother or father due to divorce. In homes with a high rate of conflict, children experience a more negative effect long-term than in discord-free postdivorce homes.

Double Divorce Dangers

The fact is that divorce alone does not generally hurt children as much as the actions of the couple that occur before the divorce and their demeanor afterward. On the one hand, mothers and fathers going through divorce already take time away from what they ought to concentrate on—their roles as parents—and that leaves a void. On the other hand, their conduct between themselves—and as individuals—can sink to the lowest standard of behavior, setting up a bad example for their daughters and damaging them.

The least you, as an about-to-be-divorced mother or father, can do is to make sure you do your "ugly" acting-out away from your daughter. Take your discord to a place away from home. Establish regular arguing hours with your spouse, if you have to, when your daughter is in school, or meet at a neutral ground like an office while you leave your girl under the supervision of a friend.

Do whatever you can to make the transition from a two-parent home to a one-parent one as smooth as possible. Divorce is widely accepted these days. Books abound on the topic; counselors are standing by. It is much better to get too much help in preparing to be a divorced mother or father than not to have enough information on hand.

Alert!

Many children of divorce report lowered academic expectations by their parents, plus less checking on their schoolwork by their mothers and fathers, and diminished parent participation in their activities and sports than children of married parents. Be aware that as a result, the kids tend to lose interest as well.

The more you are able to weather the interruption in your life that even the "best" divorce brings with it, the more you can help your daughter be strong and thrive through a difficult time for both of you. Plus, this is an opportunity for you to focus on the positives that can arise after the divorce.

You have it within you to restore your home environment to calmness and to return to your most important goal: raising your daughter to realize all her potential. You, too, have a chance to advance. Your first marriage did not work out, but you did not go through it in vain. You learned a lot and will put it to good use should you get another chance. Trust in yourself—you will.

 **Fact**

> The good news is that after a temporary dip in scholastic perfor-
> mance, school-age girls' academic scores rise when her parents
> choose divorce over staying in a bad marriage. Unfortunately, for
> boys, the results are not so positive. Many of them fall behind in aca-
> demics, and their discipline problems at school tend to spike.

Stepmothers, Stepfathers, and Stepsiblings

Some researchers report that one of every three Americans of any
age is a member of a stepfamily. Others say it is closer to one in two,
or 50 percent. That paints a rosy picture as to your chances of remar-
rying and of your girl getting a stepparent. The *step* in stepparent is
assumed to come either from the Old English word *steop*, meaning
"bereaved" or from the Indo-European root *steu*, meaning "fragment."
Just as a missing fragment that is found makes a thing whole, look
at your chance to be a stepparent as a healing process. Therefore,
think of the opportunity of adding a stepmother, stepfather, or stepsiblings—or a combination of them—as a beneficial experience for
your daughter. Instead of just having one parent after the divorce,
she can have as many as four parental figures in her life, and lots of
grandparents. She may have a mother who remarries, and a father
who remarries. Each remarriage can also bring with it the possibility
of another child—a brother or sister, or several of them, even a new
baby if the remarried couple is so inclined.

Therefore, it is important to highlight your girl's chances of suddenly living and interacting closely with all these new people, each
of whom can contribute much to her growth. Just be very sure your
daughter is not overlooked or feels deprived, in terms of attention or
financial considerations, in the process.

Step Up

Fortunately there are now support groups for every type of step-parenting arrangement imaginable. Books on the topic and innumerable Internet resources will help you make sense out of the change in your—and your daughter's—life. Discuss these changes with your daughter far in advance. Warn her about some of the minuses that could crop up if she would let them. Tell her some of the secrets for being a successful stepdaughter. Here are a few:

1. She must never forget how much you love her.
2. She must keep a written record of perceived slights and problems, and give it to you on a regular basis.
3. She must not play the custodial parent against the noncustodial parent.
4. She must not get into a competition with her stepsiblings. Why should she? She stands supreme in your heart.

 **Fact**

In the vast majority of divorces, the kids end up living with their mother. In 1990, approximately three-fourths of the children involved in custody cases were assigned to the wife. Joint custody was given in about 16 percent, and fathers received custody in 8 percent. Since then the rates of joint custody and paternal custody have risen but not that significantly.

You also have some important stepparenting strategies to keep in mind and to go by—even if you are the biological parent of the girl in the family, and your spouse and his (or her) kids are the "steps." These strategies should include the following:

- Realizing that a stepfamily is different than a first family. Your daughter may think her new father or mother will replace her old one, which can cause unrealistic expectations. Create a new family unit with new activities.
- Getting over the "you're not my dad; you're not my mom" conversation. Decide that in long-term or major matters, the biological parent makes the rules. In everyday situations, whoever is in charge at the moment will handle the discipline.
- Uniting with the stepparent—as a team—and making sure the new mother or father gets a chance to spend time with your girl alone, doing fun things.
- Not expecting an instant close attachment between your daughter and her stepparent—that takes time. But she must show respect.
- Finding alone-time with your new spouse, so that you can role-model for your daughter what a good, devoted marriage looks like.

Essential

A 1987 study on the effects of divorce on children revealed that 14 percent of kids with divorced parents needed help from a psychologist, either from one at school or one in private practice, as reported by the Center for Law and Social Policy in Washington, D.C. In contrast, only about 6 percent of children from a two-parent family needed psychological help.

If you and your new spouse discuss whatever problems could arise in regard to your daughter before they do, you will be well prepared. Ask other divorced parents of girls what they went through. By being positive that you can handle the rough spots remarriage can bring and by working on smoothing them for your daughter, you will make much progress. Anticipating step trouble is preferred to antagonizing over it. You can either allow yourself to whine over why this had to happen to you, or you can be determined to win.

Help Up

Many times one positive step forward in building your daughter's relationship with her new stepfather, stepmother, or stepsiblings seems to result in two steps back. Do not be discouraged. Stepfamilies are also called blended families. Just as the best qualities of two or three extraordinary coffees that are ground together can rise to the forefront, so can all the top talents and achievements of the individuals involved emerge in a blended family. All it takes is your daily attention to the desired result: your daughter's comfortable establishment and unhampered growth in the new family arrangement that you have formed. This new arrangement may even play out in two places, rather than in one home, as your daughter is used to.

Co-parenting

Some parents decide to co-parent their daughter. They have joint custody and pass her and her care and supervision back and forth. Just as in an Olympic relay race, one runner passes the baton smoothly to the next; the winning team usually does best because their switchover technique and progress overall are flawless.

If you and your ex have joint custody of your daughter, you must be a united front in your quest for victory in the parenting of your girl. As she travels back and forth between your homes, she should be expected to have similar rules in place in both environments. Therefore, schedule a parental planning meeting as often as possible. Or agree to the rules via e-mail and phone chats. Your daughter can benefit from growing up in two homes just as she could live half a year in the United States. and the other half on another continent. It is possible that—as a consequence—her horizon and her understanding of the world will far surpass that of other girls her age. Her exposure to other educational systems and her vacillating from one city to another—as her home base—can also benefit her academically. She may astound you with how well she can adapt. Children are amazing in the way they make the best of their traveling parental arrangements.

Your daughter can succeed, just as long as you make sure that:

- She knows she is most important in your life, whether you are with her every day or only every other week.
- She has a warm and lively connection with you that can never be severed, via daily e-mails, phone chats, and snail mail.
- She is empowered as much as possible to have a say in how and with which parent she wants to spend some of her vacations and free time. Your hurt feelings—should she prefer her other biological parent—have no place here.

When you remarry, you dream of having a second chance to have a wonderful family with your daughter riding on the crest of the new wave of happiness. Your dream can come true, but only if one step—"fragment"—fits into place at a time. Expecting grownups and kids who do not share a blood relationship or a history to feel lovey-dovey immediately is unrealistic, but every day that is filled with thoughtful parenting will bring all of you closer.

Single Parenting

Being a single parent of a daughter, whether you are of the same gender or not, can add another layer of issues to be handled. As a single father, you may not be able to grasp the growth stages of your girl and sense her moods. You may not feel comfortable to dig deeply into what worries her. You may be baffled by her taste in fashion and her choice of hair colors. You may be so busy with work and household duties that you overlook some of her needs, but at least—in most cases—you will have enough money to take care of her.

Single Moms

Single mothers have a more difficult situation. They often stand at the bottom of the income scale, unless they receive alimony or the grandparents chip in. So they often have to scrape to afford raising their daughter, in addition to taking care of all the parenting that is usually shared by two adults. Therefore, single moms have most often less free time than any other parents and can be stretched to the limit.

Alert!

One recent report examined the high school dropout rate for children from a one-parent home. It was 31 percent, as compared to 13 percent for children from a two-parent home. A similar finding was reported for the risk of teen pregnancy. In single-parent homes, it was 33 percent; in two-parent homes, it was only 11 percent.

However, study after study shows that single mothers can rise above their limited budgets and go on to do a superb job in raising their daughters. Often a powerful mother-daughter bond forms that transcends whatever difficulties arise. It is as if the girl decides not to get sidetracked with the usual teenage troubles and matures faster, achieves more, and fills the empty space in her mother's heart with top grades, school honors, and exemplary conduct.

"Chosen" Family Members

When you meet new people at work, at your place of worship, in the PTA or other organizations you join, and something about them strikes you as extraordinary, "adopt" them at once in your mind and your heart. Study what makes these adults so special. Have they overcome extraordinary difficulties? Have they risen above their meager backgrounds? Did they prevail against the odds? Have they lived each and every day to the best of their abilities and kept a smile on their face?

Family Choices

Whatever you decide that makes some people stand out in your mind, take a lesson from them by copying their attitudes, their courageous outlook, their determination to not be bowed and cowed—and impart some of it to your daughter. Even better, invite these people—whatever their age or ethnicity or accent—to your house for your daughter to learn from. You did not get to choose your biological family members. Now make a deliberate attempt to pick the best human beings you can find as your chosen family. Find yourself a substitute sister, brother, parents, cousin from among the most amazing human beings you run across. You can choose from the whole human race.

If you cannot have special people visit you, schedule an outing during which your girl can absorb—via osmosis—some of their magnificence. If your contact with them is only brief, still take away from meeting them something you can pass on to your daughter—the sparks of invincibility of the human spirit and the greatness that resides in each of us, including your daughter.

Let Girls Be Girls

When you go through divorce, or become a widow or widower, or when you break up with a long-time partner, you have a hole in your heart. It is your job to fill that hole with a new spouse or a new significant other if you decide. But never use your daughter to try to fill that emptiness that you might feel.

Daughter as Companion

You can expect your girl to help out with the extra work around your home that the absence of the other parent leaves undone. Of course, you want her to cooperate with doing the daily chores. You also appreciate her company when you watch TV together or see a suitable movie. How you laugh with her over some cartoons. You discuss current events with her, the headlines, and the highlights of the week.

Daughter as Daughter

Never steal your daughter's childhood or girlhood by transplanting her into the footprints of your lost partner or share intimate things. Do not run down her biological father or mother even if you have to bite your tongue—hard. Do not discuss your yearning for a passionate romance. Do not give her the details of the dates you are going on. Find a place to experience affection again, but do not bring home one of those dates and have that person spend the night. What are you thinking? That your girl cannot see what you are doing? Or that she does not remember? That she won't pattern her life after yours to the nth degree? Naturally, after a lengthy period, you can change that rule.

Daughter Uninterrupted

Keep in mind that your daughter will copy your life, little by little. She will especially follow you in whatever way you do not want her to follow you. Therefore, act in her best interest as you struggle through whatever discord your spouse or partner slings in your direction. You are the best parent of your daughter that you can be, and you will not sink to the level of the less capable parent. You will summon your energy, take up the challenge, and make sure your daughter—and you—come through this parenting test as aces.

"Although there are many trial marriages . . . there is no such thing as a trial child," said author Gail Sheehy. Always remember as you raise your daughter, that there are no rehearsals in this field—none. You only get one chance to raise your girl, so apply to this task all your energy, experience, and effort. The result will astound you.

From Girl to Woman

There will come a day when all the many tough, ticklish, and terrific lessons you have taught your daughter come together to produce a wonderful young human being—your girl all grown up. As she grew from infancy to her tween and teen stages, you were there for her, supporting her and loving her. Now she is becoming an adult capable of making her own decisions and mapping her own journey through life. This is the time you can begin to let go and admire the young woman you have raised.

Your Daughter as a Young Woman

As a young woman, your daughter is self-reliant, confident, and independent thinking. She is ready to venture into the world and make good choices. You have loved her from the moment she was born, all through her baby years, her elementary school experiences—on and on, until she advanced to her grown-up stage.

During these years you taught her all you know, and with this knowledge she can now stand on her own two feet. She may make some mistakes, but that is the only downside of life, that even a grown daughter can make an error now and then.

But without making a mistake and figuring out what went wrong, your daughter would not have a chance to progress. If she were "perfect" in every way, she would

be a marble statue, not the warmhearted, strong, and determined example of the best of young womanhood.

Essential

Be sure to tell your daughter that success for a woman has many definitions. It may mean great accomplishments, such as earning a graduate degree, publishing articles in international journals, and speaking to thousands. Or it may be growing a vegetable garden and taking the tomatoes to the soup kitchen. Or perhaps it will be reading to a sick child in a hospital room. The trick is learning who you are as a woman and being thrilled about it.

You want your daughter to grow in confidence through her mistakes. That means she must believe in herself and have opinions. What makes girls strong and independent minded is their ability to form ideas, consider them, and let others hear them.

Competing in the World

What you are doing is miraculous; you are raising a good girl who wants to succeed and proves it every day. She is indeed willing to do her best to achieve and does not shirk from competition, and the news could not be better in this regard. This is the century of the smart, independent-thinking, productive girl.

Going to College

One example to prove that this century is the best era ever for girls is the scene on today's American college campuses. For the first time the tide has turned; female students now outnumber male students by four to three. In fact, women receive 57 percent of the bachelor's degrees these days while men only get 43 percent.

This development will make college a very welcoming and inviting place for your daughter when she is ready for it. Many of her classes will be female oriented. Many of the organizations at the university she might attend will be run by girls or even be dominated by them. Even her chances of getting into a field she likes may increase because more women-oriented courses of study will be added. In short, the era of the "Big Man on Campus" has just turned into the era of the "Wonderful Woman on Campus."

Fact

Christina Hoff Sommers, a resident scholar at the American Enterprise Institute and the author of *The War Against Boys: How Misguided Feminism Is Harming Our Young Men*, says that a gender switch has been thrown, and that now we will have many more females who are more educated and well informed than we have males with the same attributes.

Your daughter is fortunate to be part of the new girls in power movement that shows itself more and more in high school and truly emerges in college. While the admission deans have to worry about how to get more boys to apply, your daughter has nothing but advantages awaiting her once she gets there. Of course, more girls than ever before going to college may mean the competition is getting stiffer. But your daughter will welcome this challenge when she is old enough for it. She will be well prepared because you have gotten her primed in advance.

Girls' Top Tactics

You and your daughter may have discussed her going to college someday. If she seems interested in college, start talking now, no matter what grade she is in, and encourage her studies. Her academic training, bolstered by your interest and guidance at home, will help her get there. Of course, she has to have a high grade-point average and do well on the required admission tests.

Long before your girl needs to take the SAT or the ACT, or both, allow her to look at those tests, or at least a section of them. Take away the fear of the unknown for her by keeping a practice book lying around on the kitchen table. Mark the book up, dog-ear the pages, and rip out a word list or two. Every so often pick out a question at random and together with your daughter, answer it—or try to. Demystify the college application process by telling your girl that all her good work inside the classroom and out will be considered and not only her GPA.

Alert!

While girls usually make higher grades in high school than boys, boys usually score higher on their SATs. One reason for that is that girls can get too concerned about finding the perfect test answer while boys guess more accurately and overall use the test time period more wisely.

Also try your best to get your daughter over the notion that she cannot make a mistake when she applies. Her essay should not sound as though it was written by a brilliant robot but by a real girl. One essay option offered to prospective students by a college recently was, "Tell us about something you did that was just plain fun." So, make sure your girl's life is filled with a good combination of studying and enjoyable activities. Also, get on the Internet and have admission officers from numerous schools send you their glossy brochures and their facts on financial aid packages, and let them compete for your tuition cash. It is fun to look at the inviting pictures with your girl and to highlight the strengths the various schools have to offer and at what price—in other words, to comparison-shop.

Competing in Business

For too long, parents have been ambivalent about making their daughters competitive in the world of work. On the one hand, they want their girls to be able to compete with their male counterparts, but on the other, they do not want them to become too pushy and hard. What the parents forget is that all they need to do is tell their daughters to do their personal best.

 **Fact**

Most people consider childhood to last from birth to age eighteen. Richard Bromfield, Ph.D., says that childhood consists of close to a million minutes during which our country could have had as many as four different presidents. Think of the almost two decades you put in raising your girl as your best job ever.

That personal best varies from daughter to daughter, but your girl knows what it is for her, and that is all that matters. Therefore, she should really know how to compete in academics and athletics, in applying for college and scholarships, in job interviews, in the workplace, and in whatever other opportunities may crop up. To ensure that your daughter can handle the competition, explain the following:

- She should know that this world is made up of many competitive environments.
- She should be able to accept whatever pressures these competitive environments place on her.
- She should learn to de-pressurize whatever competitive environment she ends up in.
- She should go with her own design and opt out of any competitive environment any time she chooses.

That is another huge advantage of being a girl these days; she can leap at whatever competitive endeavors she likes and log off any time she has had enough. Your daughter can change her plans, a little or a lot, and nobody can stop her. She is empowered to be herself.

As she grows, your daughter may change. Your daughter must always feel free to fight her battles and put her competitive drive into high gear—or to make peace, slow down, and choose her own winding path. As a girl today, she has more choices than any previous generation, male or female.

Dealing with Setbacks

If your daughter's first college or career plan does not pan out, she should not feel a sense of dread. Obviously, she is meant for something else, something better. Many girls have so many talents that it is a joy for the parent to watch them explore one after the other. Just as food tastes better with an exotic spice added in now and then, your daughter's life will perk up even more when she tries her hand at one job and then another, or when she switches from one major to another in college.

Tell your girl about the many times you have changed your mind about something; it meant your mind was alive and working. Tell her about the journey she is making from girl to woman. There may be some side trips and meandering along the way in order to enjoy the infinite variety of her possibilities. Girls who never have a setback will be ill equipped in a quickly changing world that each day adds more options to everyone's menu. The ultimate test of any activity and endeavor for your daughter is to ask herself if it fits her. If it does, that's great; if it does not, that's even better. Let the next stage of her life's sojourn begin with all its new chances.

Mentoring Your Daughter-Friend

To be a mentor means to be an experienced adviser and supporter, and you are that. As a parent with close to twenty years of experience, there is no one more qualified than you to give advice to your daughter, watch over her, and foster her progress. In business, mentoring connects the most successful employee with a new and inexperienced colleague. In politics, acting, and athletics, mentoring is very much en vogue. In fact, many of the most successful people in the world have gained enormously from a mentor.

Fact

In ancient Greek mythology, Mentor was a friend of Odysseus. When Odysseus left to fight in the Trojan War, he asked Mentor to look after his son Telemachus and his possessions. The first modern use of *mentor* is thought to have occurred in 1699 when the popular book *Les Adventures de Telemaque* by François Fénelon was published in France.

Think what it means to be your daughter's mentor. These days you often hear this word on TV or in the news. The five-time Tour de France winner Eddy Merckx mentored Lance Armstrong, the seven-time Tour de France winner. Now is your turn. Most likely, you will not mentor the next world-class athlete. But you will mentor someone more outstanding, your own flesh and blood reconfigured in your daughter. Therefore, take your mentor role as seriously as you can and share with your daughter all your secrets for successful living.

Internet Mentoring

You have a great advantage in mentoring your daughter: the latest technology. Therefore, you do not have to write out lengthy letters, take them to the post office, hope she checks her mailbox once in a while, and then wait for her to reply if she can ever find the time with all the new activities and demands that fill her life away from home. You have a better way of staying in touch with your daughter by simply:

- Texting her, e-mailing her your best advice, or leaving your deepest thought of the day on her voice mail.
- Forwarding her book write-ups, articles, and blogs of interest.
- Giving her a prepaid phone card or including her in a family-plan cell phone deal.
- Scheduling regular visits with her, or meeting halfway between your locations every month for brunch.

The best thing about the Web mentoring of your daughter is that you can present her with new ways of thinking, a path to new opportunities, and tons of fresh resources at a distance. So no hurt feelings while she decides whether to take your wise counsel. You know you have made the offer. That is all you can do. She has to choose for herself what fits with her life's format and future. The next day you can send more advice her way. In fact, by using all the plus points of cyberspace, you can reduce the space separating you and your daughter to nothing more than the split second it takes to click the mouse.

Empty Nest Equals Wider Circle

Some parents begin lamenting the "empty nest syndrome" they fear they will experience when their daughter leaves, starting with the time she enters high school. All parents have their own modus operandi, so to speak. Many, however, seem to enjoy the past more than the moment of parental achievement. They also suffer forward and wallow in anticipation of a daughterless home, rather than realize that all they need to do is widen their home front. They should incorporate the college campus where their daughter resides or the new town she has chosen to work in into their lives. In fact, instead of having an empty nest, parents whose girl has gone off into the world simply have a bigger nest.

No Regrets

It is human nature to want what you know you cannot have either in the years to come or by wishing you had another chance to live your past over. Especially parents who fear that they did not give their best efforts in raising their daughter tend to regret their lost opportunities and bemoan the fact that she flew the coop far too soon. What parenting chances that Moms and Dads let slip away are indeed gone, but it is never too late to start over. Even disengaged fathers and mothers can make a new start. Parenting is not a one-time act but a continuum during which parents can decide to re-engage in their child rearing and give their best efforts to their daughter from this moment on. What can prevent some parents from doing this is they get too caught up in feeling sorry for themselves once their daughter leaves. They find themselves crying for no reason, snapping at people, being melancholy, or feeling that life is passing them by.

New Season

There is nothing wrong with being wistful and thoughtful, even wishful, as a parent. Now you are alone at home and have no extra laundry to do or a big mess to clean up. So enjoy your fewer chores, welcome this new season, and live it up. Take time now to do the following:

- Express some of those long-neglected talents you have; take a class or join a new group.
- Indulge in the dreams and desires you have tabled for so long; work on yourself or new hobbies.
- Enjoy getting a new lease on life and experience a sense of freedom and peace. Sleep later than usual and have long, lazy weekends.
- Realize your wish to travel and to see more of the world, starting with the many scenic destinations in your own state.

This is your time to embrace the new you and pack your own life full with zest. This time of life can show parents that they have a much greater potential than they thought they had. They thought that in rearing their girl they spent themselves, got worn down, and were coming face-to-face with their own mortality. On the contrary, now they can discover that they are awakening and reviving, and enjoying their realization of immortality: their adult daughter and all she has to offer the world.

Enjoy Your "Masterpiece"

Although your daughter is not a little girl anymore, she continues to crave your love and acceptance. As always, she wants you to be proud of her now and in the years to come. That means you have to show her that you trust her and that you have faith in her. You have taught her to master the basic living skills and you have instilled good values in her over the years. Now as she shows by her actions how much she has learned from you, you need to trust in yourself and feel good about all you have done.

Remember this: You were her master teacher throughout her childhood and youth. Although there are many more lessons you can still teach her, as she moves on, take some time to do the following:

- Relive the wonderful years you had raising your girl.
- Flip through your photo albums and look at the mementoes of the journey.
- Exhale more deeply than ever before; your big job is done!
- Appreciate the feeling of victory and be grateful that you had the chance to pass on so much of your best—all of it!—to your daughter.

Not enough parents pause for a week or several, or a month or several, to simply rejoice in having done a masterful job in raising their daughter.

Thankful Job

Here is the most amazing thing: Every minute you concerned yourself with parenting your girl, you did it out of duty, because you loved your child, and because you were her mother or father—and for no other reason. Yet nothing you ever did went unrecorded. Your girl made a mental note of everything. You see, in matters of gratitude a daughter may be different than a son. In many cases, she remembers each and every one of the small gestures you made over the years to raise her right.

Alert!

JoAnn Deak, Ph.D., says that girls are made in such a way that they want to please, want to fit in, and want to connect with the world. Therefore, girls tend to make it a point to be more agreeable and to adjust to their surroundings. They also want to verbalize their feelings, are better at it, and can better express their thankfulness.

There is not a single parent of a girl who did not sacrifice something in raising her, but it is not forgotten! Everything you did is etched into the mind and heart of your daughter. There is not one single good thing you ever did for your daughter that she will not repay you for later in life. If your daughter has not yet started, it is only a matter of time before she will.

Celebrate New Traditions

No matter how old your daughter gets, she will cherish all the special occasions you spend together. While family traditions are often passed from generation to generation, do not feel bound by them. You raised the latest version of a great girl, so feel free to adjust old family traditions to fit the new circumstances you find yourself in.

Honor your relationship with your daughter and involve her in deciding how to observe family celebrations and the red-letter days on the calendar. Respect that your daughter is now an adult and before you make any plans involving her, find out:

1. What time she is available. Be willing to shift the celebration to a time more convenient for her.
2. Where she wants to celebrate—at home or in a restaurant, for example—and adjust your plans accordingly.
3. How she wants to celebrate—in a small circle, with the extended family, or by her bringing home a new friend.
4. Also invite suggestions from the rest of the family and have them contribute their prize culinary creations.

Take as much time and effort as possible to make a big deal out of your daughter's birthday, job anniversaries, college highlights, and special days. The bond you have with your daughter is incredibly strong, but it can still benefit from one more golden thread of love woven in, now and then.

 **Essential**

While shopping, gift-giving, choosing the appropriate music and decorations for family get-togethers, and parties can be a favorite part of your holidays, the cost, choosing gifts, the busy schedule, extra cooking and baking, and the entertaining can also make your holidays the most stressful times of the year. An older daughter can take over many of these extra tasks.

Welcome to Your Best Life

You celebrate the successful raising of your daughter every day as you look at the framed photo of her that sits on your desk or hangs on the wall. You also rejoice in your good fortune of having ushered her to her young-adult stage when you tell your friends or neighbors of your girl's latest experiences or escapades on campus or her first few exciting months on the job. Raising a daughter brings a sense of fulfillment and of having been rewarded more than you ever imagined. When you give your daughter the tools to achieve her dream career, to handle competition at work, and to be smart about her income, you have infused her with such power that she will exceed your expectations. In her adult life, she will accomplish many great things because you taught her that nothing is impossible.

APPENDIX A

Bibliography

Biederman, Jerry, and Lorin Biederman, eds. *Parent School: Simple Lessons from the Leading Experts on Being a Mom and Dad* (New York: M. Evans and Co., 2002).

Buchanan, Andrea J., ed. *It's a Girl* (Emeryville, CA: Seal Press, 2006).

Chess, Stella, M.D., and Alexander Thomas, M.D. *Know Your Child* (New York: Basic Books, 1987).

Deak, Joann, Ph.D. *Girls Will Be Girls* (New York: Hyperion, 2002).

Erwin, Cheryl L., M.A. *The Everything® Parent's Guide to Raising Boys* (Avon, MA: Adams Media, 2006).

Frontline. *Inside the Teenage Brain* (PBS Video, Public Broadcasting Service, 2004).

Gadeberg, Jeanette. *Raising Strong Daughters* (Minneapolis, MN: Fairview Press, 1995).

Harrison, Melissa, and Harry H. Harrison Jr. *Mother to Daughter* (New York: Workman Publishing, 2005).

Hartlet-Brewer, Elizabeth. *Raising Confident Girls* (Cambridge, MA: Da Capo Press, 2000).

Healy, Jane M., Ph.D. *Endangered Minds: Why Children Don't Think and What We Can Do about It* (New York: Touchstone, 1990).

Hersch, Patricia. *A Tribe Apart: A Journey into the Heart of American Adolescence* (New York: Ballantine, 1998).

Holmes, Melissa, M.D., and Trish Hutchison, M.D. *Girlology: A Girl's Guide to Stuff that Matters* (Deerfield Beach, FL: Health Communications, Inc., 2005).

Karres, Erika, Ed.D. *Crushes, Flirts, & Friends* (Avon, MA: Adams Media, 2006).

———. *Fab Friends and Best Buds* (Avon, MA: Adams Media, 2005).

———. *Make Your Kids Smarter* (Kansas City, MO: Andrews McMeel Publishing, 2002).

———. *Mean Chicks, Cliques, and Dirty Tricks* (Avon, MA: Adams Media, 2004).

———. *Violence Proof Your Kids Now* (Berkeley, CA: Conari Press, 2000).

Nelson, Jane, Ed.D., Cheryl Erwin, M.A., and Carol Delzer, M.A., J.D. *Positive Discipline for Single Parents: Nurturing, Cooperation, Respect and Joy in Your Single-Parent Family,* rev. 2nd ed. (Rocklin, CA: Prima, 1999).

Ricci, Isolina, Ph.D. *Mom's House, Dad's House: Making Two Homes for Your Child,* rev. ed. (New York: Fireside, 1997).

Siegel, Daniel, M.D., and Mary Hartzell, M.Ed. *Parenting from the Inside Out: How a Deeper Self-Understanding Can Help You Raise Children Who Thrive* (New York: Jeremy P. Tarcher/Putnam, 2003).

APPENDIX B

Additional Resources

Use these Web sites for general information and as overall resources.

Parenting Resources

National PTA
✎ *www.pta.org*

Girl Scouts of the USA
✎ *www.girlscouts.org*

Positive Discipline Association
✎ *www.posdis.org*

Parents' Action for Children
✎ *www.parentsaction.org*

Zero to Three
✎ *www.zerotothree.org*

Tufts University Child & Family Web Guide
✎ *www.cfw.tufts.edu*

Child Care

National Association for the Education of Young Children
✎ *www.naeyc.org*

Child Care Aware
⊜ www.childcareaware.org

Development and Health

KidsHealth
⊜ www.kidshealth.org

Medline Plus
⊜ www.nlm.nih.gov/medlineplus/parenting.html

Child Development Institute
⊜ www.childdevelopmentinfo.com

Media, Violence, and Culture

National Institute on Media and the Family
⊜ www.mediafamily.org

Talk with Your Kids
⊜ www.talkwithkids.org

Common Sense Media
⊜ www.commonsensemedia.org

Index

THE EVERYTHING®
PARENT'S GUIDES SERIES

Expert Advice for Parents
in Need of Answers

All titles are trade paperback, 6" x 9", $14.95

THE EVERYTHING® PARENT'S GUIDES SERIES (CONTINUED).

The Everything® Parent's Guide to the Strong-Willed Child
ISBN 10: 1-59337-381-3; ISBN 13: 978-1-59337-381-8

The Everything® Parent's Guide to Raising Siblings
ISBN 10: 1-59337-537-9; ISBN 13: 978-1-59337-537-9

The Everything® Parent's Guide to Sensory Integration Disorder
ISBN 10: 1-59337-714-2; ISBN 13: 978-1-59337-714-4

The Everything® Parent's Guide to Children and Divorce
ISBN 10: 1-59337-418-6; ISBN 13: 978-1-59337-418-1

The Everything® Parent's Guide to Raising Boys
ISBN 10: 1-59337-587-5; ISBN 13: 978-1-59337-587-4

The Everything® Parent's Guide to Childhood Illnesses
ISBN 10: 1-59869-239-9; ISBN 13: 978-1-59869-239-6

The Everything® Parent's Guide to Raising Girls
ISBN 10: 1-59869-247-X; ISBN 13: 978-1-59869-247-1

The Everything® Parent's Guide to Children with Juvenile Diabetes
ISBN 10: 1-59869-246-1; ISBN 13: 978-1-59869-246-4

The Everything® Parent's Guide to Children with Depression
ISBN 10: 1-59869-264-X; ISBN 13: 978-1-59869-264-8